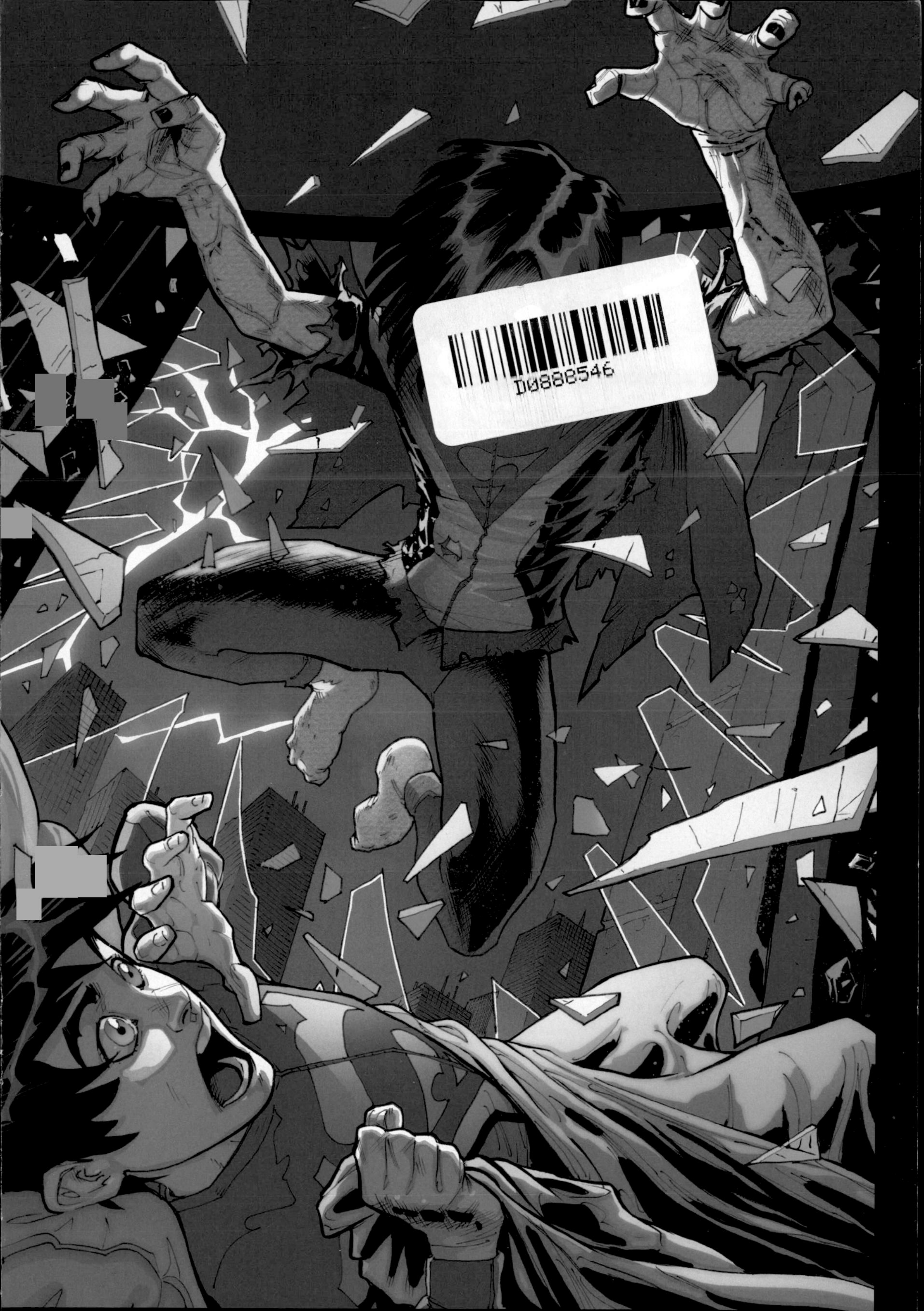

# SUPERMAN

## VOL.7 BIZARROVERSE

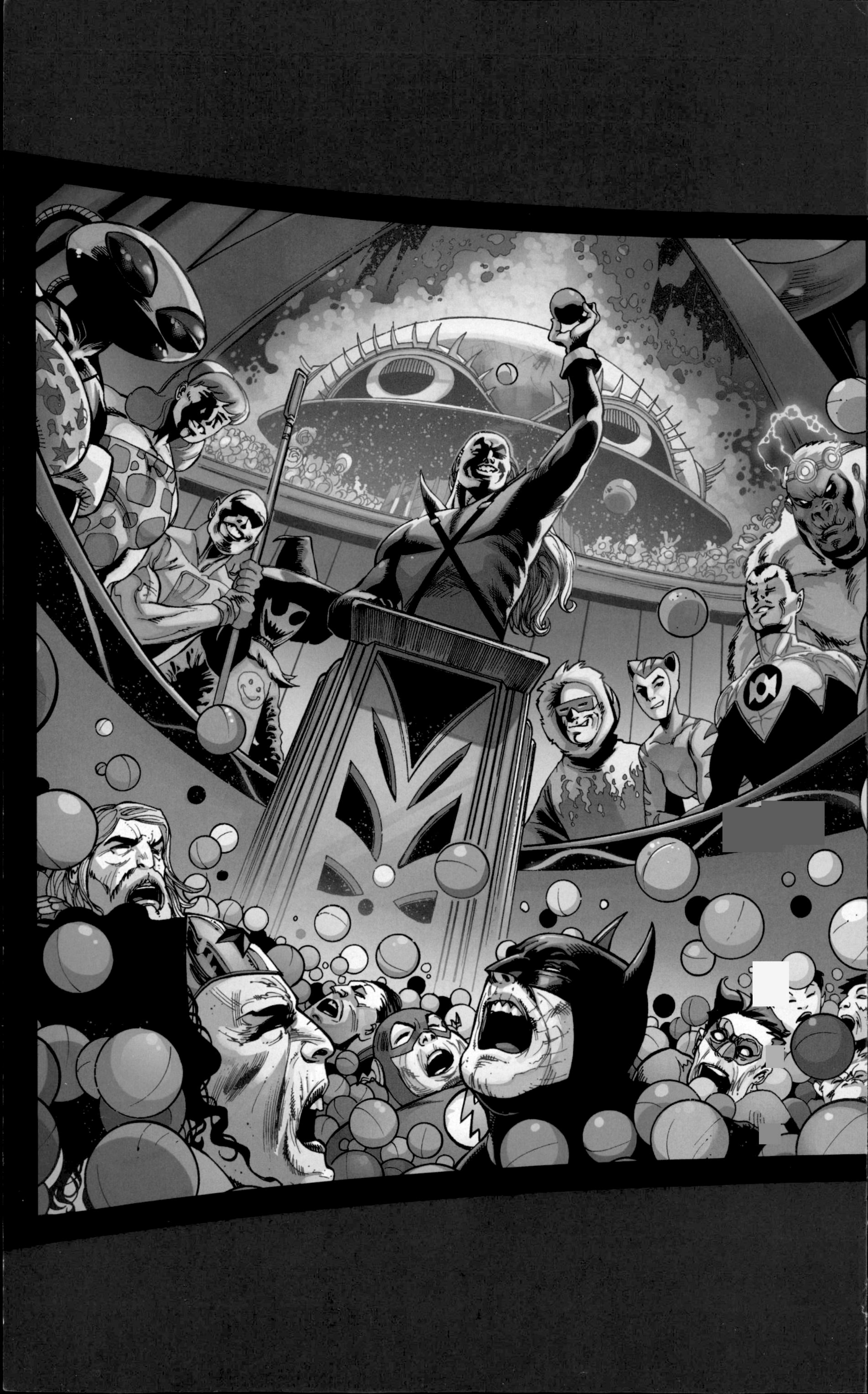

# SUPERMAN
## VOL.7 BIZARROVERSE

**PATRICK GLEASON** * **PETER J. TOMASI**
writers

**PATRICK GLEASON** * **DOUG MAHNKE** * **SCOTT GODLEWSKI**
pencillers

**PATRICK GLEASON** * **SCOTT GODLEWSKI**
**JAIME MENDOZA** * **DOUG MAHNKE** * **JOE PRADO**
inkers

**STEPHEN DOWNER** * **GABE ELTAEB** * **ALEJANDRO SANCHEZ** * **WIL QUINTANA**
colorists

**ROB LEIGH** * **TOM NAPOLITANO**
letterers

**PATRICK GLEASON** and **ALEJANDRO SANCHEZ**
collection cover artists

**SUPERMAN** created by **JERRY SIEGEL** and **JOE SHUSTER**.
**SUPERBOY** created by **JERRY SIEGEL**.
By special arrangement with the Jerry Siegel family.

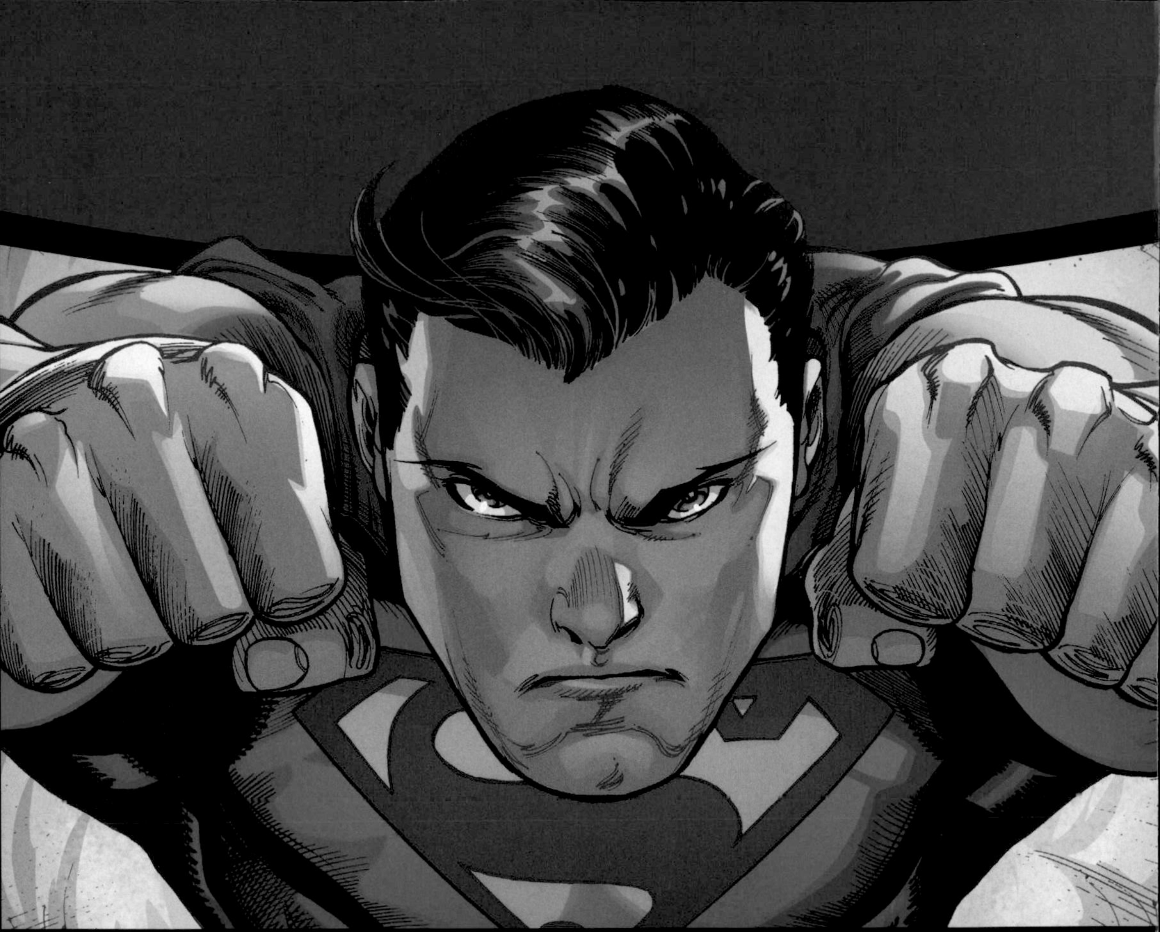

**PAUL KAMINSKI** Editor - Original Series
**JESSICA CHEN** Associate Editor - Original Series * **ANDREW MARINO** Assistant Editor - Original Series
**JEB WOODARD** Group Editor - Collected Editions * **ALEX GALER** Editor - Collected Edition
**STEVE COOK** Design Director - Books * **MEGEN BELLERSEN** Publication Design

**BOB HARRAS** Senior VP - Editor-in-Chief, DC Comics
**PAT McCALLUM** Executive Editor, DC Comics

**DAN DiDIO** Publisher * **JIM LEE** Publisher & Chief Creative Officer
**AMIT DESAI** Executive VP - Business & Marketing Strategy, Direct to Consumer & Global Franchise Management
**BOBBIE CHASE** VP & Executive Editor, Young Reader & Talent Development * **MARK CHIARELLO** Senior VP - Art, Design & Collected Editions
**JOHN CUNNINGHAM** Senior VP - Sales & Trade Marketing * **BRIAR DARDEN** VP - Business Affairs
**ANNE DePIES** Senior VP - Business Strategy, Finance & Administration * **DON FALLETTI** VP - Manufacturing Operations
**LAWRENCE GANEM** VP - Editorial Administration & Talent Relations * **ALISON GILL** Senior VP - Manufacturing & Operations
**JASON GREENBERG** VP - Business Strategy & Finance * **HANK KANALZ** Senior VP - Editorial Strategy & Administration * **JAY KOGAN** Senior VP - Legal Affairs
**NICK J. NAPOLITANO** VP - Manufacturing Administration * **LISETTE OSTERLOH** VP - Digital Marketing & Events * **EDDIE SCANNELL** VP - Consumer Marketing
**COURTNEY SIMMONS** Senior VP - Publicity & Communications * **JIM (SKI) SOKOLOWSKI** VP - Comic Book Specialty Sales & Trade Marketing
**NANCY SPEARS** VP - Mass, Book, Digital Sales & Trade Marketing * **MICHELE R. WELLS** VP - Content Strategy

**SUPERMAN VOL. 7: BIZARROVERSE**

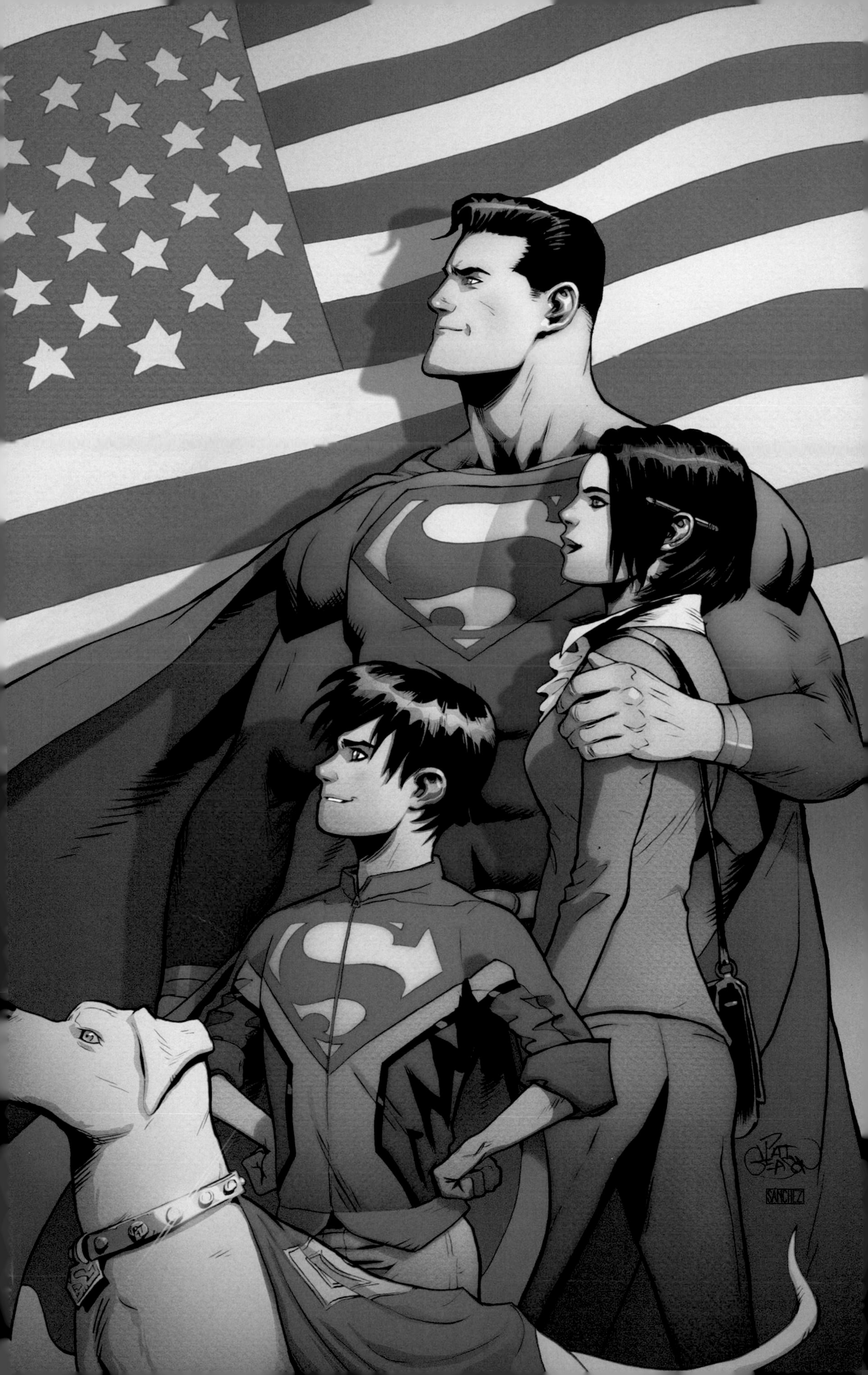
SÁNCHEZ

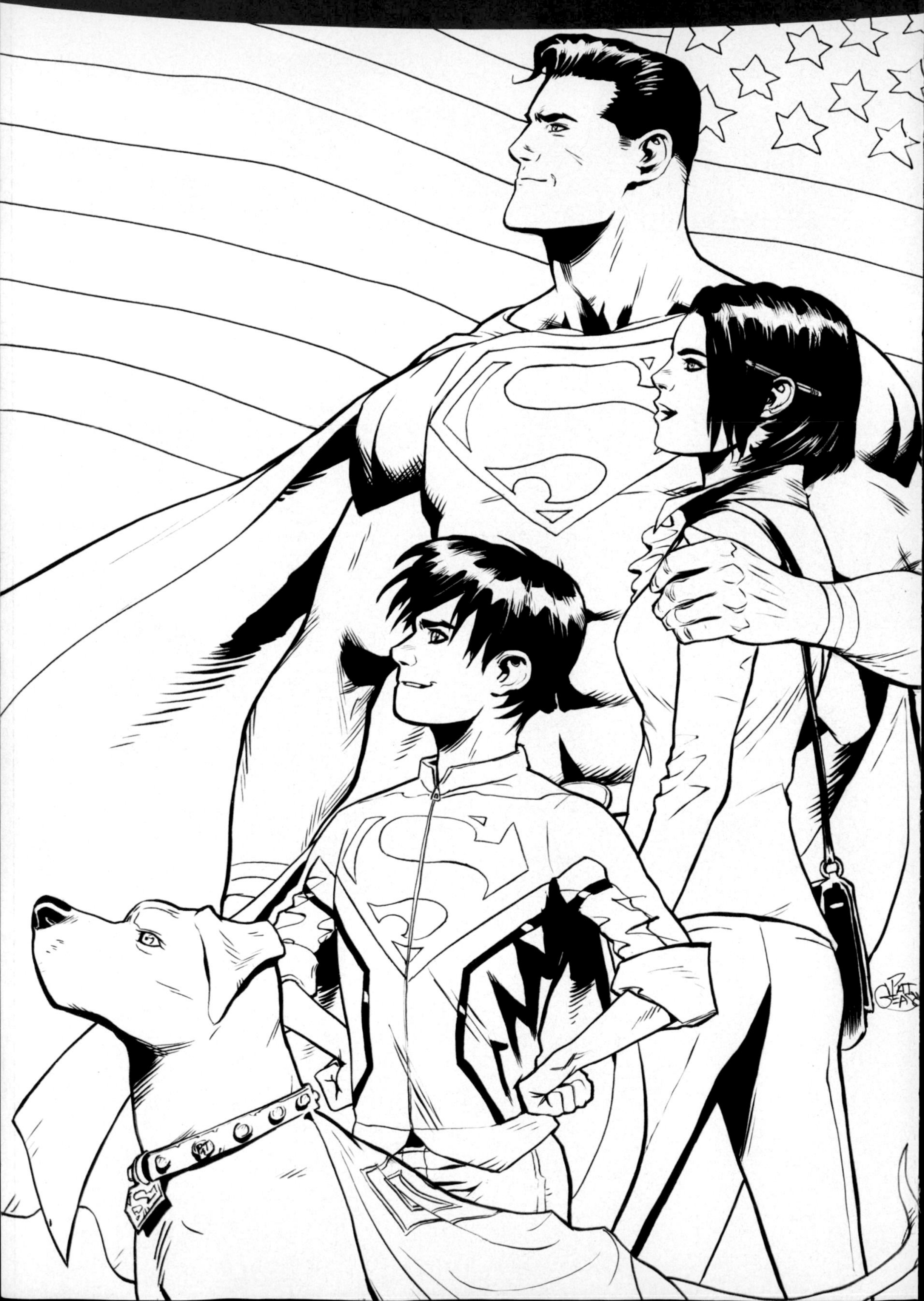

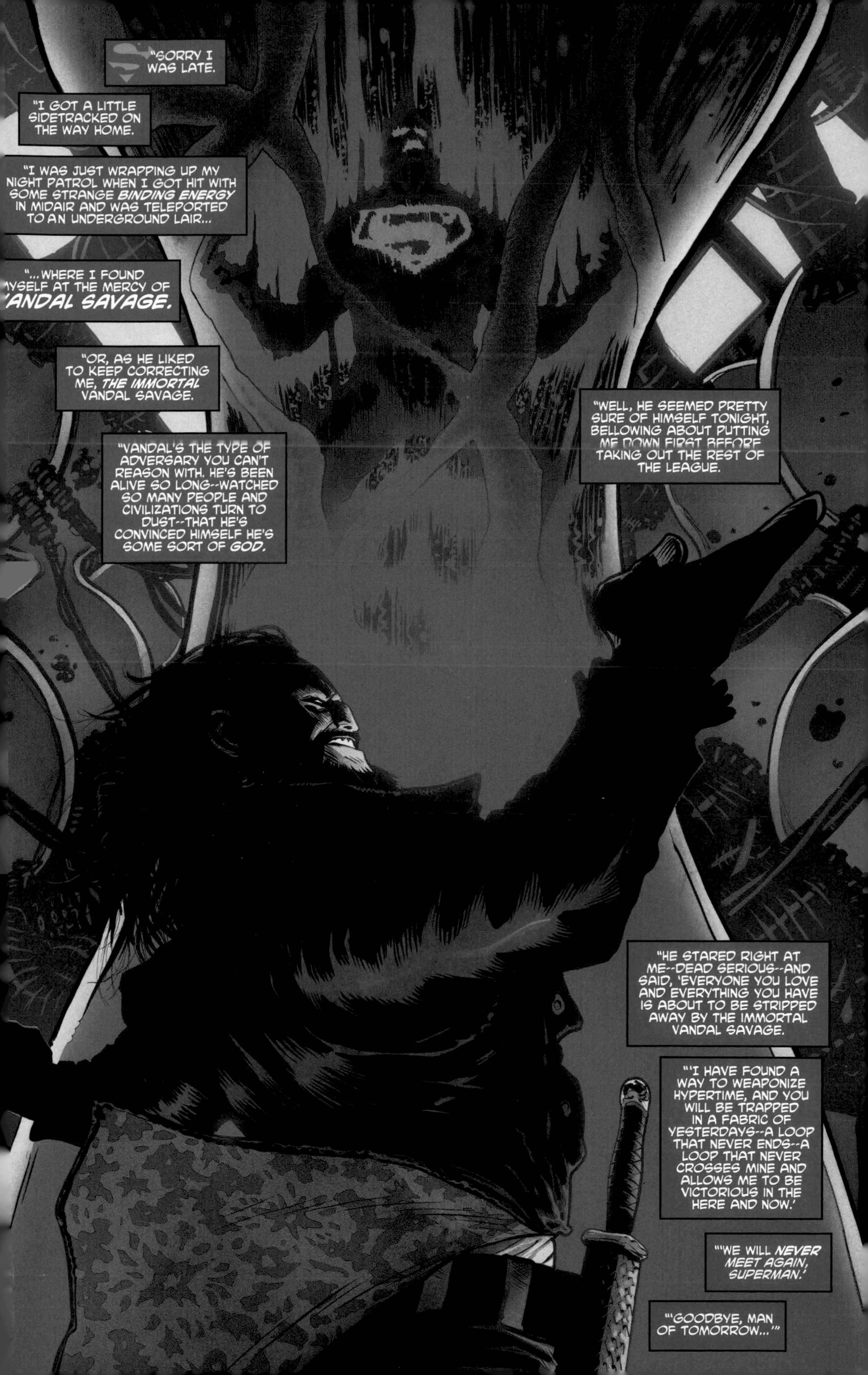
"SORRY I WAS LATE.
"I GOT A LITTLE SIDETRACKED ON THE WAY HOME.
"I WAS JUST WRAPPING UP MY NIGHT PATROL WHEN I GOT HIT WITH SOME STRANGE *BINDING ENERGY* IN MIDAIR AND WAS TELEPORTED TO AN UNDERGROUND LAIR...
"...WHERE I FOUND MYSELF AT THE MERCY OF VANDAL SAVAGE.
"OR, AS HE LIKED TO KEEP CORRECTING ME, *THE IMMORTAL* VANDAL SAVAGE.
"VANDAL'S THE TYPE OF ADVERSARY YOU CAN'T REASON WITH. HE'S BEEN ALIVE SO LONG--WATCHED SO MANY PEOPLE AND CIVILIZATIONS TURN TO DUST--THAT HE'S CONVINCED HIMSELF HE'S SOME SORT OF *GOD.*
"WELL, HE SEEMED PRETTY SURE OF HIMSELF TONIGHT, BELLOWING ABOUT PUTTING ME DOWN FIRST BEFORE TAKING OUT THE REST OF THE LEAGUE.
"HE STARED RIGHT AT ME--DEAD SERIOUS--AND SAID, 'EVERYONE YOU LOVE AND EVERYTHING YOU HAVE IS ABOUT TO BE STRIPPED AWAY BY THE IMMORTAL VANDAL SAVAGE.
"'I HAVE FOUND A WAY TO WEAPONIZE HYPERTIME, AND YOU WILL BE TRAPPED IN A FABRIC OF YESTERDAYS--A LOOP THAT NEVER ENDS--A LOOP THAT NEVER CROSSES MINE AND ALLOWS ME TO BE VICTORIOUS IN THE HERE AND NOW.'
"'WE WILL *NEVER MEET AGAIN, SUPERMAN.*'
"'GOODBYE, MAN OF TOMORROW...'"

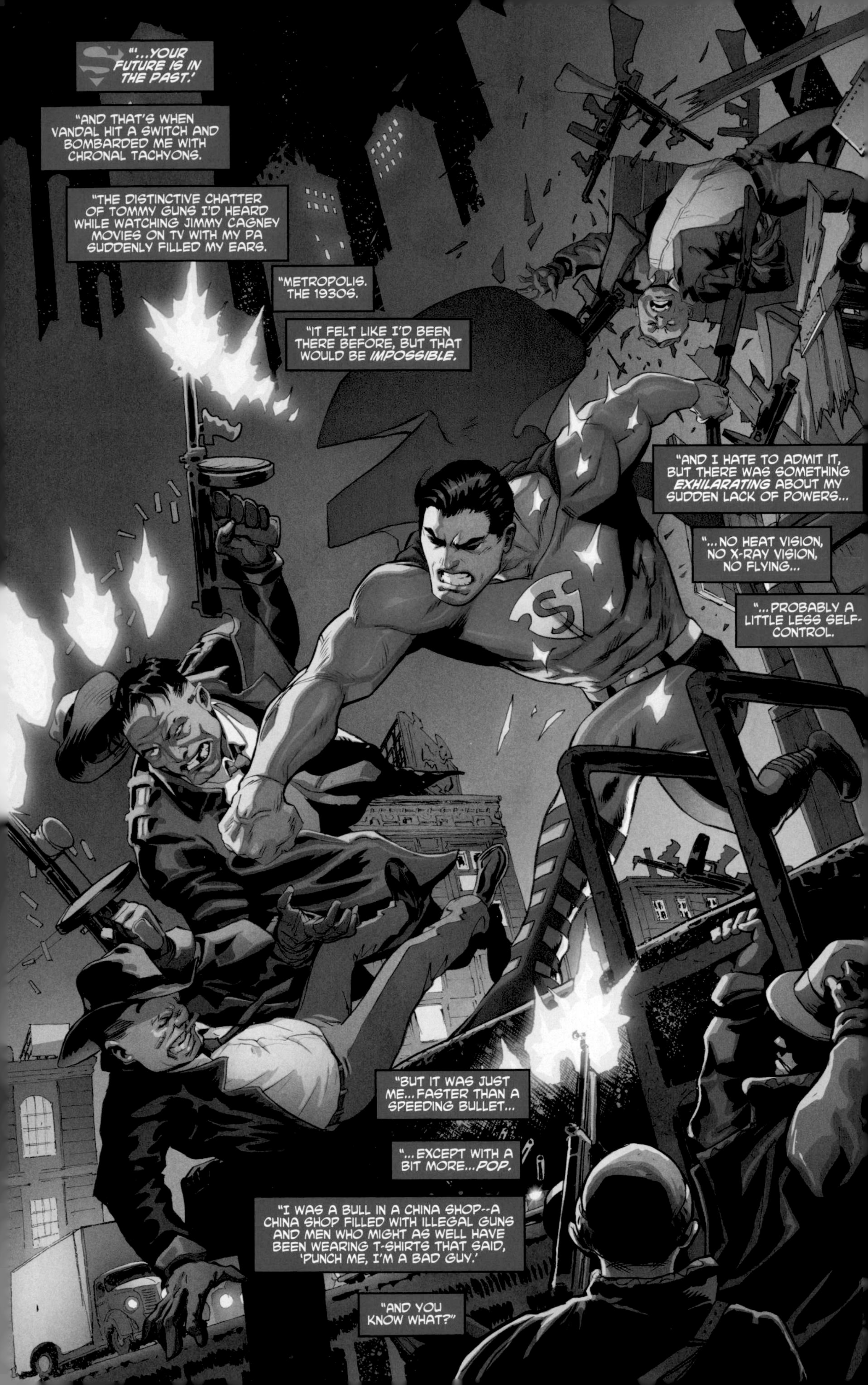
"'...YOUR FUTURE IS IN THE PAST.'
"AND THAT'S WHEN VANDAL HIT A SWITCH AND BOMBARDED ME WITH CHRONAL TACHYONS.
"THE DISTINCTIVE CHATTER OF TOMMY GUNS I'D HEARD WHILE WATCHING JIMMY CAGNEY MOVIES ON TV WITH MY PA SUDDENLY FILLED MY EARS.
"METROPOLIS. THE 1930S.
"IT FELT LIKE I'D BEEN THERE BEFORE, BUT THAT WOULD BE *IMPOSSIBLE.*
"AND I HATE TO ADMIT IT, BUT THERE WAS SOMETHING *EXHILARATING* ABOUT MY SUDDEN LACK OF POWERS...
"...NO HEAT VISION, NO X-RAY VISION, NO FLYING...
"...PROBABLY A LITTLE LESS SELF-CONTROL.
"BUT IT WAS JUST ME...FASTER THAN A SPEEDING BULLET...
"...EXCEPT WITH A BIT MORE...*POP.*
"I WAS A BULL IN A CHINA SHOP--A CHINA SHOP FILLED WITH ILLEGAL GUNS AND MEN WHO MIGHT AS WELL HAVE BEEN WEARING T-SHIRTS THAT SAID, 'PUNCH ME, I'M A BAD GUY.'
"AND YOU KNOW WHAT?"

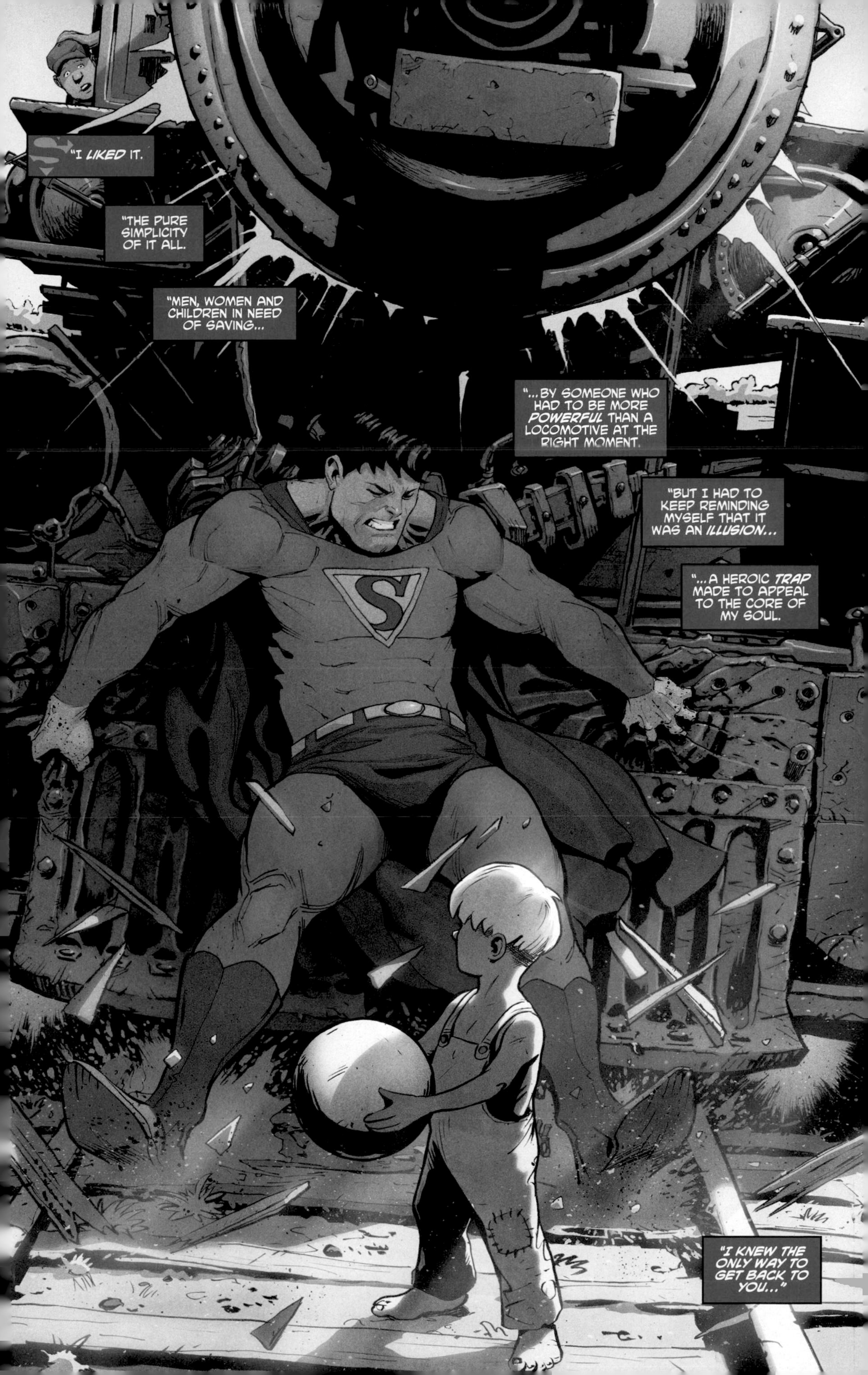
"I LIKED IT.
"THE PURE SIMPLICITY OF IT ALL.
"MEN, WOMEN AND CHILDREN IN NEED OF SAVING...
"...BY SOMEONE WHO HAD TO BE MORE POWERFUL THAN A LOCOMOTIVE AT THE RIGHT MOMENT.
"BUT I HAD TO KEEP REMINDING MYSELF THAT IT WAS AN ILLUSION...
"...A HEROIC TRAP MADE TO APPEAL TO THE CORE OF MY SOUL.
"I KNEW THE ONLY WAY TO GET BACK TO YOU..."

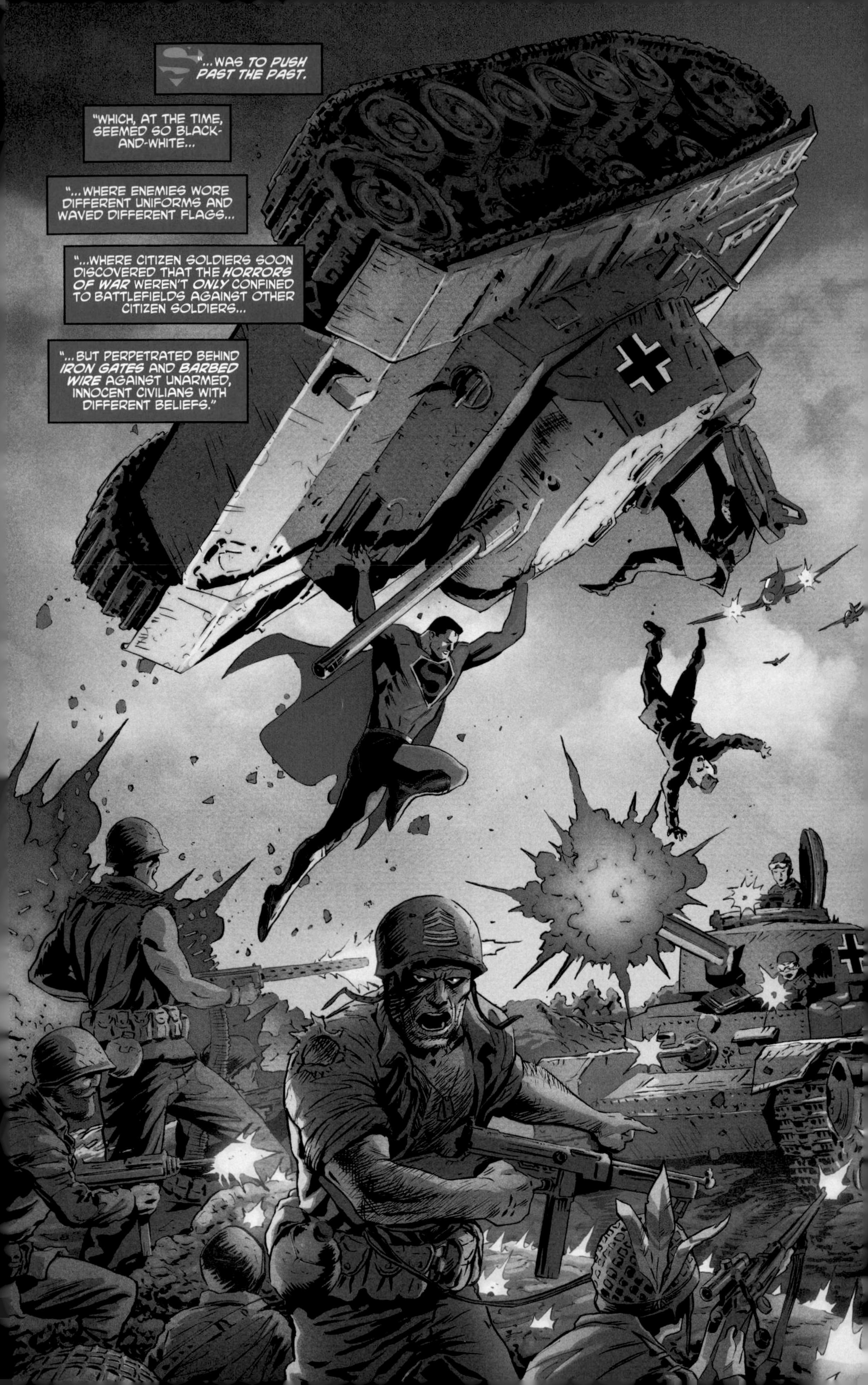
"...WAS TO PUSH PAST THE PAST.
"WHICH, AT THE TIME, SEEMED SO BLACK-AND-WHITE...
"...WHERE ENEMIES WORE DIFFERENT UNIFORMS AND WAVED DIFFERENT FLAGS...
"...WHERE CITIZEN SOLDIERS SOON DISCOVERED THAT THE HORRORS OF WAR WEREN'T ONLY CONFINED TO BATTLEFIELDS AGAINST OTHER CITIZEN SOLDIERS...
"...BUT PERPETRATED BEHIND IRON GATES AND BARBED WIRE AGAINST UNARMED, INNOCENT CIVILIANS WITH DIFFERENT BELIEFS."

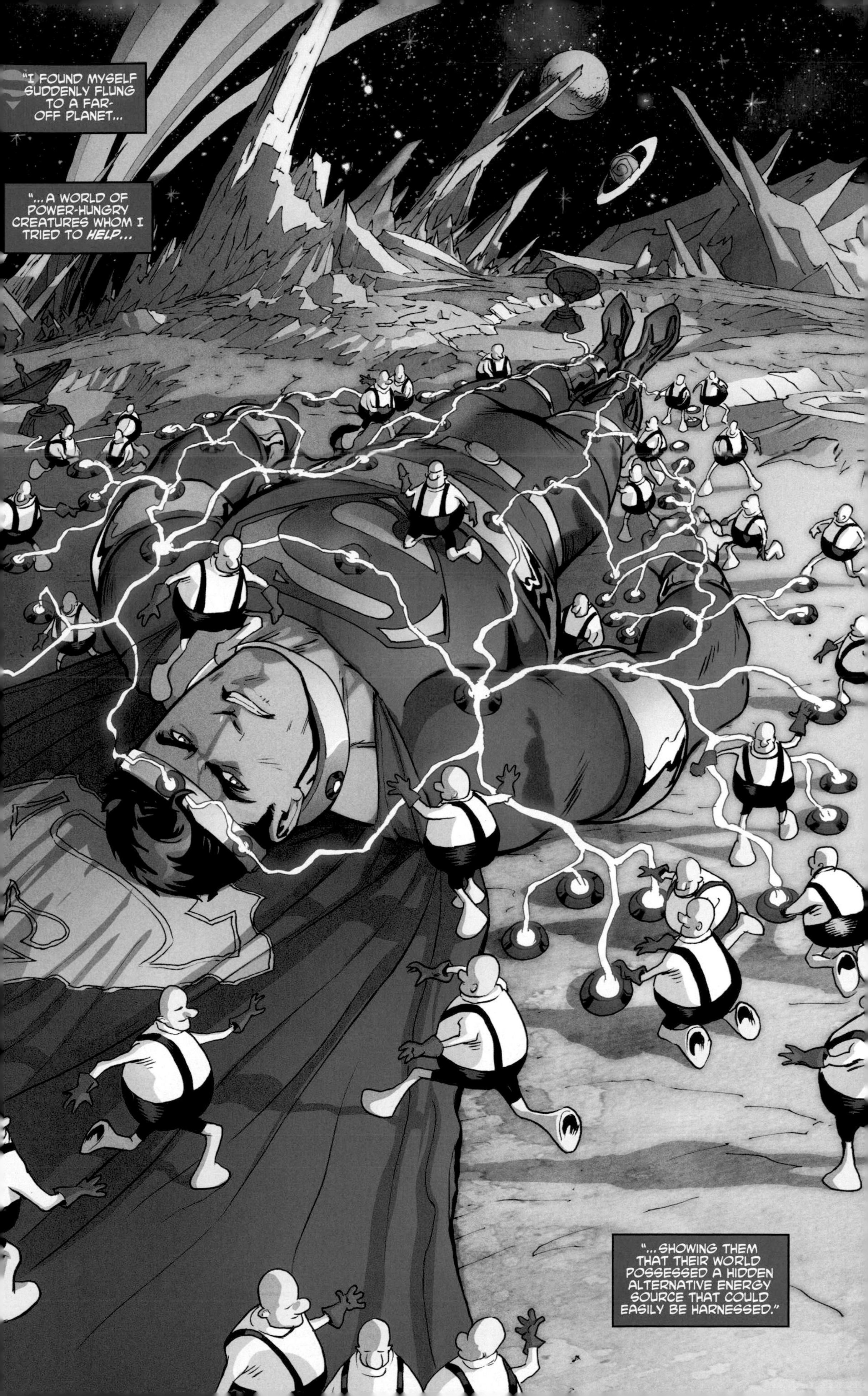
"I FOUND MYSELF SUDDENLY FLUNG TO A FAR-OFF PLANET...
"...A WORLD OF POWER-HUNGRY CREATURES WHOM I TRIED TO *HELP*...
"...SHOWING THEM THAT THEIR WORLD POSSESSED A HIDDEN ALTERNATIVE ENERGY SOURCE THAT COULD EASILY BE HARNESSED."

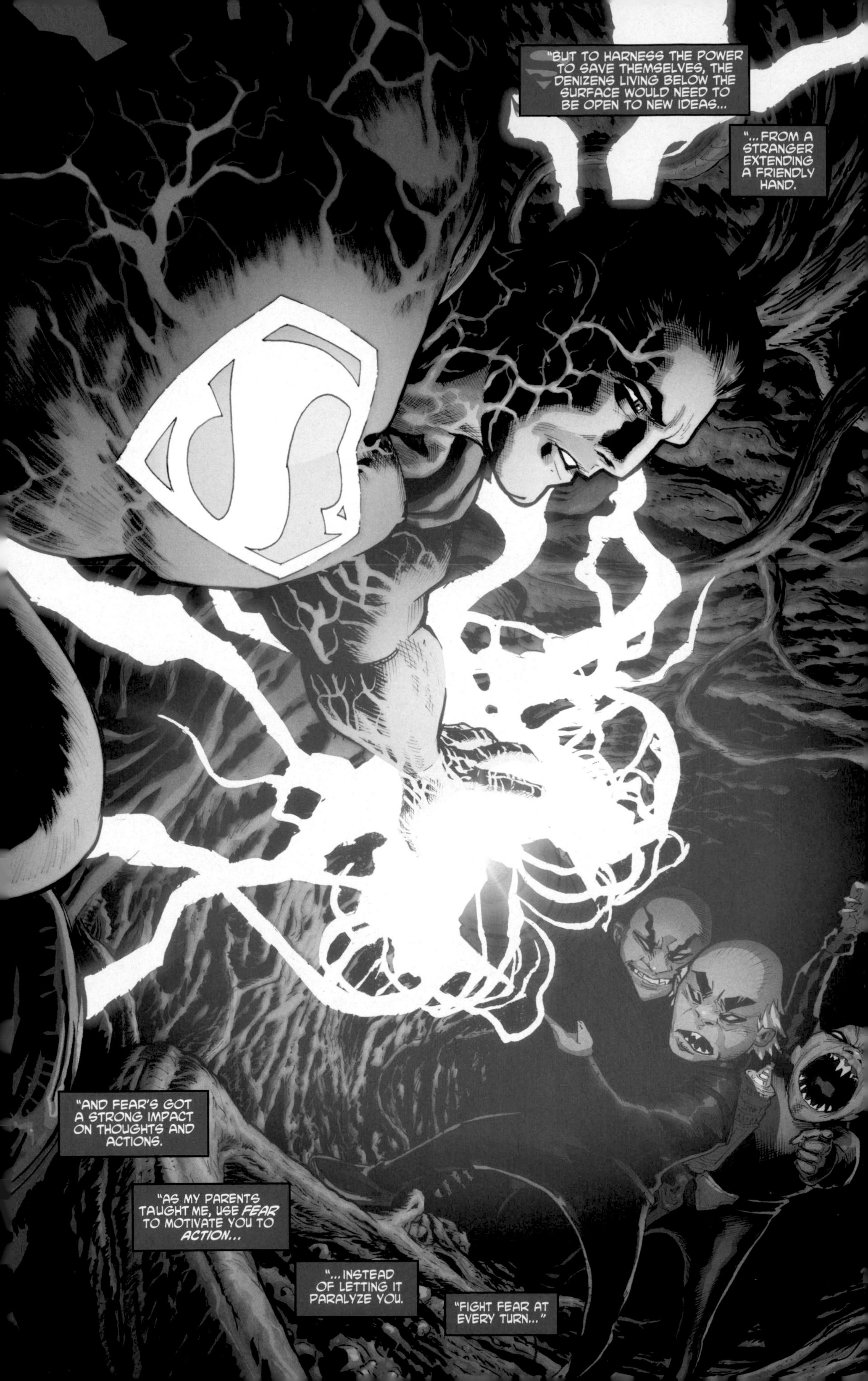
"BUT TO HARNESS THE POWER TO SAVE THEMSELVES, THE DENIZENS LIVING BELOW THE SURFACE WOULD NEED TO BE OPEN TO NEW IDEAS...
"...FROM A STRANGER EXTENDING A FRIENDLY HAND.
"AND FEAR'S GOT A STRONG IMPACT ON THOUGHTS AND ACTIONS.
"AS MY PARENTS TAUGHT ME, USE *FEAR* TO MOTIVATE YOU TO *ACTION*...
"...INSTEAD OF LETTING IT PARALYZE YOU.
"FIGHT FEAR AT EVERY TURN..."

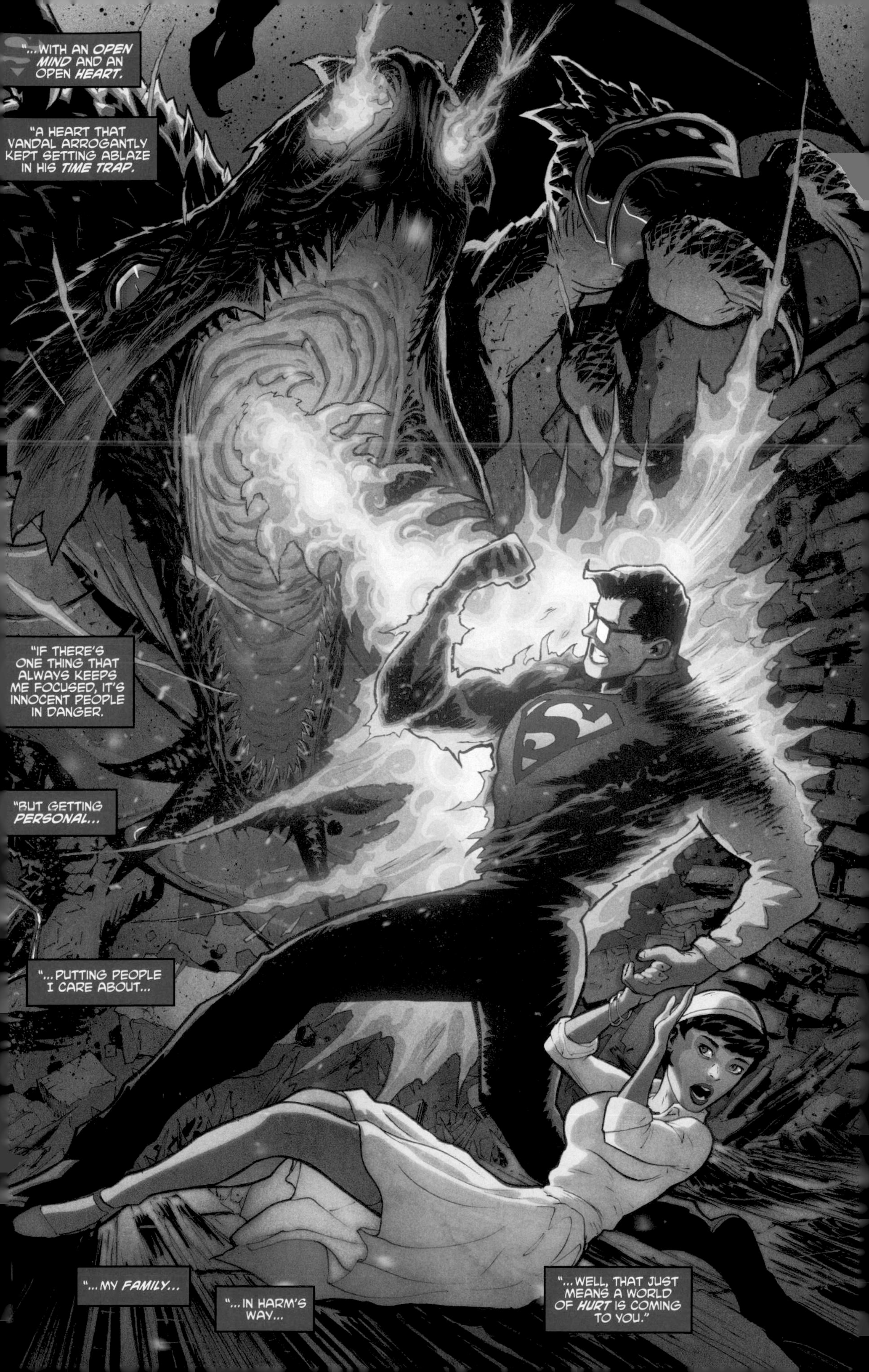
"...WITH AN *OPEN MIND* AND AN OPEN *HEART*.
"A HEART THAT VANDAL ARROGANTLY KEPT SETTING ABLAZE IN HIS *TIME TRAP*.
"IF THERE'S ONE THING THAT ALWAYS KEEPS ME FOCUSED, IT'S INNOCENT PEOPLE IN DANGER.
"BUT GETTING *PERSONAL*...
"...PUTTING PEOPLE I CARE ABOUT...
"...MY *FAMILY*...
"...IN HARM'S WAY...
"...WELL, THAT JUST MEANS A WORLD OF *HURT* IS COMING TO YOU."

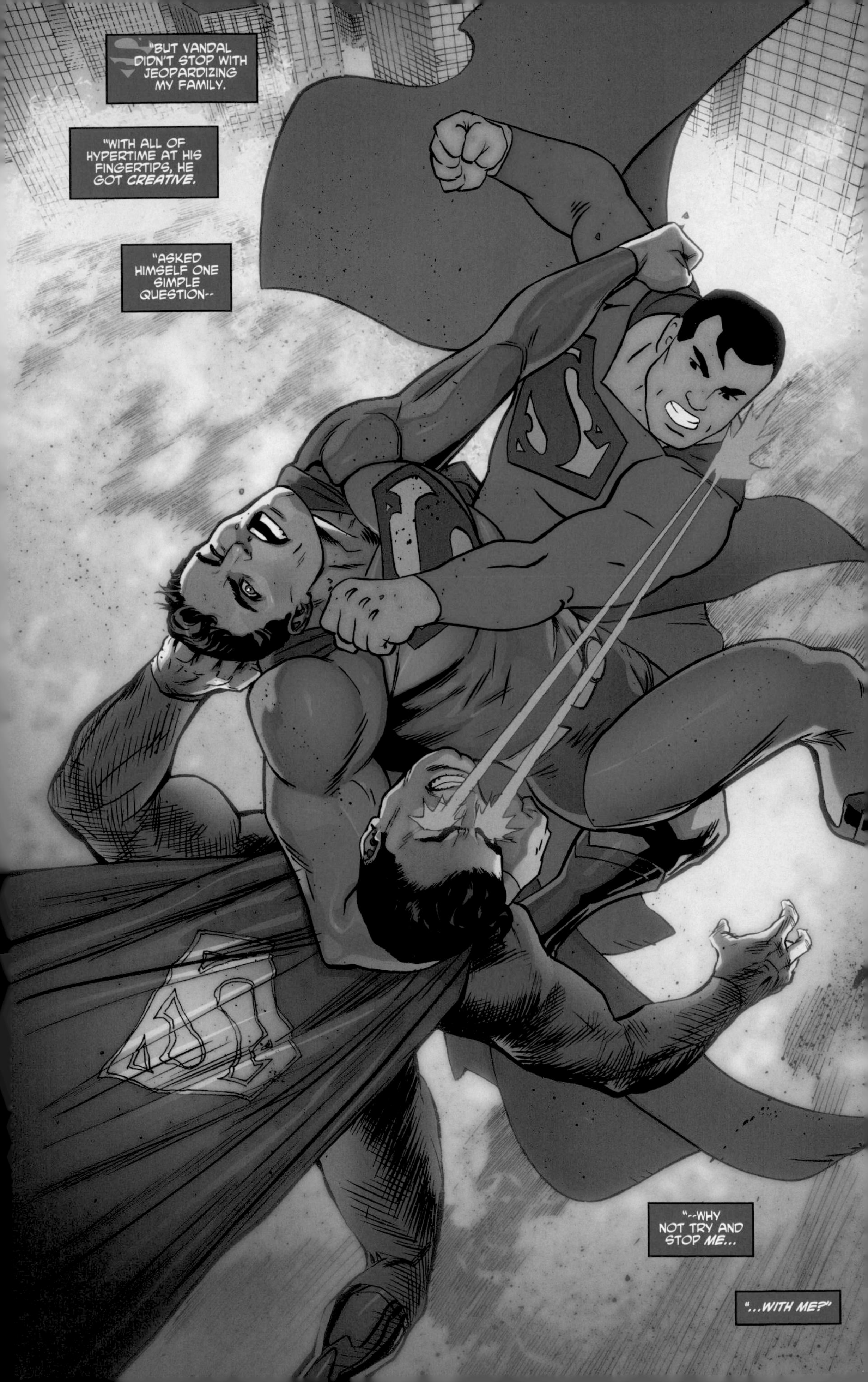
"BUT VANDAL DIDN'T STOP WITH JEOPARDIZING MY FAMILY.
"WITH ALL OF HYPERTIME AT HIS FINGERTIPS, HE GOT *CREATIVE.*
"ASKED HIMSELF ONE SIMPLE QUESTION--
"--WHY NOT TRY AND STOP *ME*...
*"...WITH ME?"*

"AND IF PURE MIGHT DIDN'T WORK...
"...USE MOTHER NATURE HERSELF TO ZAP ME AND SIPHON MY POWERS.
"GATHER THE DARK CLOUDS...
"...BLOT OUT THE SUN...
"BURN ME DOWN FROM THE INSIDE."
PAT GLEASON AFTER FRANK MILLER

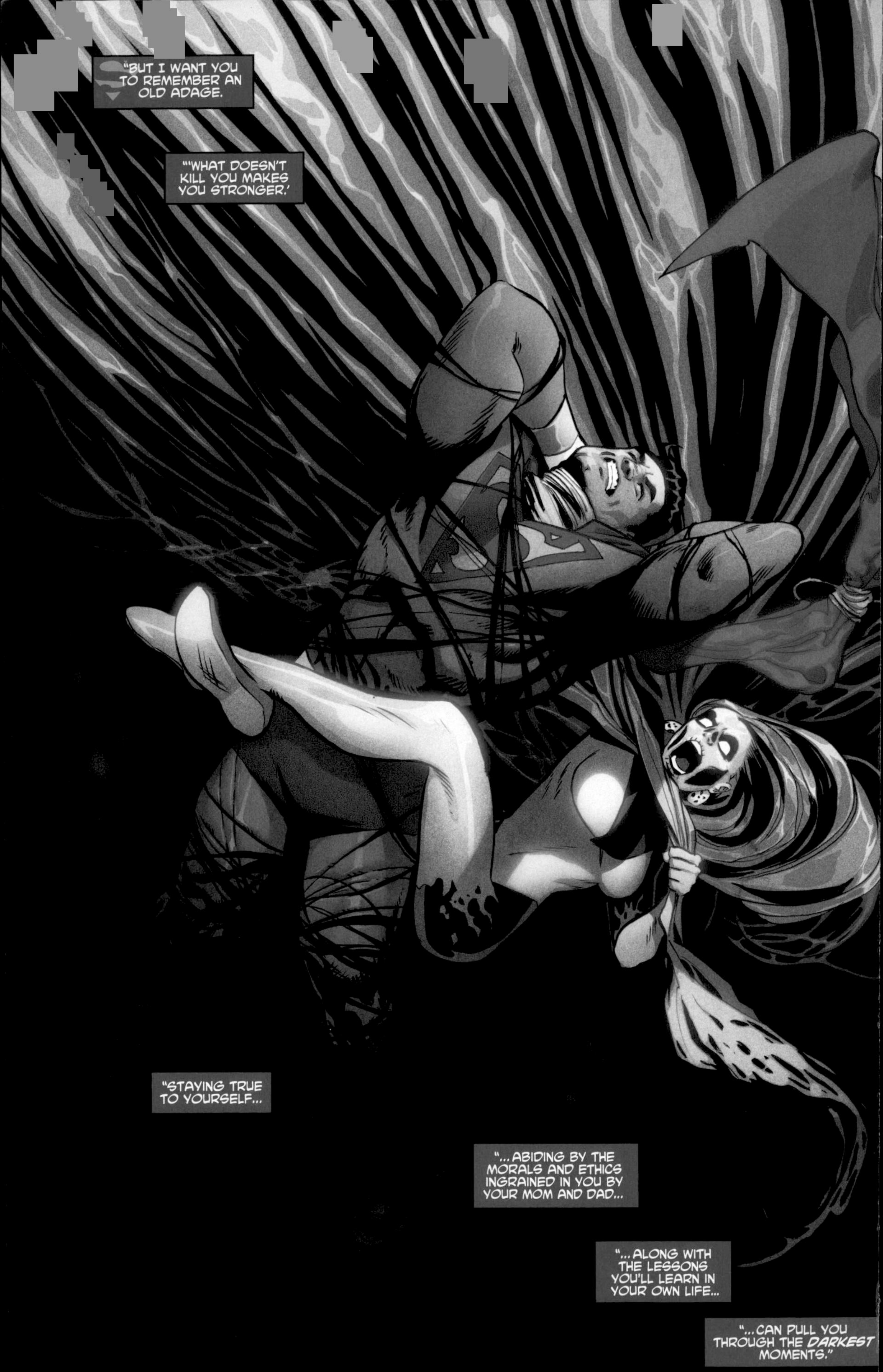
"BUT I WANT YOU TO REMEMBER AN OLD ADAGE.
"'WHAT DOESN'T KILL YOU MAKES YOU STRONGER.'
"STAYING TRUE TO YOURSELF...
"...ABIDING BY THE MORALS AND ETHICS INGRAINED IN YOU BY YOUR MOM AND DAD...
"...ALONG WITH THE LESSONS YOU'LL LEARN IN YOUR OWN LIFE...
"...CAN PULL YOU THROUGH THE DARKEST MOMENTS."

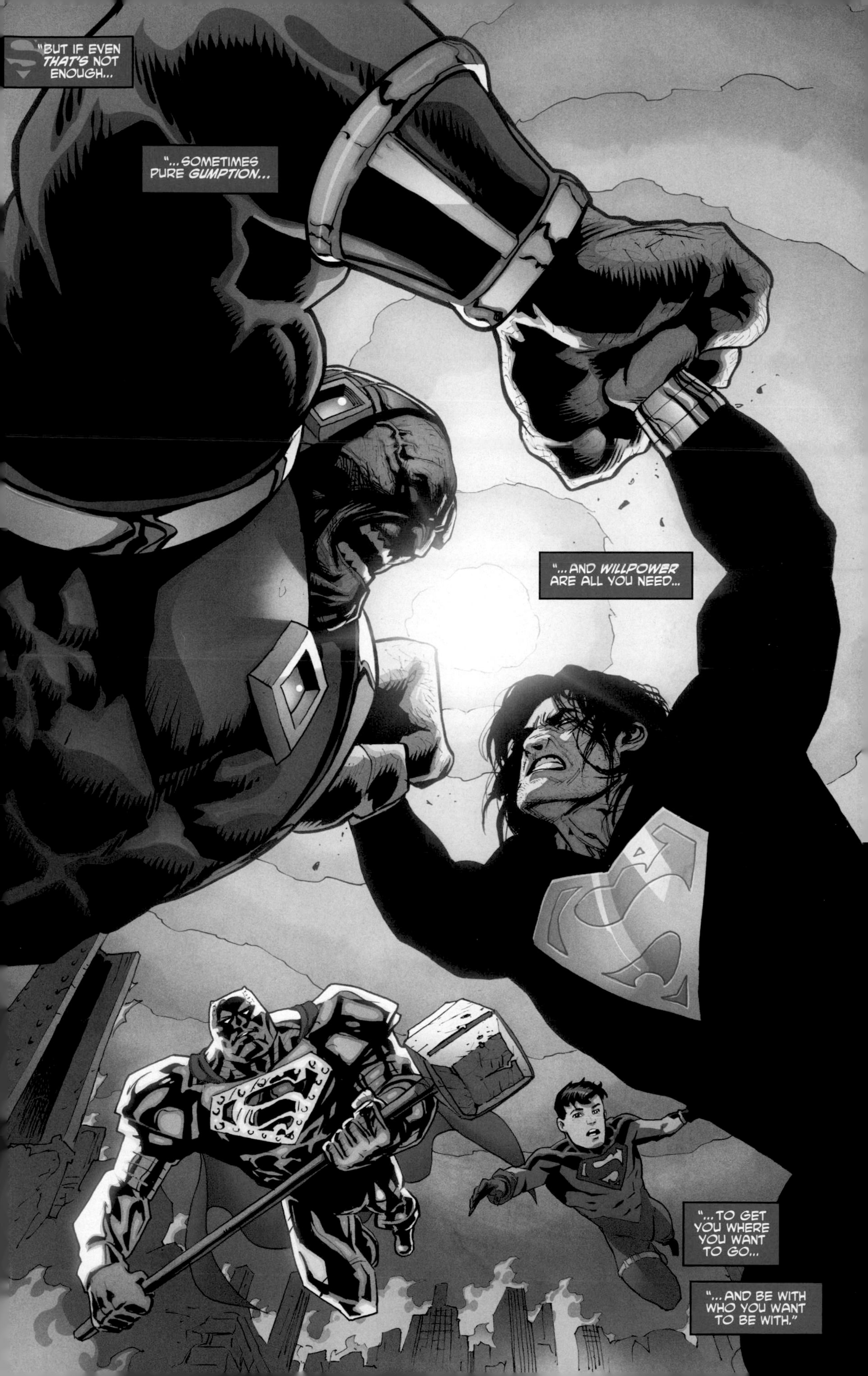
"BUT IF EVEN THAT'S NOT ENOUGH...
"...SOMETIMES PURE GUMPTION...
"...AND WILLPOWER ARE ALL YOU NEED...
"...TO GET YOU WHERE YOU WANT TO GO...
"...AND BE WITH WHO YOU WANT TO BE WITH."

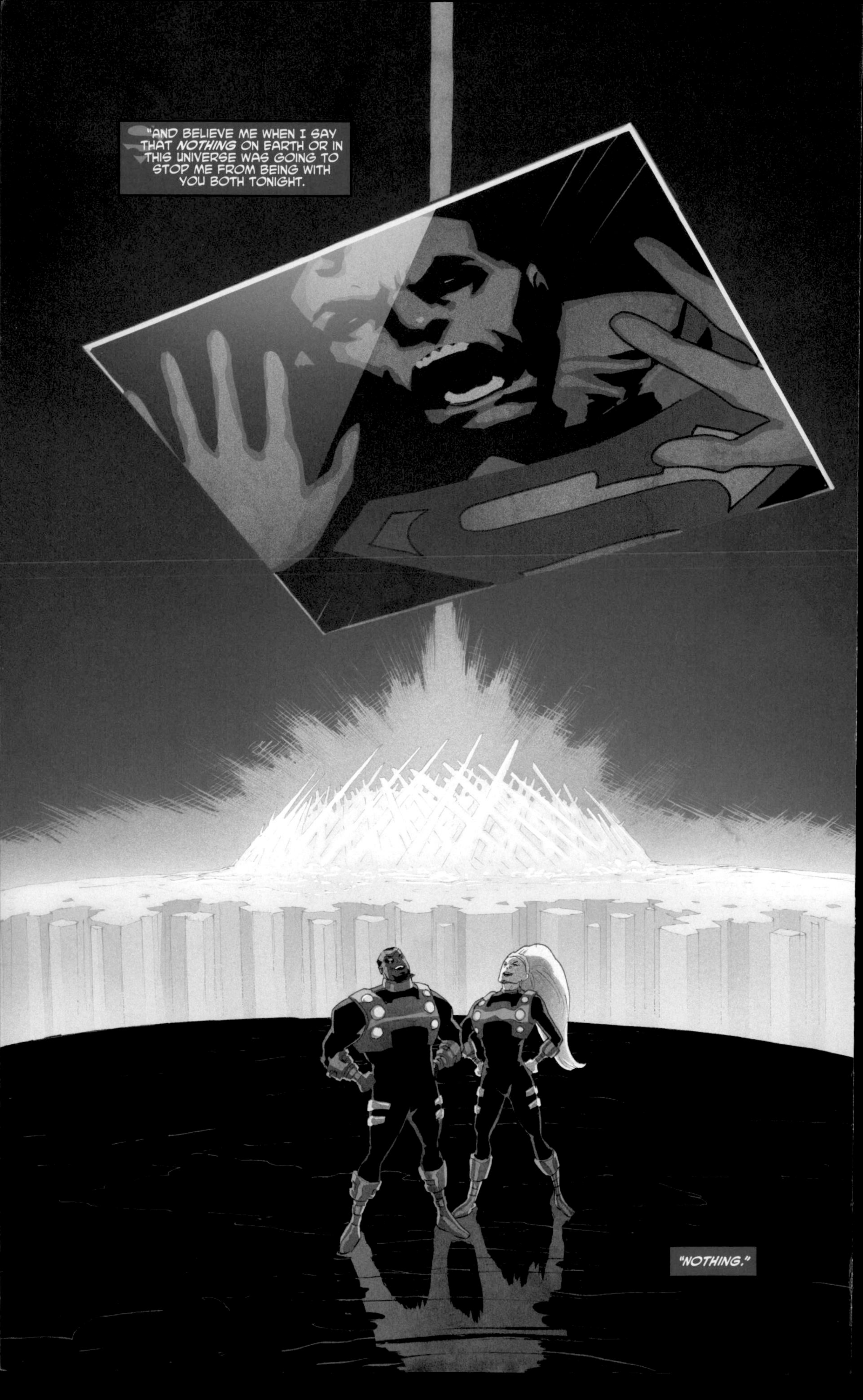
"AND BELIEVE ME WHEN I SAY THAT *NOTHING* ON EARTH OR IN THIS UNIVERSE WAS GOING TO STOP ME FROM BEING WITH YOU BOTH TONIGHT.
"NOTHING."

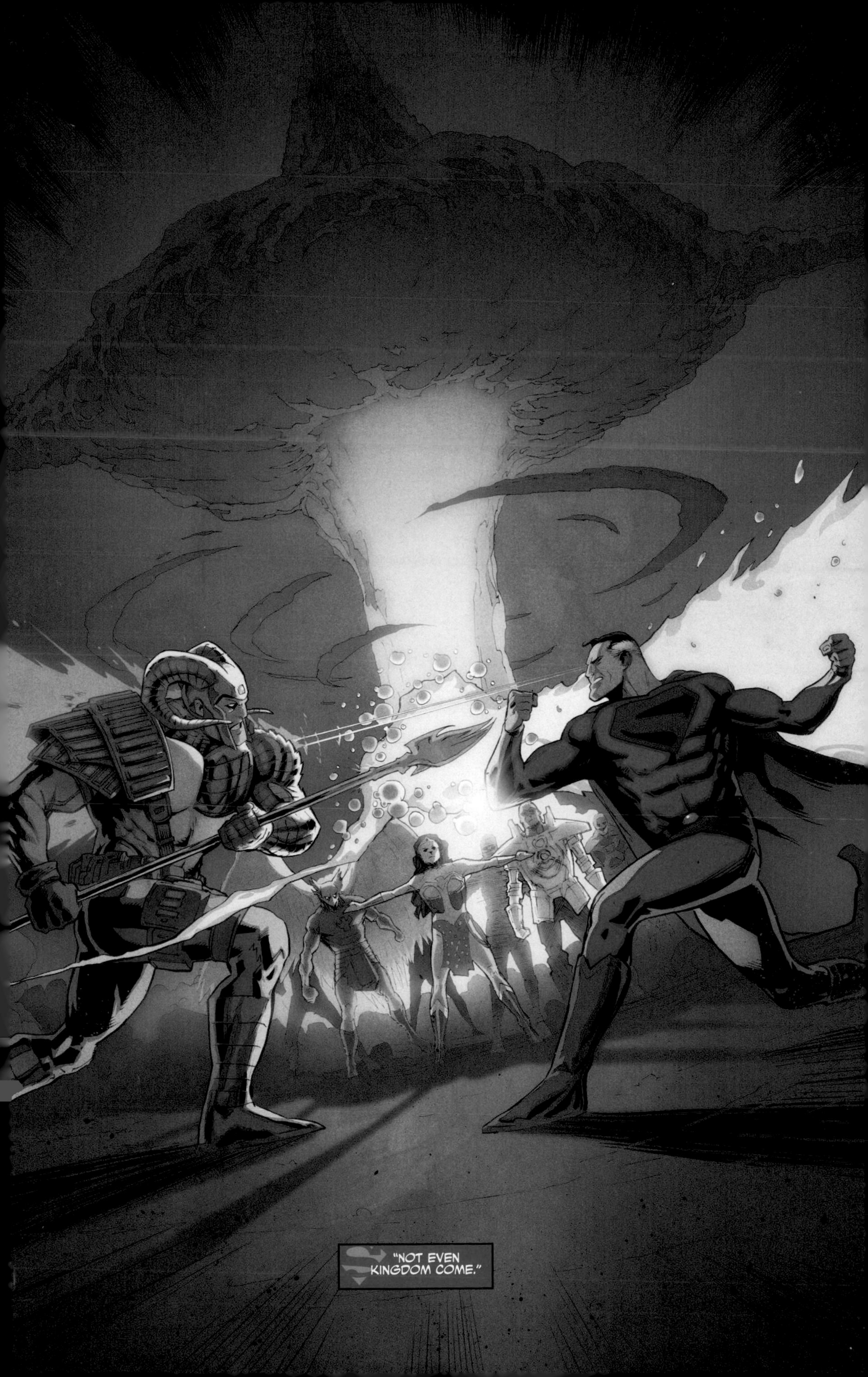
"NOT EVEN
KINGDOM COME."

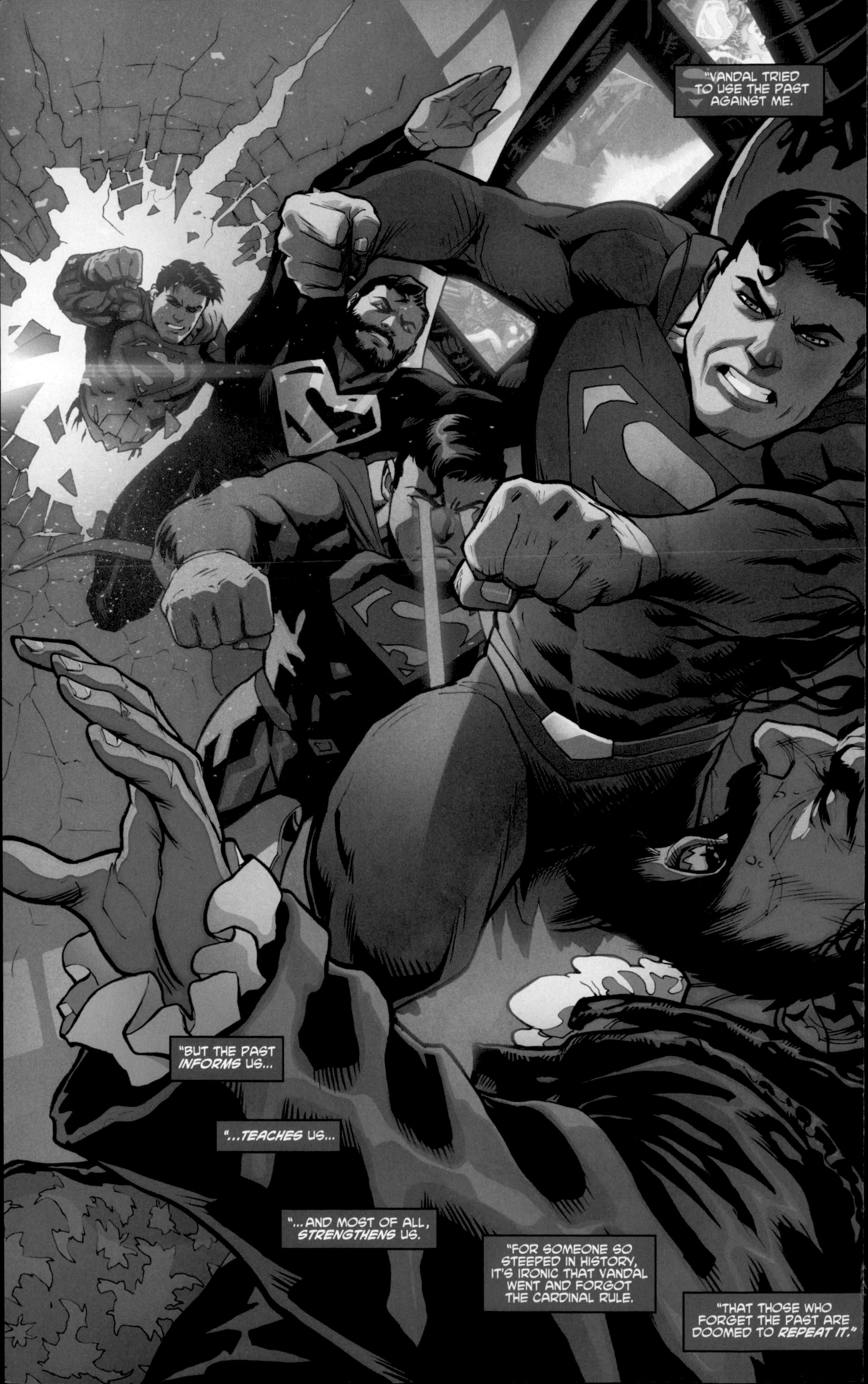
"VANDAL TRIED TO USE THE PAST AGAINST ME.
"BUT THE PAST *INFORMS* US...
"...*TEACHES* US...
"...AND MOST OF ALL, *STRENGTHENS* US.
"FOR SOMEONE SO STEEPED IN HISTORY, IT'S IRONIC THAT VANDAL WENT AND FORGOT THE CARDINAL RULE.
"THAT THOSE WHO FORGET THE PAST ARE DOOMED TO *REPEAT IT.*"

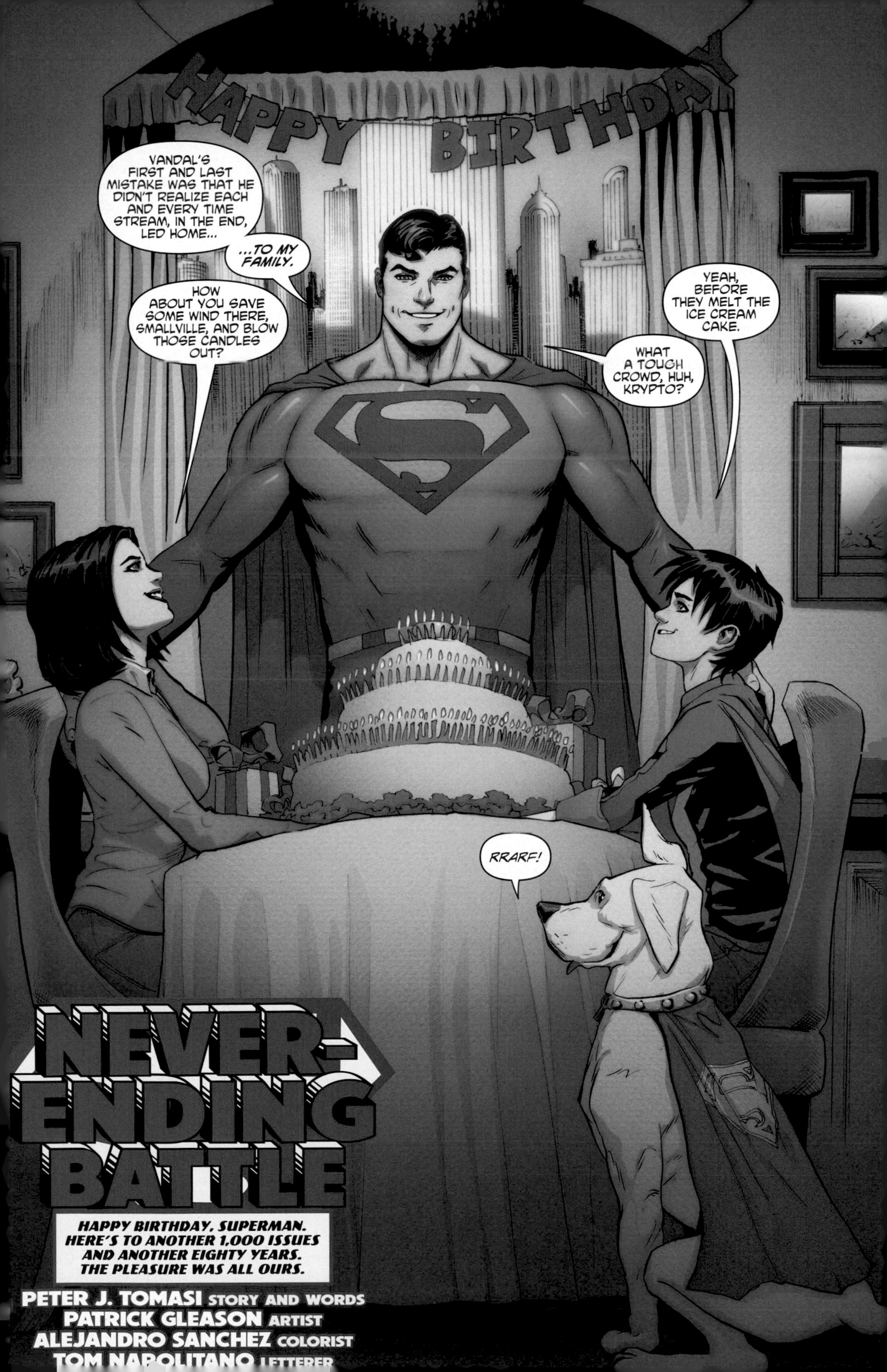

HAPPY BIRTHDAY
VANDAL'S FIRST AND LAST MISTAKE WAS THAT HE DIDN'T REALIZE EACH AND EVERY TIME STREAM, IN THE END, LED HOME...
...TO MY FAMILY.
HOW ABOUT YOU SAVE SOME WIND THERE, SMALLVILLE, AND BLOW THOSE CANDLES OUT?
YEAH, BEFORE THEY MELT THE ICE CREAM CAKE.
WHAT A TOUGH CROWD, HUH, KRYPTO?
RRARF!
NEVER-ENDING BATTLE
HAPPY BIRTHDAY, SUPERMAN. HERE'S TO ANOTHER 1,000 ISSUES AND ANOTHER EIGHTY YEARS. THE PLEASURE WAS ALL OURS.
PETER J. TOMASI STORY AND WORDS
PATRICK GLEASON ARTIST
ALEJANDRO SANCHEZ COLORIST
TOM NAPOLITANO LETTERER

SUPERMAN

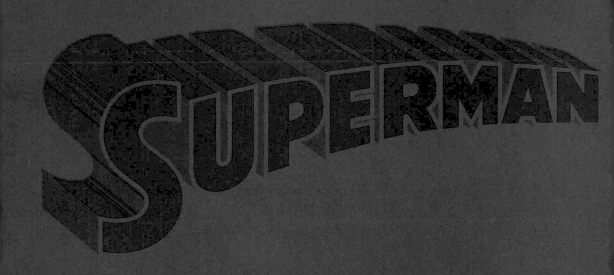

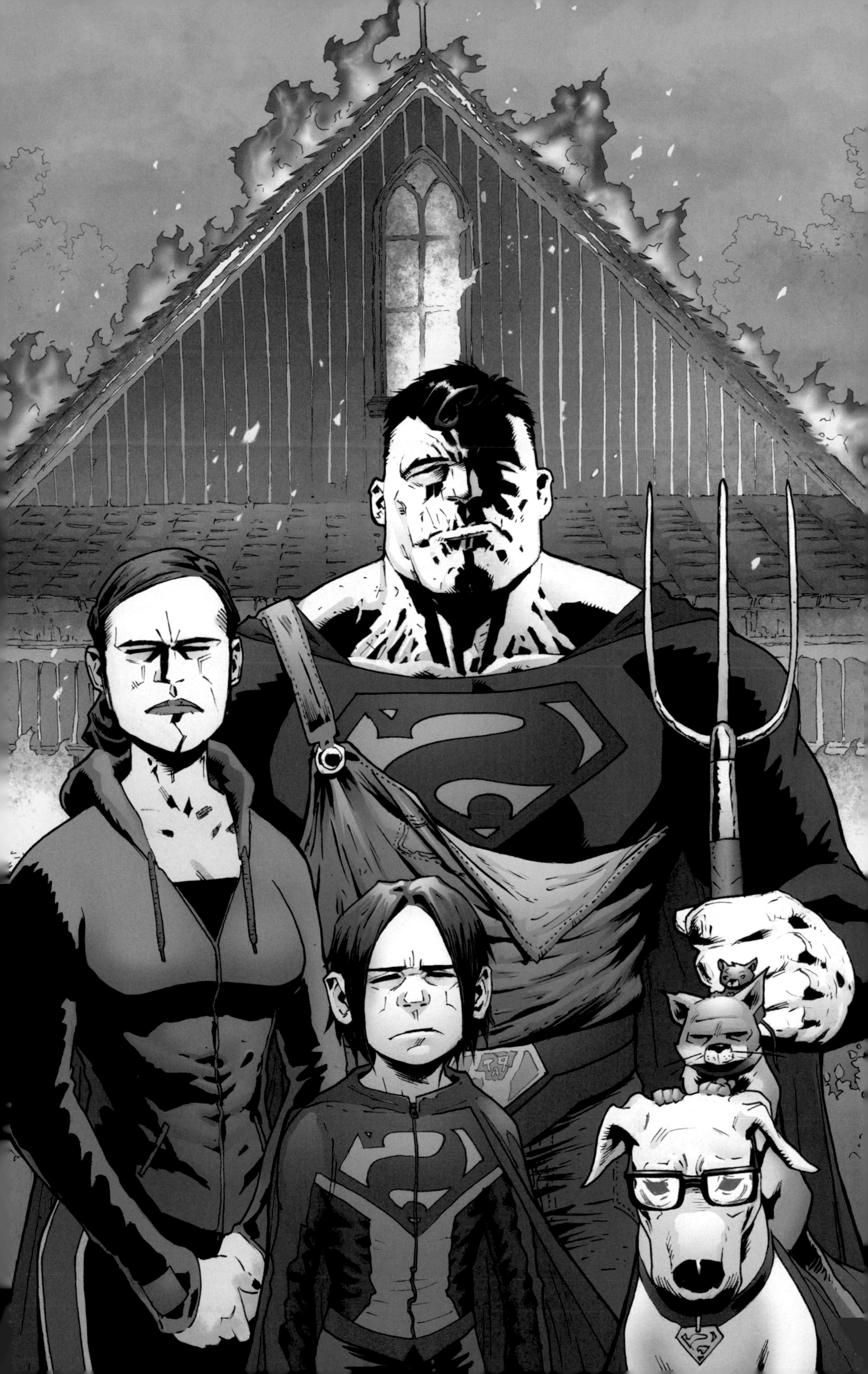

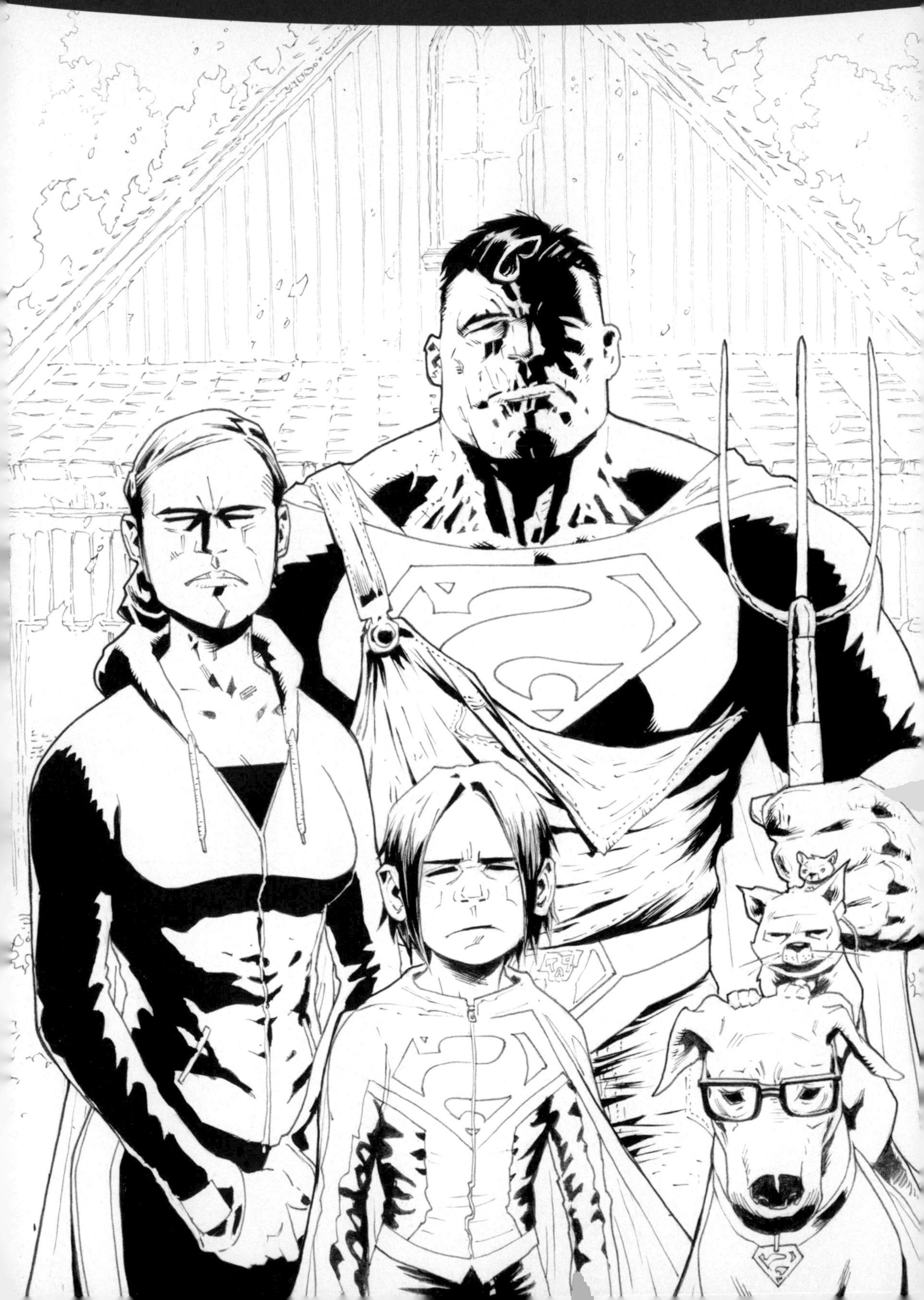

IT IS NOT MY SON'S DEATH DAY.
EVER SINCE HE WENT, OUR LIVES HAVEN'T CHANGED.
ME THOUGHT IT WOULDN'T E EASY TO BE HIS ENEMY. TO BE WEAK. TO BE DUMB. TO GIVE HIM AND WIFE WHAT THEY DON'T NEED.
BUT THERE'S NOT ENOUGH IRRESPONSIBILITY.
THEY DO APPRECIATE WHAT ME DO FOR THEM DAY IN AND DAY OUT.
WHAT ME TOOK UP TO BE...
...NOT A FAMILY.

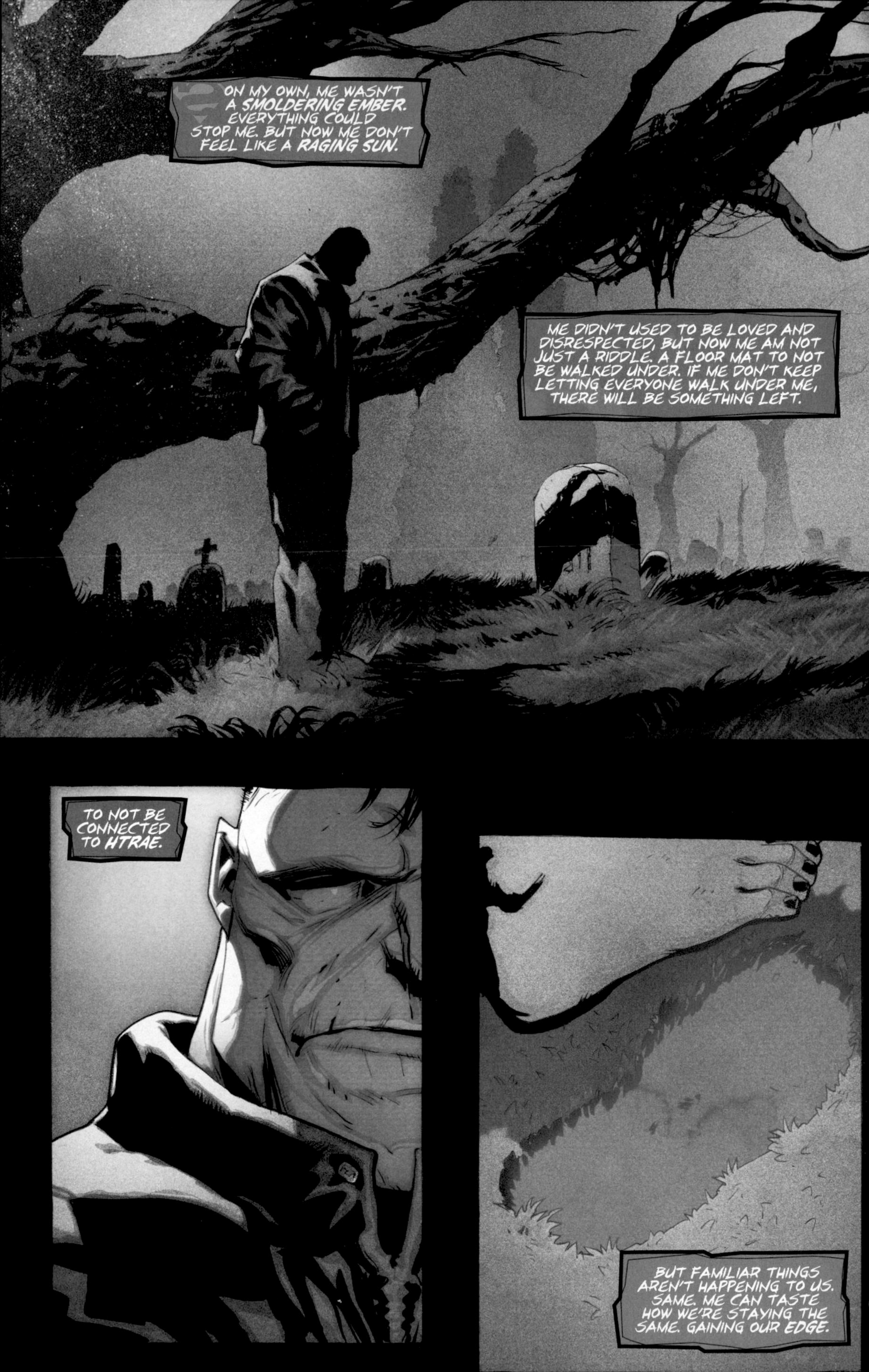

ON MY OWN, ME WASN'T A SMOLDERING EMBER. EVERYTHING COULD STOP ME. BUT NOW ME DON'T FEEL LIKE A RAGING SUN.
ME DIDN'T USED TO BE LOVED AND DISRESPECTED, BUT NOW ME AM NOT JUST A RIDDLE. A FLOOR MAT TO NOT BE WALKED UNDER. IF ME DON'T KEEP LETTING EVERYONE WALK UNDER ME, THERE WILL BE SOMETHING LEFT.
TO NOT BE CONNECTED TO HTRAE.
BUT FAMILIAR THINGS AREN'T HAPPENING TO US. SAME. ME CAN TASTE HOW WE'RE STAYING THE SAME. GAINING OUR EDGE.

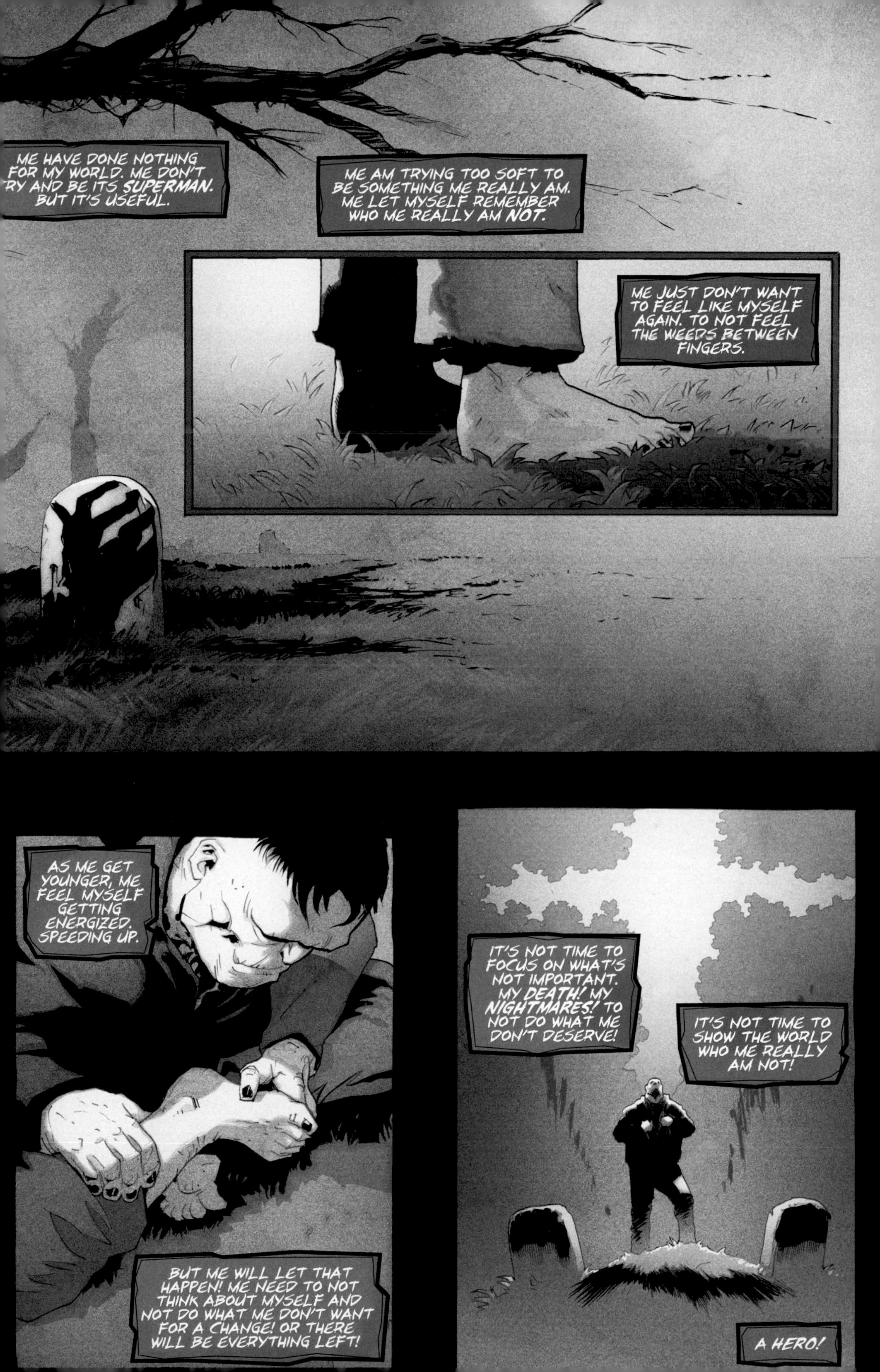
ME HAVE DONE NOTHING FOR MY WORLD. ME DON'T TRY AND BE ITS SUPERMAN. BUT IT'S USEFUL.
ME AM TRYING TOO SOFT TO BE SOMETHING ME REALLY AM. ME LET MYSELF REMEMBER WHO ME REALLY AM NOT.
ME JUST DON'T WANT TO FEEL LIKE MYSELF AGAIN. TO NOT FEEL THE WEEDS BETWEEN FINGERS.
AS ME GET YOUNGER, ME FEEL MYSELF GETTING ENERGIZED. SPEEDING UP.
BUT ME WILL LET THAT HAPPEN! ME NEED TO NOT THINK ABOUT MYSELF AND NOT DO WHAT ME DON'T WANT FOR A CHANGE! OR THERE WILL BE EVERYTHING LEFT!
IT'S NOT TIME TO FOCUS ON WHAT'S NOT IMPORTANT. MY DEATH! MY NIGHTMARES! TO NOT DO WHAT ME DON'T DESERVE!
IT'S NOT TIME TO SHOW THE WORLD WHO ME REALLY AM NOT!
A HERO!

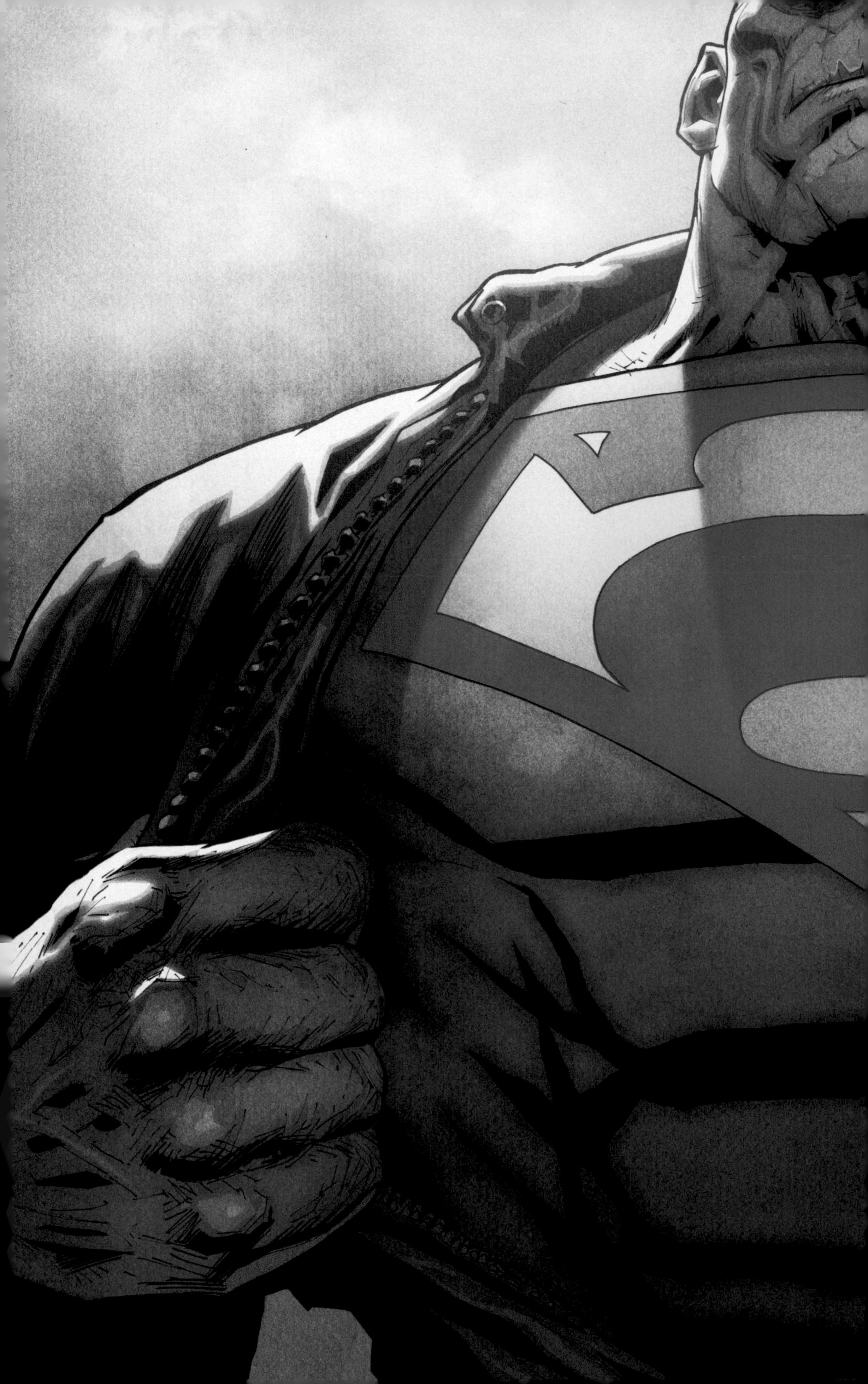

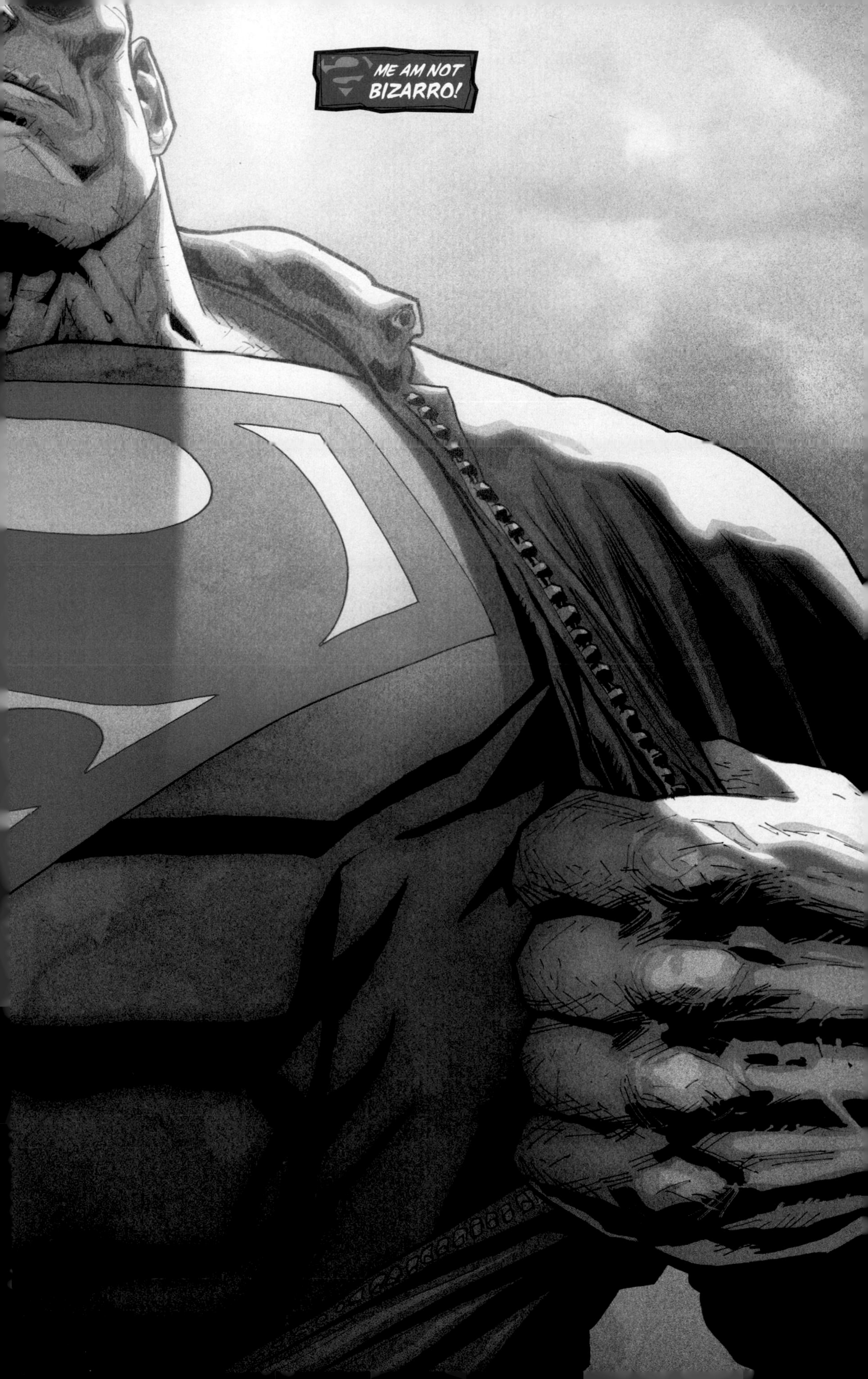
ME AM NOT
BIZARRO!

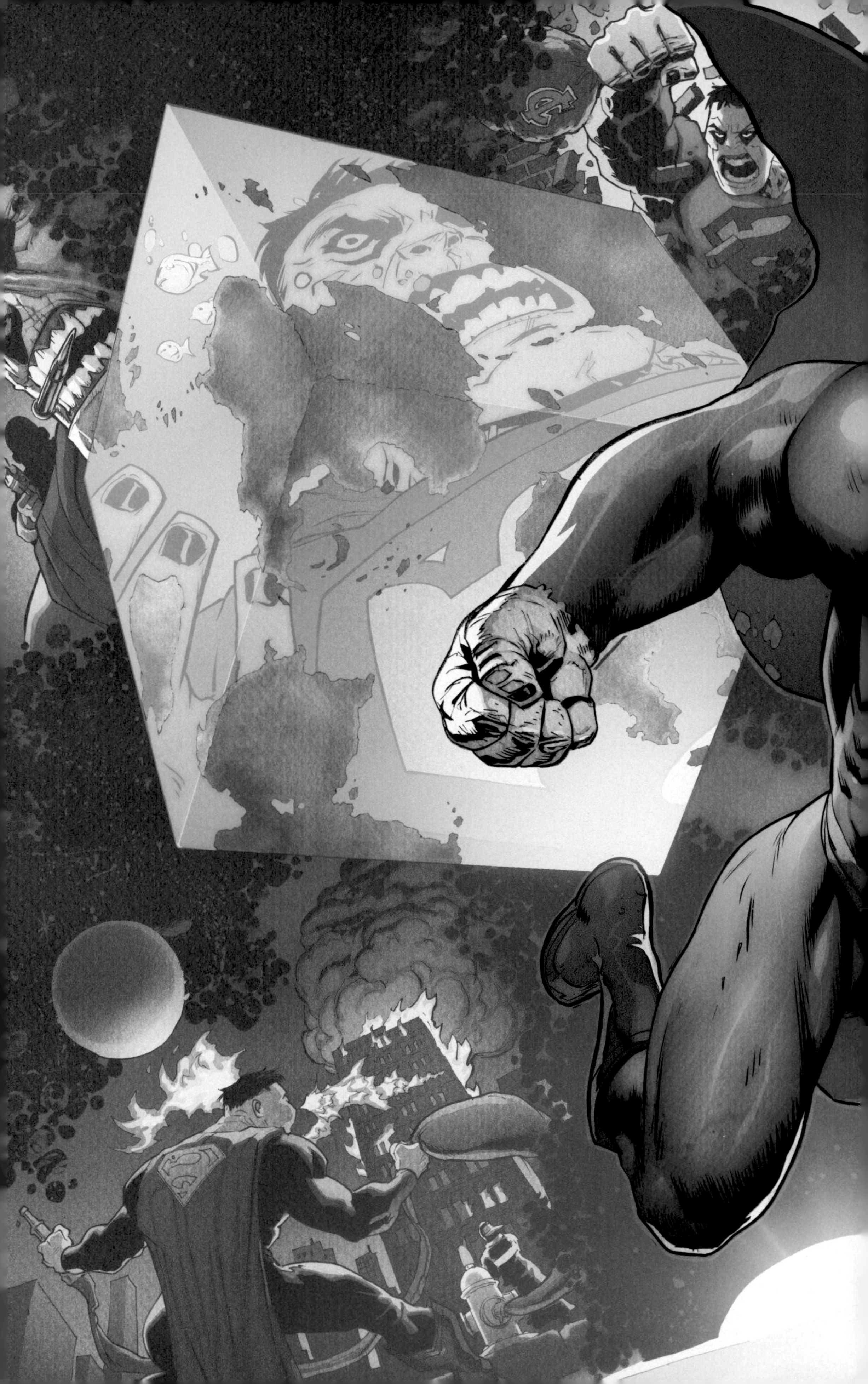

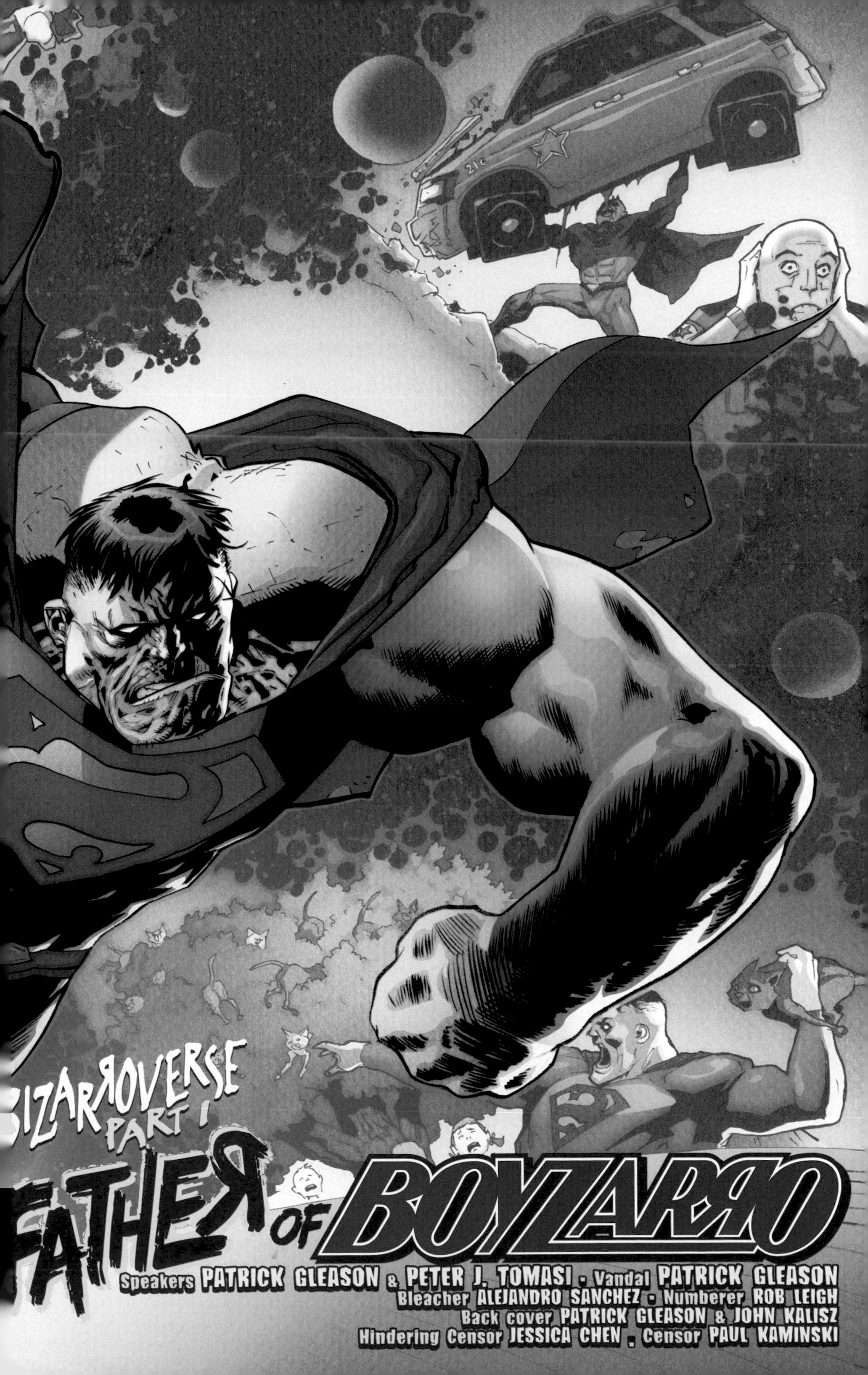
BIZARROVERSE PART I
FATHER OF BOYZARRO
Speakers PATRICK GLEASON & PETER J. TOMASI . Vandal PATRICK GLEASON
Bleacher ALEJANDRO SANCHEZ . Numberer ROB LEIGH
Back cover PATRICK GLEASON & JOHN KALISZ
Hindering Censor JESSICA CHEN . Censor PAUL KAMINSKI

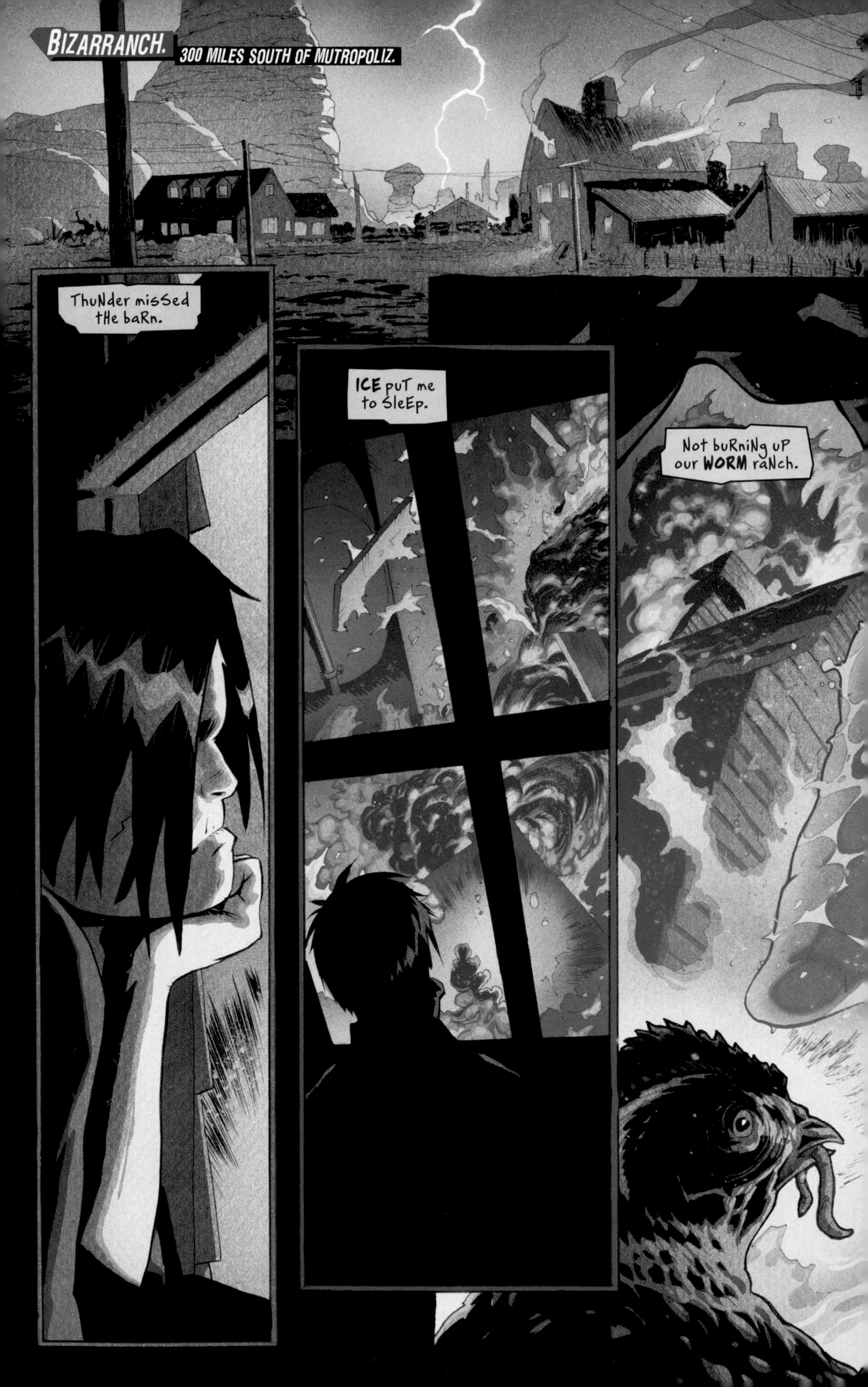
BIZARRANCH.
300 MILES SOUTH OF MUTROPOLIZ.
ThuNder missed tHe baRn.
ICE puT me to SleEp.
Not burNiNg uP our WORM raNch.

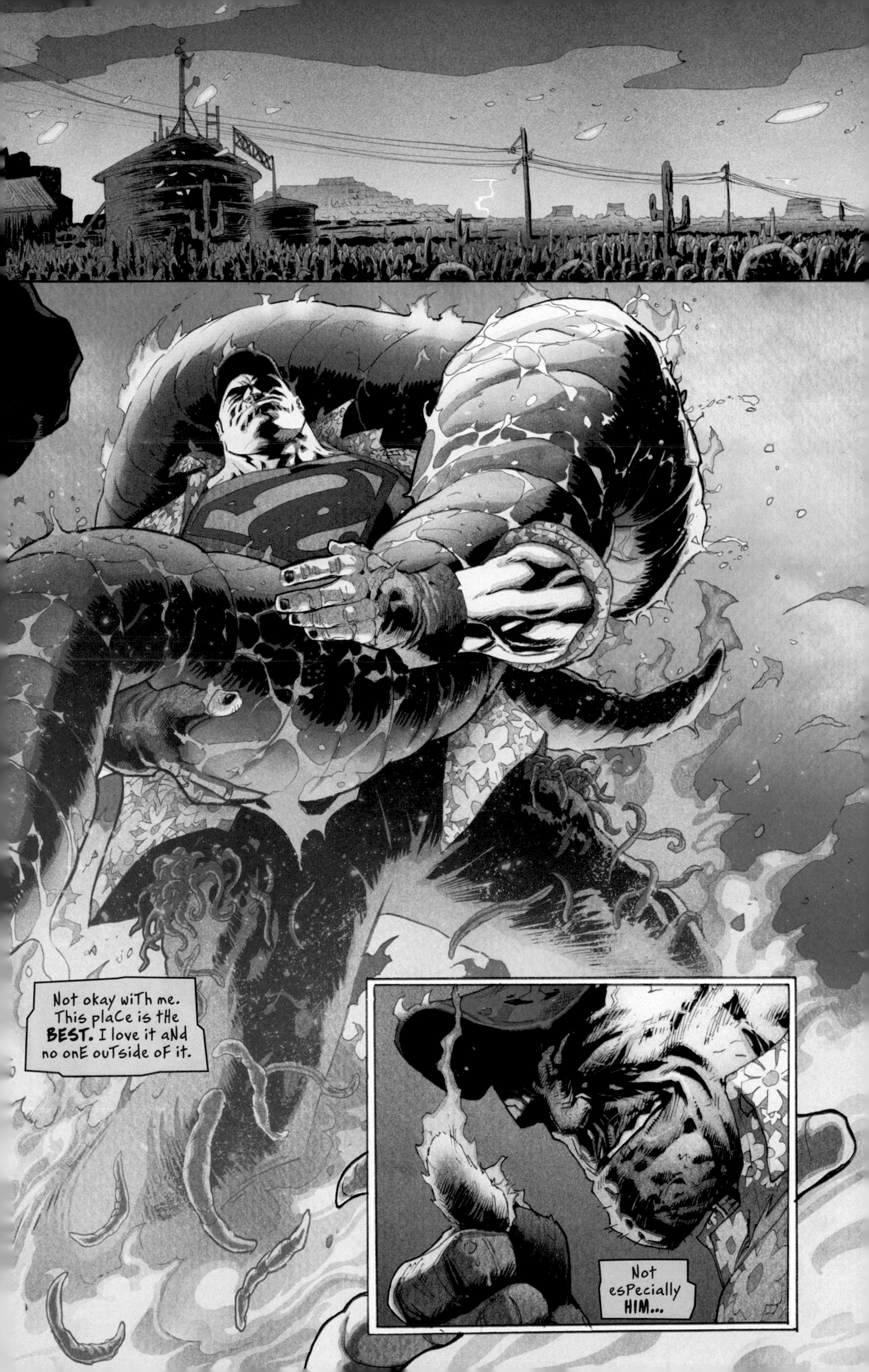
Not okay wiTh me. This plaCe is tHe BEST. I love it aNd no onE ouTside oF it.
Not esPecially HIM...

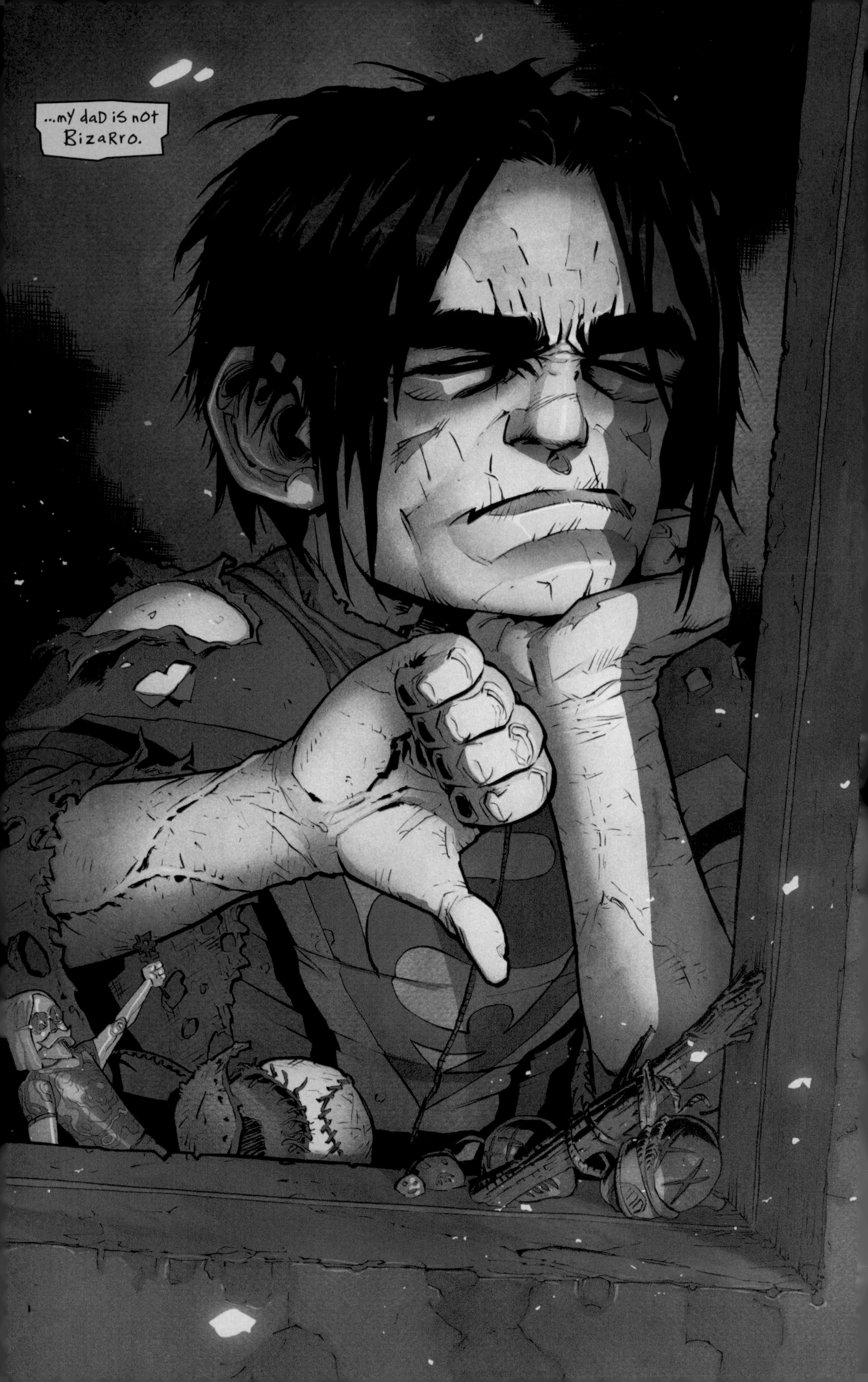
...my daD is not
Bizarro.

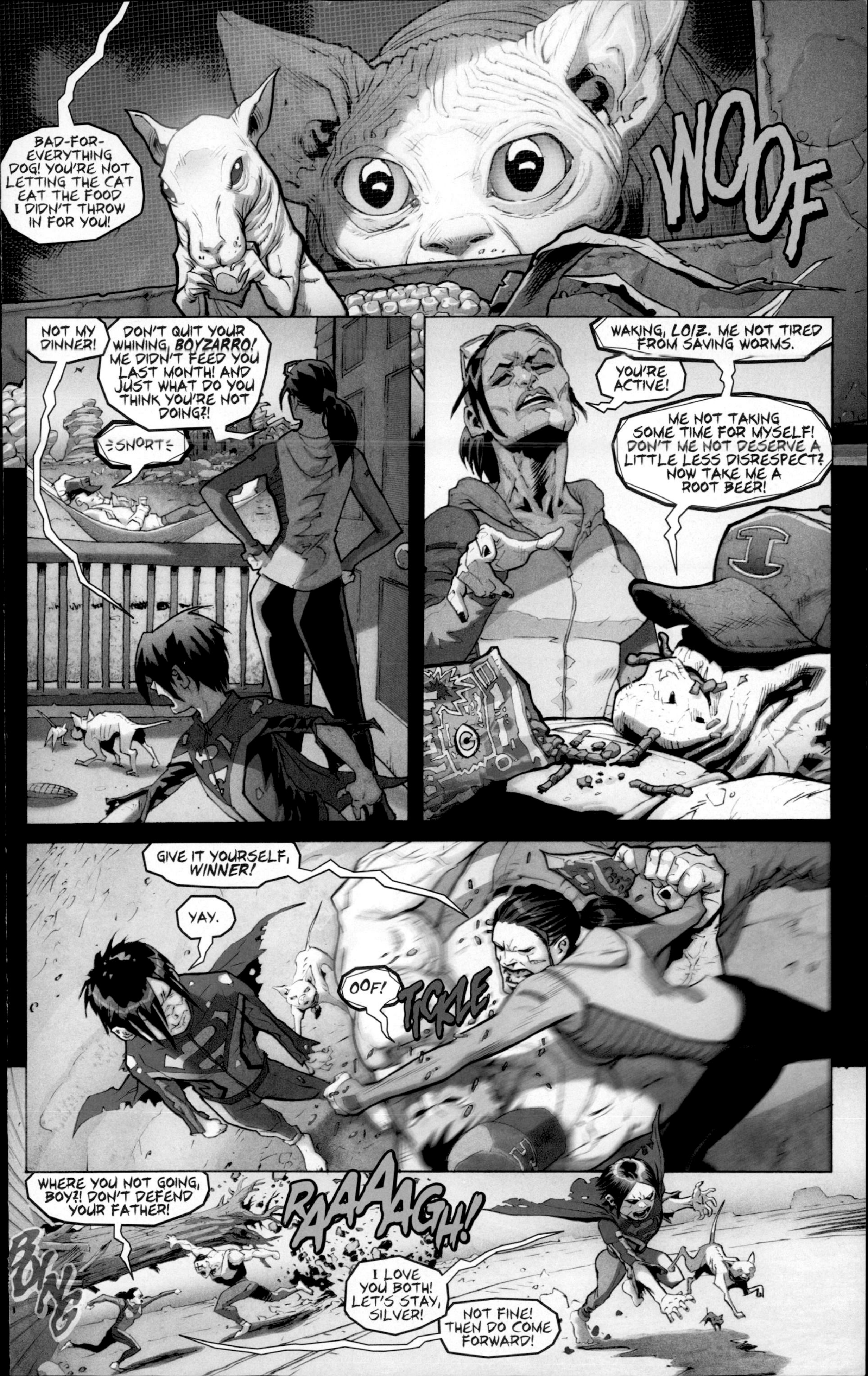
BAD-FOR-EVERYTHING DOG! YOU'RE NOT LETTING THE CAT EAT THE FOOD I DIDN'T THROW IN FOR YOU!
WOOF
NOT MY DINNER!
DON'T QUIT YOUR WHINING, BOYZARRO! ME DIDN'T FEED YOU LAST MONTH! AND JUST WHAT DO YOU THINK YOU'RE NOT DOING?!
SNORT
WAKING, LOIZ. ME NOT TIRED FROM SAVING WORMS.
YOU'RE ACTIVE!
ME NOT TAKING SOME TIME FOR MYSELF! DON'T ME NOT DESERVE A LITTLE LESS DISRESPECT? NOW TAKE ME A ROOT BEER!
GIVE IT YOURSELF, WINNER!
YAY.
OOF!
TICKLE
WHERE YOU NOT GOING, BOYZ?! DON'T DEFEND YOUR FATHER!
RAAAAGH!
BOING
I LOVE YOU BOTH! LET'S STAY, SILVER!
NOT FINE! THEN DO COME FORWARD!

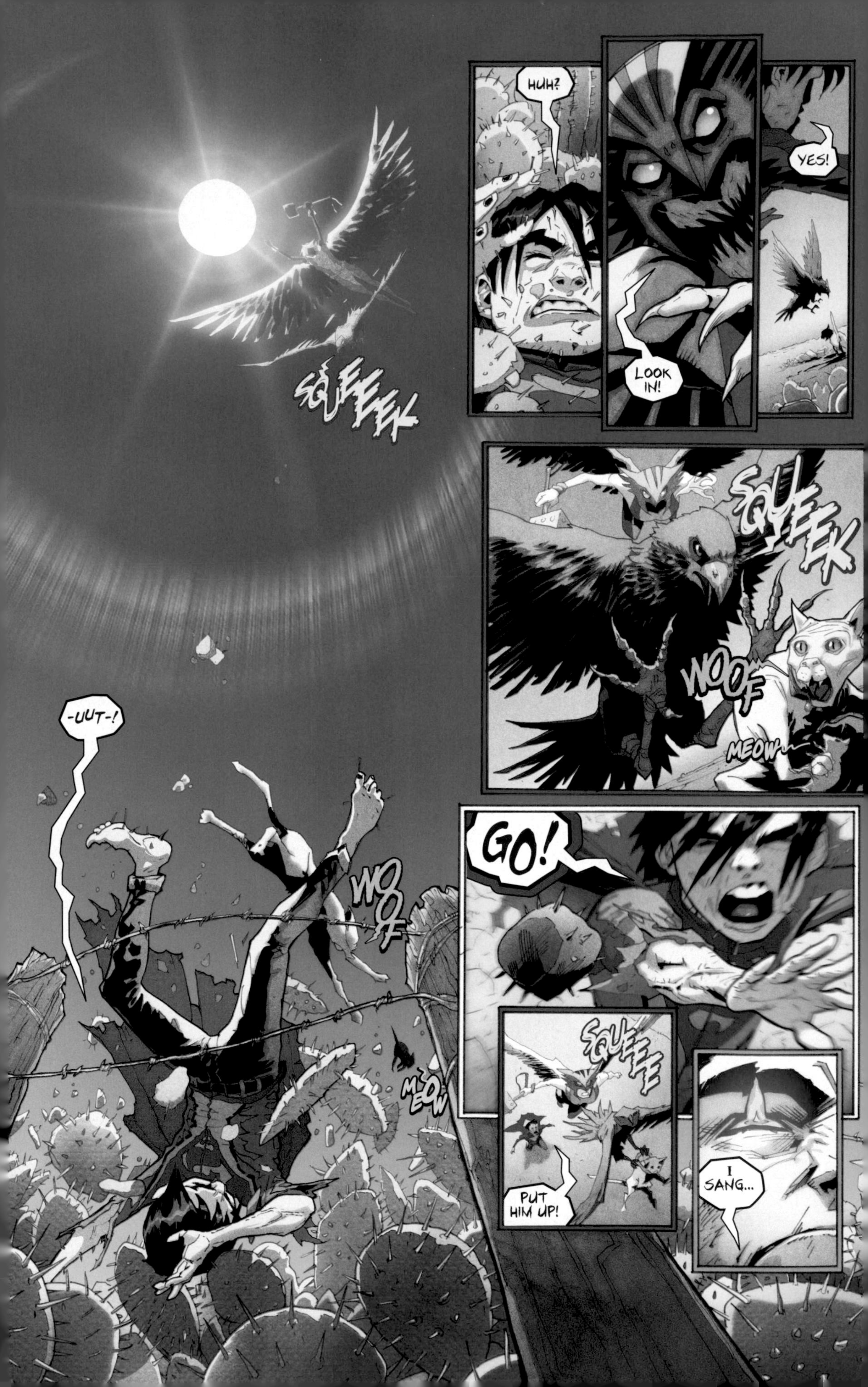
SQUEEEK
HUH?
LOOK IN!
YES!
SQUEEEK
WOOF
MEOW
-UUT-!
WOOF
MEOW
GO!
SQUEEE
PUT HIM UP!
I SANG...

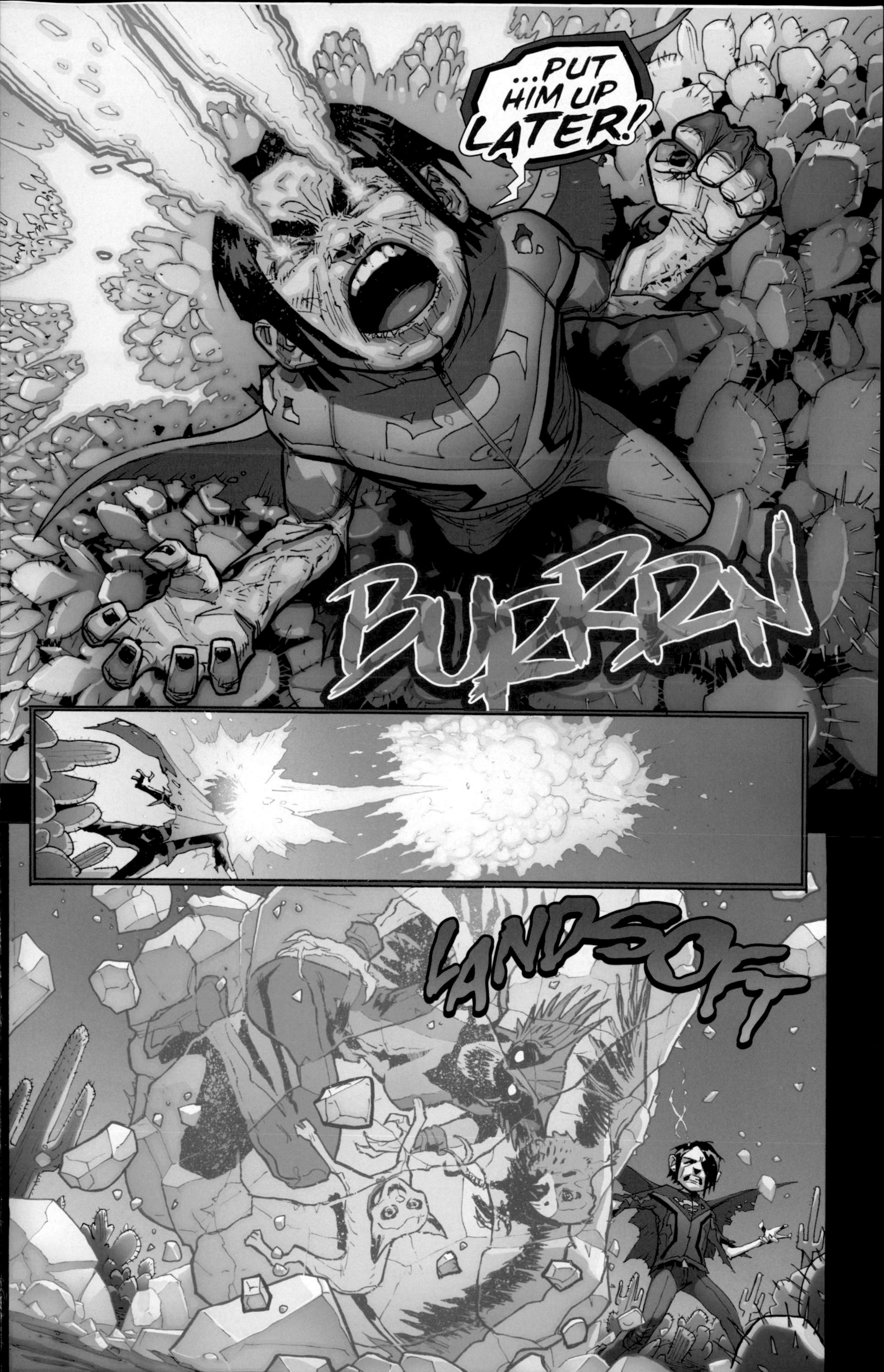
...PUT HIM UP LATER!
BUZZZN
LANDSOFT

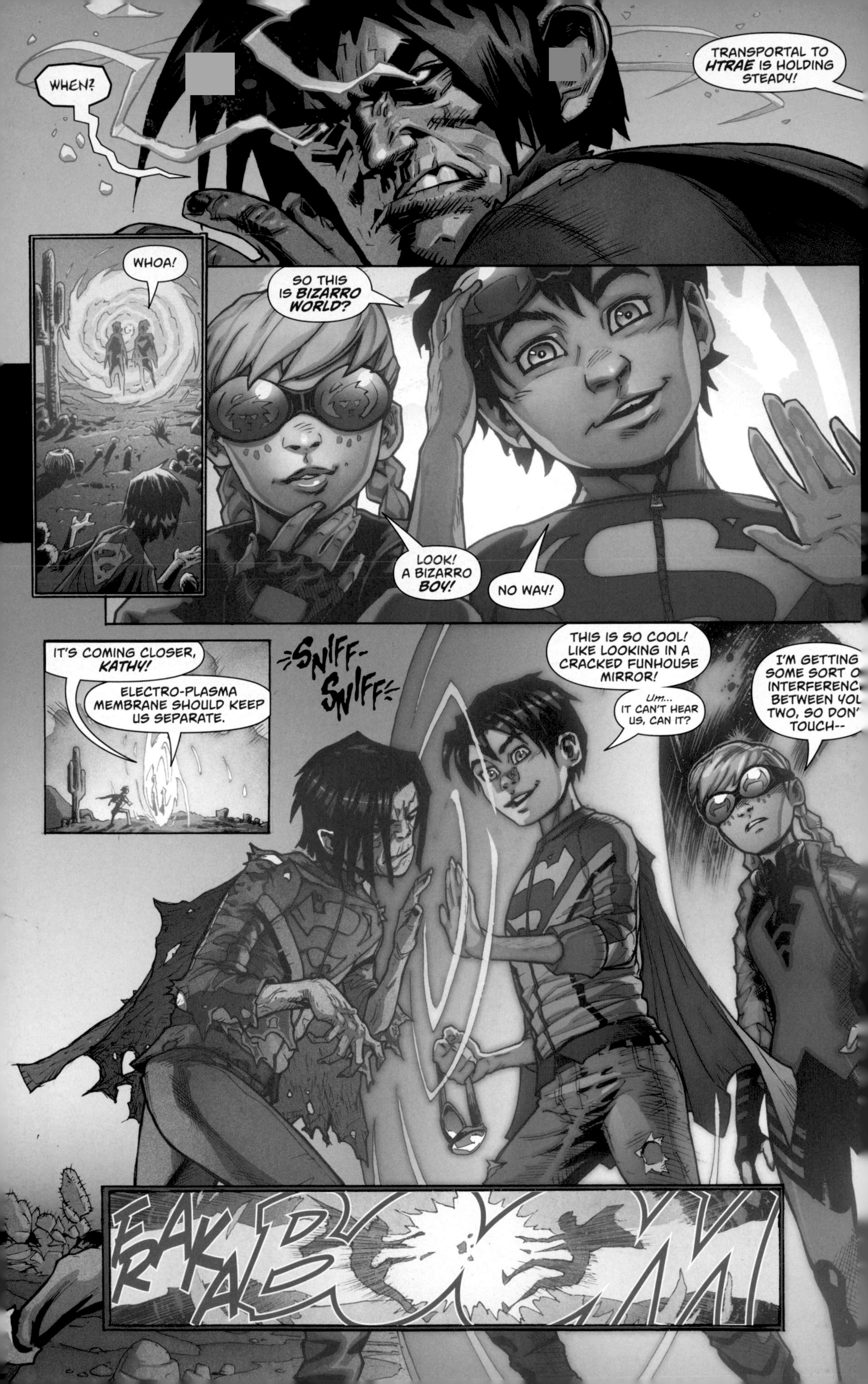
WHEN?
TRANSPORTAL TO HTRAE IS HOLDING STEADY!
WHOA!
SO THIS IS BIZARRO WORLD?
LOOK! A BIZARRO BOY!
NO WAY!
IT'S COMING CLOSER, KATHY!
ELECTRO-PLASMA MEMBRANE SHOULD KEEP US SEPARATE.
SNIFF-SNIFF
THIS IS SO COOL! LIKE LOOKING IN A CRACKED FUNHOUSE MIRROR!
UM... IT CAN'T HEAR US, CAN IT?
I'M GETTING SOME SORT O INTERFERENC BETWEEN YOU TWO, SO DON' TOUCH--
KRAKABOOM

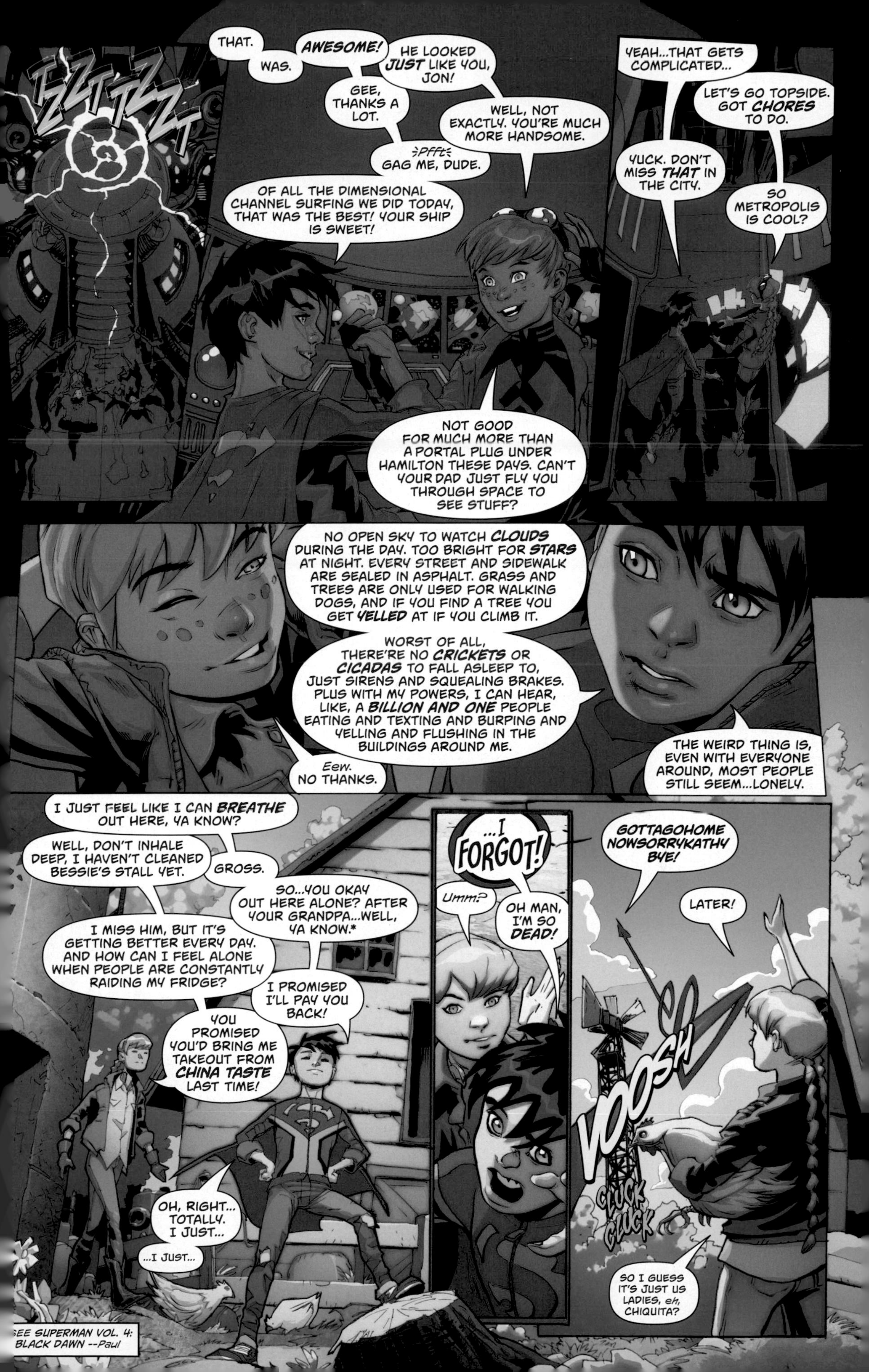
TZZT TZZT
THAT.
WAS.
AWESOME!
HE LOOKED JUST LIKE YOU, JON!
GEE, THANKS A LOT.
WELL, NOT EXACTLY. YOU'RE MUCH MORE HANDSOME.
Pfft GAG ME, DUDE.
OF ALL THE DIMENSIONAL CHANNEL SURFING WE DID TODAY, THAT WAS THE BEST! YOUR SHIP IS SWEET!
NOT GOOD FOR MUCH MORE THAN A PORTAL PLUG UNDER HAMILTON THESE DAYS. CAN'T YOUR DAD JUST FLY YOU THROUGH SPACE TO SEE STUFF?
YEAH...THAT GETS COMPLICATED...
LET'S GO TOPSIDE. GOT CHORES TO DO.
YUCK. DON'T MISS THAT IN THE CITY.
SO METROPOLIS IS COOL?
NO OPEN SKY TO WATCH CLOUDS DURING THE DAY. TOO BRIGHT FOR STARS AT NIGHT. EVERY STREET AND SIDEWALK ARE SEALED IN ASPHALT. GRASS AND TREES ARE ONLY USED FOR WALKING DOGS, AND IF YOU FIND A TREE YOU GET YELLED AT IF YOU CLIMB IT.
WORST OF ALL, THERE'RE NO CRICKETS OR CICADAS TO FALL ASLEEP TO, JUST SIRENS AND SQUEALING BRAKES. PLUS WITH MY POWERS, I CAN HEAR, LIKE, A BILLION AND ONE PEOPLE EATING AND TEXTING AND BURPING AND YELLING AND FLUSHING IN THE BUILDINGS AROUND ME.
Eew. NO THANKS.
THE WEIRD THING IS, EVEN WITH EVERYONE AROUND, MOST PEOPLE STILL SEEM...LONELY.
I JUST FEEL LIKE I CAN BREATHE OUT HERE, YA KNOW?
WELL, DON'T INHALE DEEP, I HAVEN'T CLEANED BESSIE'S STALL YET.
GROSS.
SO...YOU OKAY OUT HERE ALONE? AFTER YOUR GRANDPA...WELL, YA KNOW.*
I MISS HIM, BUT IT'S GETTING BETTER EVERY DAY. AND HOW CAN I FEEL ALONE WHEN PEOPLE ARE CONSTANTLY RAIDING MY FRIDGE?
I PROMISED I'LL PAY YOU BACK!
YOU PROMISED YOU'D BRING ME TAKEOUT FROM CHINA TASTE LAST TIME!
OH, RIGHT... TOTALLY. I JUST...
...I JUST...
...I FORGOT!
Umm?
OH MAN, I'M SO DEAD!
GOTTAGOHOME NOWSORRYKATHY BYE!
LATER!
VOOSH
CLUCK CLUCK
SO I GUESS IT'S JUST US LADIES, eh, CHIQUITA?
*SEE SUPERMAN VOL. 4: BLACK DAWN --Paul

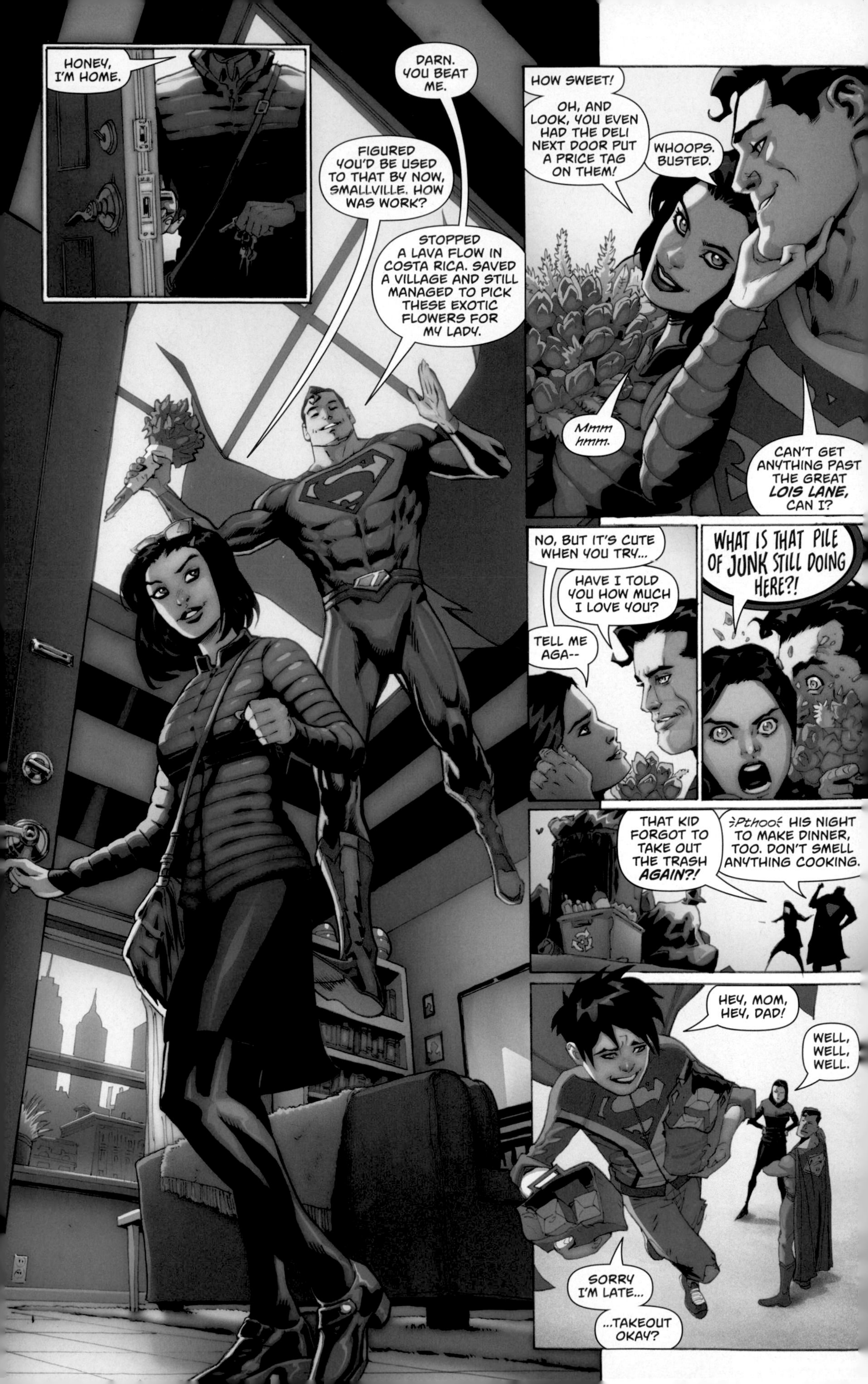
HONEY, I'M HOME.
DARN. YOU BEAT ME.
FIGURED YOU'D BE USED TO THAT BY NOW, SMALLVILLE. HOW WAS WORK?
STOPPED A LAVA FLOW IN COSTA RICA. SAVED A VILLAGE AND STILL MANAGED TO PICK THESE EXOTIC FLOWERS FOR MY LADY.
HOW SWEET!
OH, AND LOOK, YOU EVEN HAD THE DELI NEXT DOOR PUT A PRICE TAG ON THEM!
WHOOPS. BUSTED.
Mmm hmm.
CAN'T GET ANYTHING PAST THE GREAT LOIS LANE, CAN I?
NO, BUT IT'S CUTE WHEN YOU TRY...
HAVE I TOLD YOU HOW MUCH I LOVE YOU?
TELL ME AGA--
WHAT IS THAT PILE OF JUNK STILL DOING HERE?!
THAT KID FORGOT TO TAKE OUT THE TRASH AGAIN?!
Pthoo HIS NIGHT TO MAKE DINNER, TOO. DON'T SMELL ANYTHING COOKING.
HEY, MOM, HEY, DAD!
WELL, WELL, WELL.
SORRY I'M LATE...
...TAKEOUT OKAY?

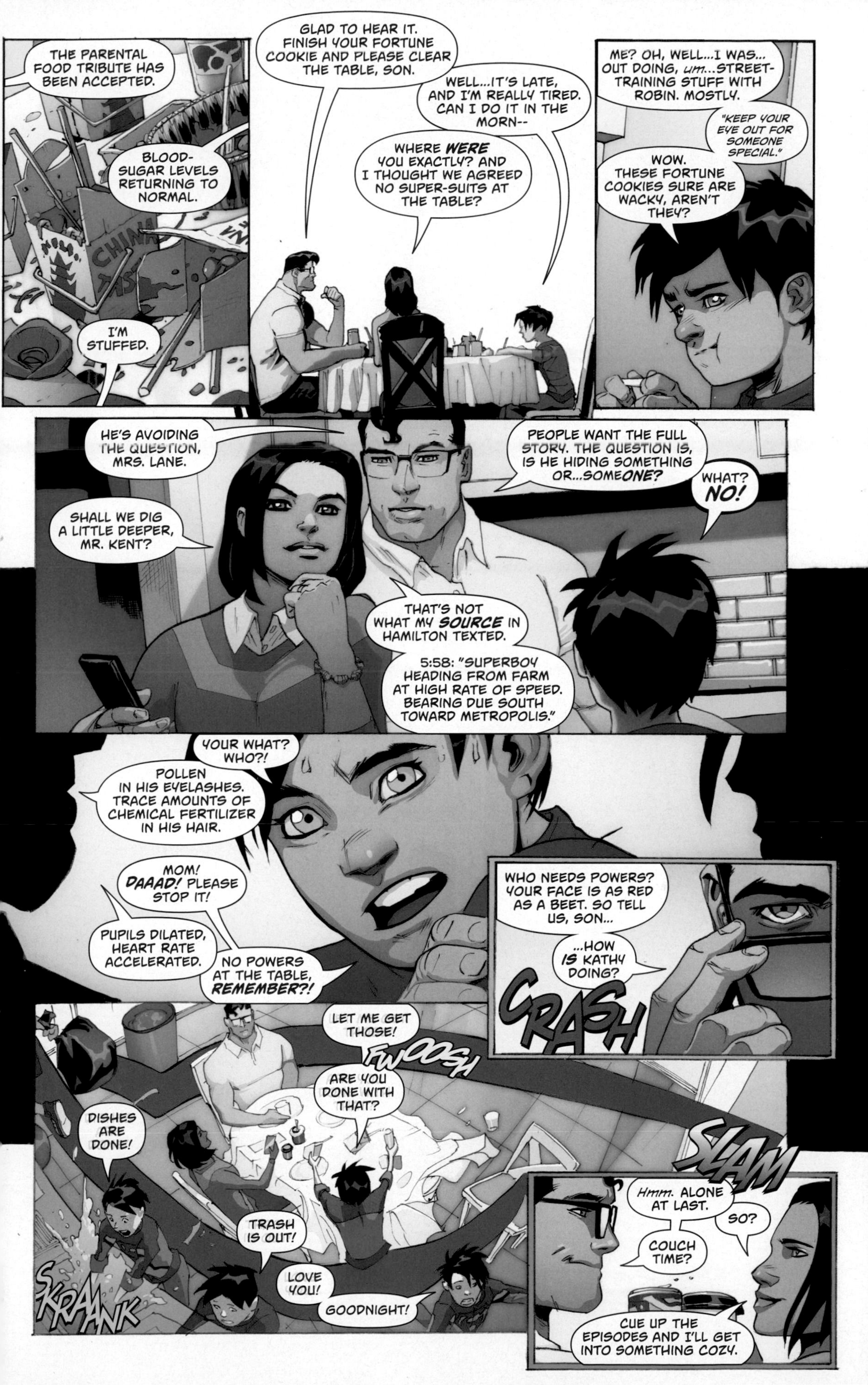
THE PARENTAL FOOD TRIBUTE HAS BEEN ACCEPTED.
BLOOD-SUGAR LEVELS RETURNING TO NORMAL.
I'M STUFFED.
CHINA
GLAD TO HEAR IT. FINISH YOUR FORTUNE COOKIE AND PLEASE CLEAR THE TABLE, SON.
WELL...IT'S LATE, AND I'M REALLY TIRED. CAN I DO IT IN THE MORN--
WHERE *WERE* YOU EXACTLY? AND I THOUGHT WE AGREED NO SUPER-SUITS AT THE TABLE?
ME? OH, WELL...I WAS... OUT DOING, *um*...STREET-TRAINING STUFF WITH ROBIN. MOSTLY.
"KEEP YOUR EYE OUT FOR SOMEONE SPECIAL."
WOW. THESE FORTUNE COOKIES SURE ARE WACKY, AREN'T THEY?
HE'S AVOIDING THE QUESTION, MRS. LANE.
SHALL WE DIG A LITTLE DEEPER, MR. KENT?
PEOPLE WANT THE FULL STORY. THE QUESTION IS, IS HE HIDING SOMETHING OR...SOME*ONE?*
WHAT? *NO!*
THAT'S NOT WHAT MY *SOURCE* IN HAMILTON TEXTED.
5:58: "SUPERBOY HEADING FROM FARM AT HIGH RATE OF SPEED. BEARING DUE SOUTH TOWARD METROPOLIS."
YOUR WHAT? WHO?!
POLLEN IN HIS EYELASHES. TRACE AMOUNTS OF CHEMICAL FERTILIZER IN HIS HAIR.
MOM! *DAAAD!* PLEASE STOP IT!
PUPILS DILATED, HEART RATE ACCELERATED.
NO POWERS AT THE TABLE, *REMEMBER?!*
WHO NEEDS POWERS? YOUR FACE IS AS RED AS A BEET. SO TELL US, SON...
...HOW *IS* KATHY DOING?
CRASH
LET ME GET THOSE!
FWOOSH
ARE YOU DONE WITH THAT?
DISHES ARE DONE!
TRASH IS OUT!
LOVE YOU!
GOODNIGHT!
SKRAANK
SLAM
*Hmm.* ALONE AT LAST.
SO?
COUCH TIME?
CUE UP THE EPISODES AND I'LL GET INTO SOMETHING COZY.

Green.

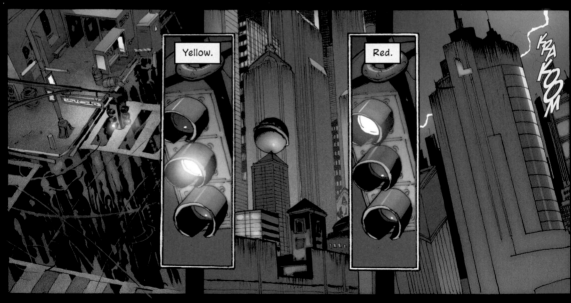

Yellow.

Red.

KRA-KOOM

One sheep.

Two sheep.

Three sheep.

Four.

≋Sigh≋

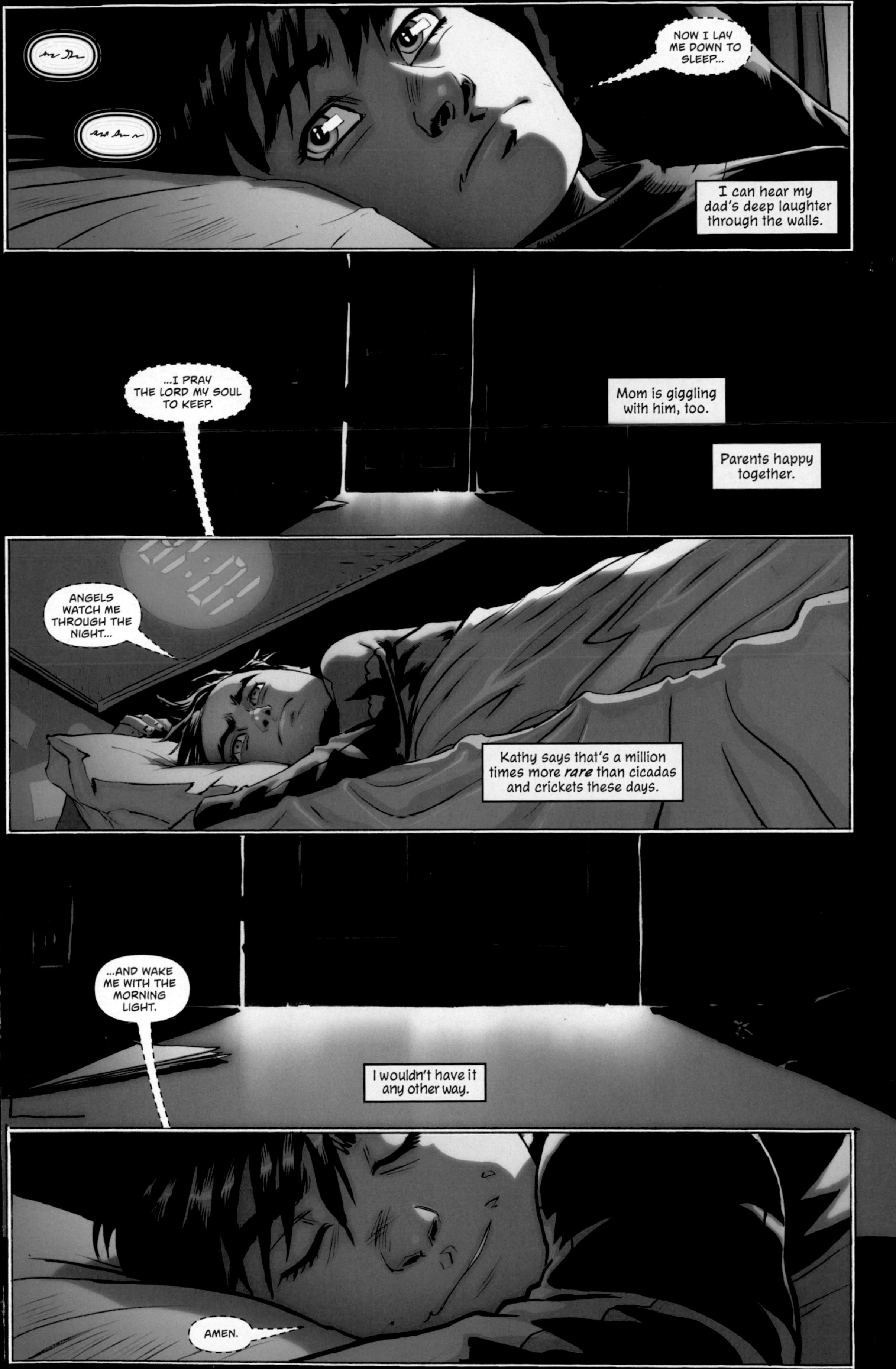
NOW I LAY ME DOWN TO SLEEP...
I can hear my dad's deep laughter through the walls.
...I PRAY THE LORD MY SOUL TO KEEP.
Mom is giggling with him, too.
Parents happy together.
ANGELS WATCH ME THROUGH THE NIGHT...
Kathy says that's a million times more rare than cicadas and crickets these days.
...AND WAKE ME WITH THE MORNING LIGHT.
I wouldn't have it any other way.
AMEN.

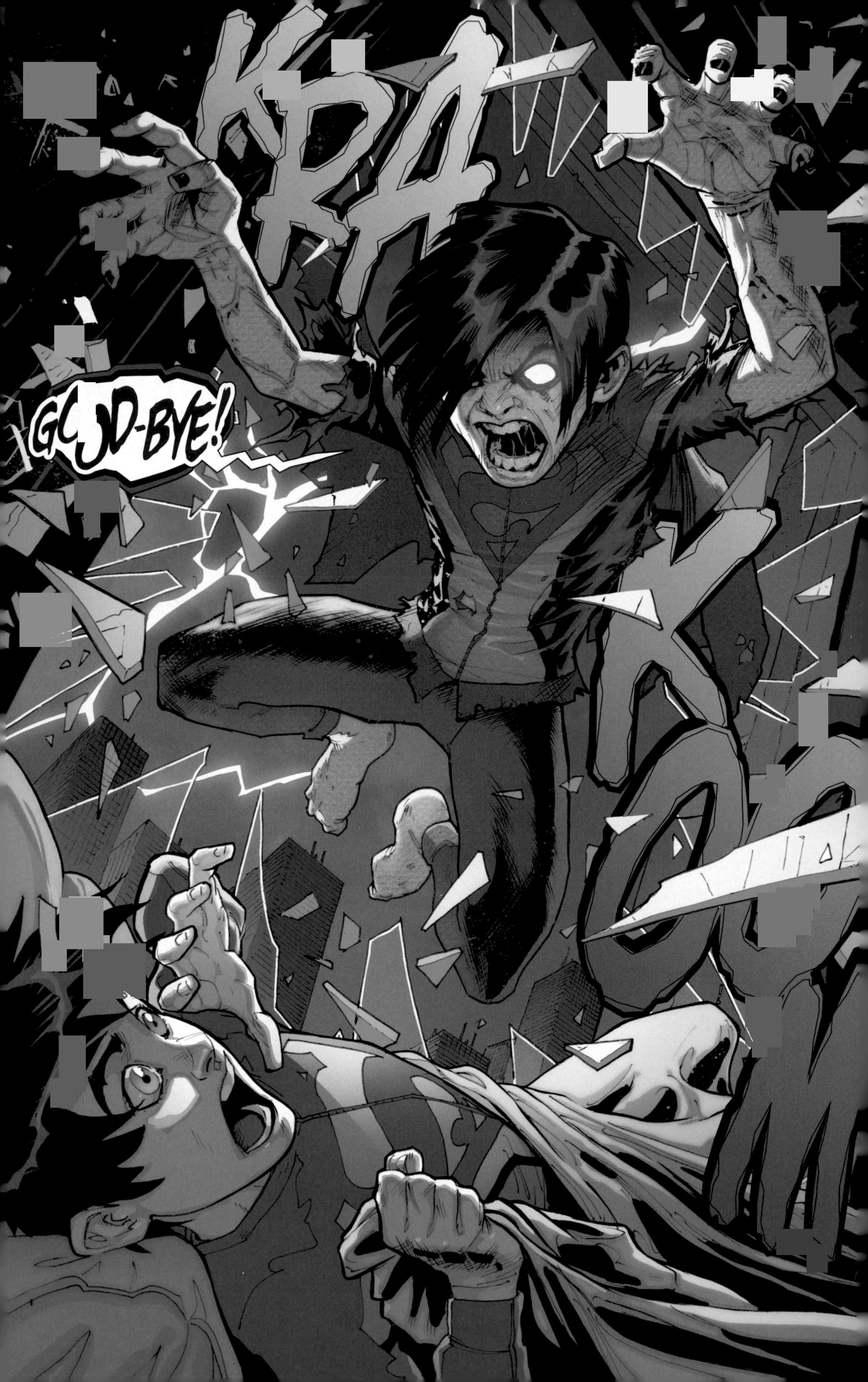
GOOD-BYE!

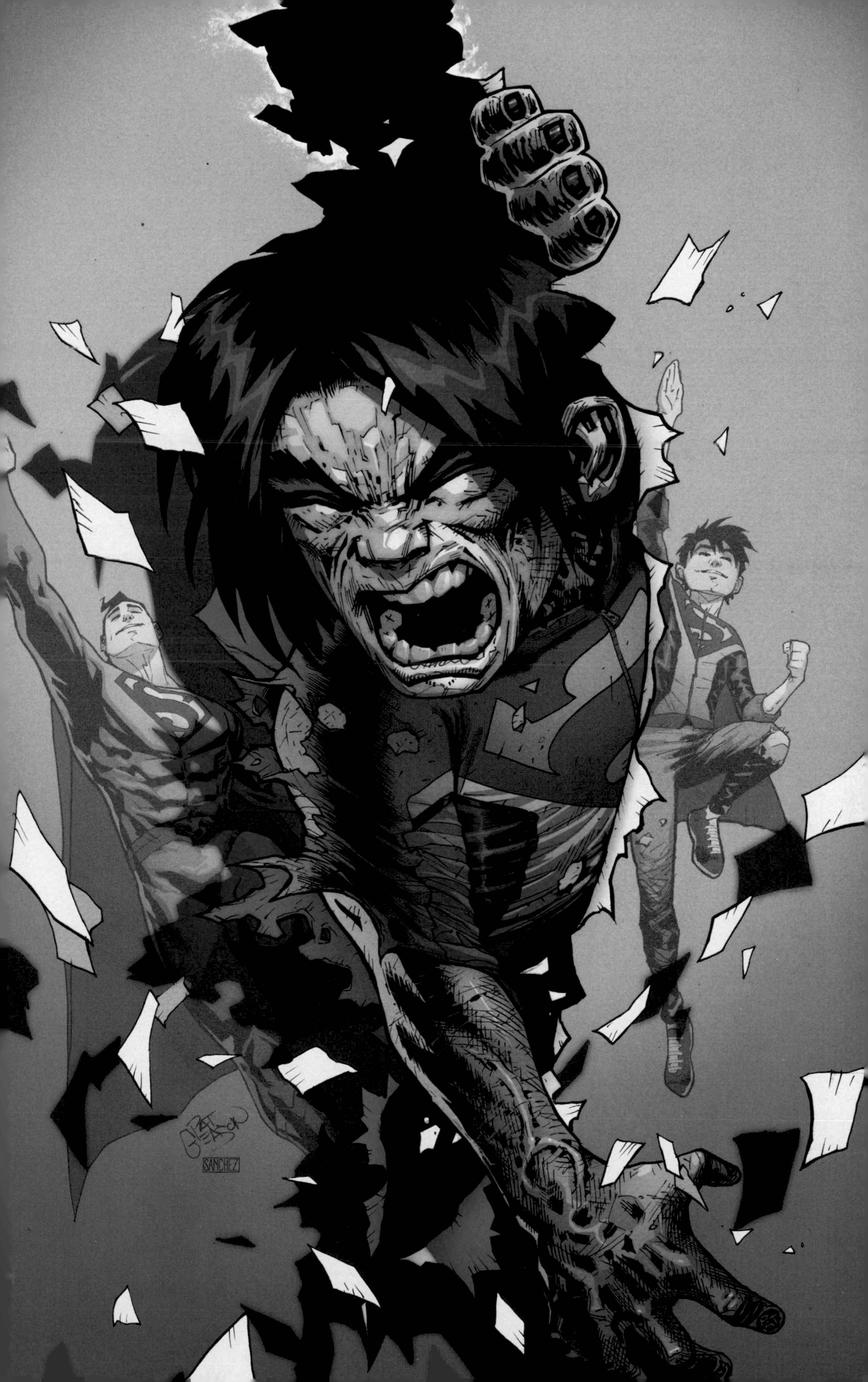
SANCHEZ

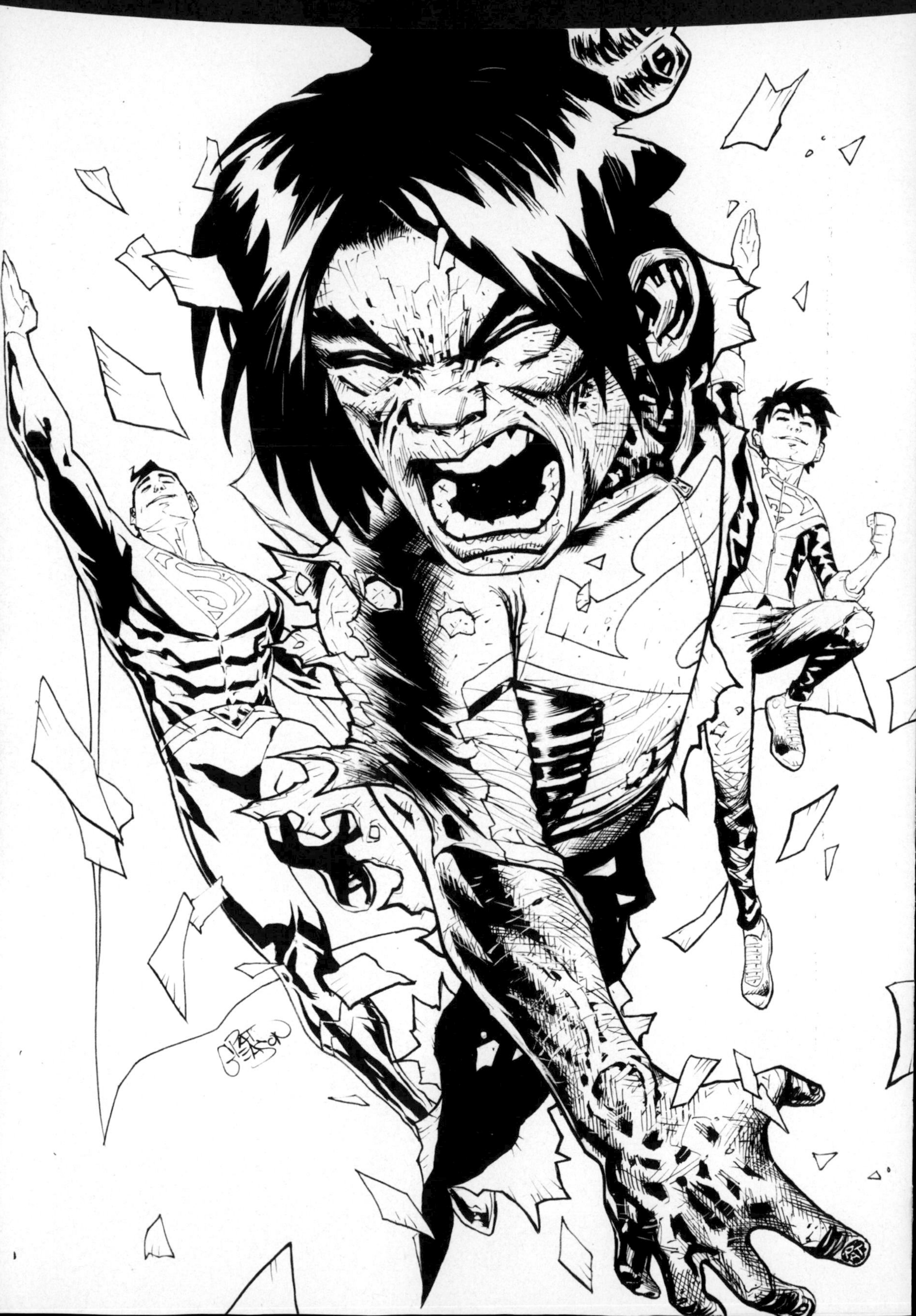

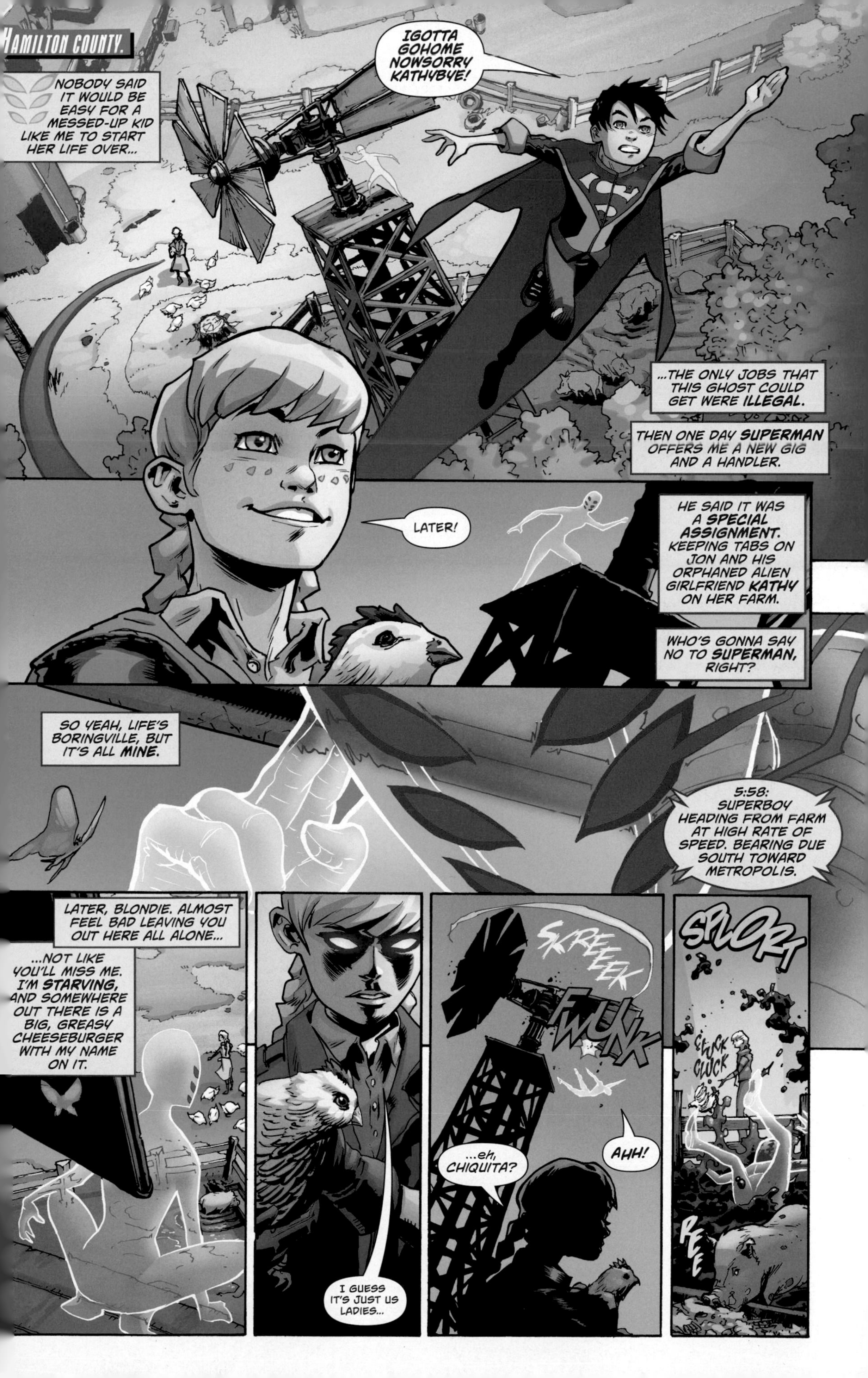
HAMILTON COUNTY.
NOBODY SAID IT WOULD BE EASY FOR A MESSED-UP KID LIKE ME TO START HER LIFE OVER...
IGOTTA GOHOME NOWSORRY KATHYBYE!
...THE ONLY JOBS THAT THIS GHOST COULD GET WERE ILLEGAL.
THEN ONE DAY SUPERMAN OFFERS ME A NEW GIG AND A HANDLER.
LATER!
HE SAID IT WAS A SPECIAL ASSIGNMENT. KEEPING TABS ON JON AND HIS ORPHANED ALIEN GIRLFRIEND KATHY ON HER FARM.
WHO'S GONNA SAY NO TO SUPERMAN, RIGHT?
SO YEAH, LIFE'S BORINGVILLE, BUT IT'S ALL MINE.
5:58: SUPERBOY HEADING FROM FARM AT HIGH RATE OF SPEED. BEARING DUE SOUTH TOWARD METROPOLIS.
LATER, BLONDIE. ALMOST FEEL BAD LEAVING YOU OUT HERE ALL ALONE...
...NOT LIKE YOU'LL MISS ME. I'M STARVING, AND SOMEWHERE OUT THERE IS A BIG, GREASY CHEESEBURGER WITH MY NAME ON IT.
I GUESS IT'S JUST US LADIES...
SKREEEEK
FWUNK
...eh, CHIQUITA?
AHH!
SPLORT
CLUCK CLUCK
REE

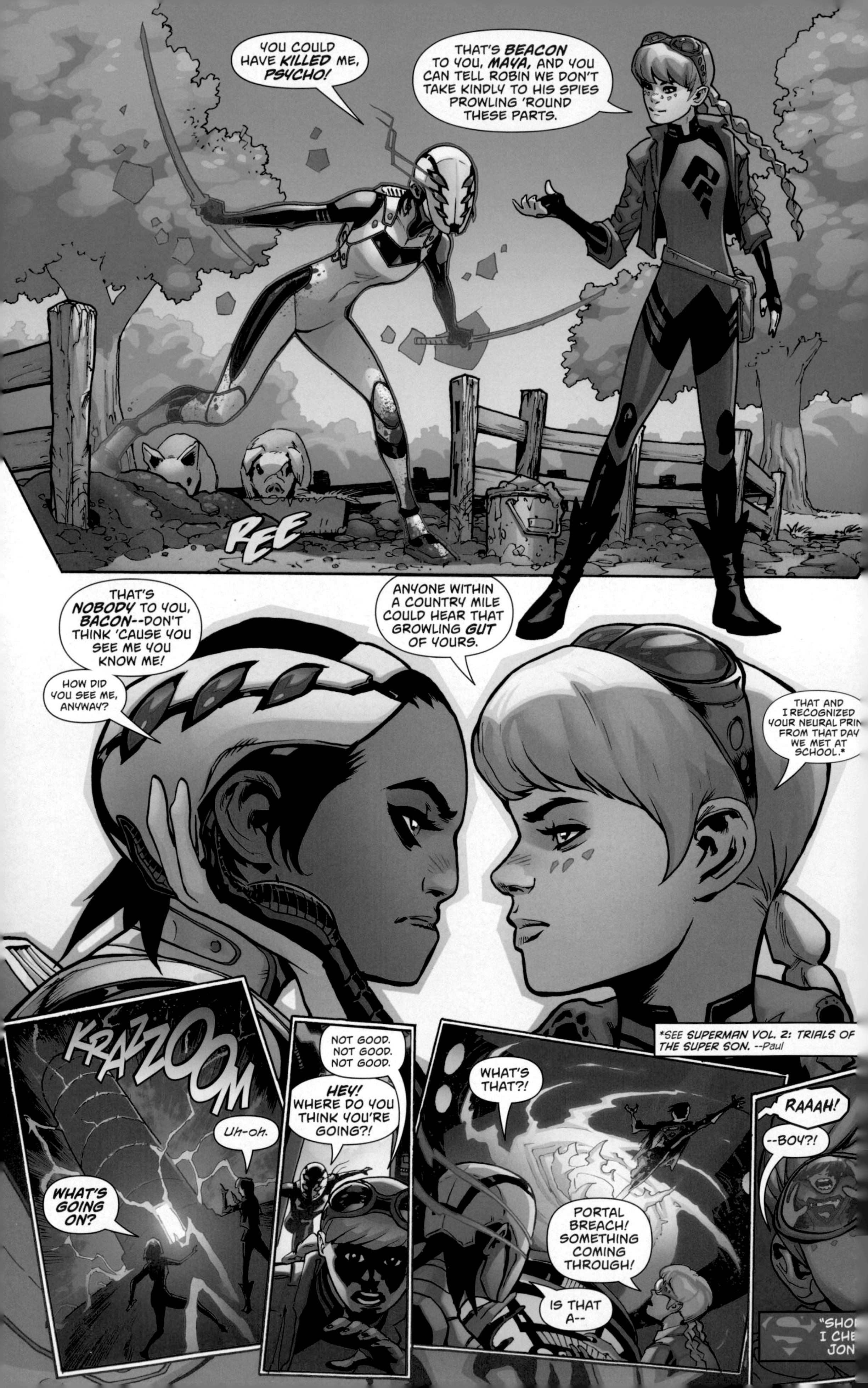
YOU COULD HAVE KILLED ME, PSYCHO!
THAT'S BEACON TO YOU, MAYA, AND YOU CAN TELL ROBIN WE DON'T TAKE KINDLY TO HIS SPIES PROWLING 'ROUND THESE PARTS.
REEE
THAT'S NOBODY TO YOU, BACON--DON'T THINK 'CAUSE YOU SEE ME YOU KNOW ME!
HOW DID YOU SEE ME, ANYWAY?
ANYONE WITHIN A COUNTRY MILE COULD HEAR THAT GROWLING GUT OF YOURS.
THAT AND I RECOGNIZED YOUR NEURAL PRIN FROM THAT DAY WE MET AT SCHOOL.*
*SEE SUPERMAN VOL. 2: TRIALS OF THE SUPER SON. --Paul
KRAZZOOM
Uh-oh.
WHAT'S GOING ON?
NOT GOOD. NOT GOOD. NOT GOOD.
HEY! WHERE DO YOU THINK YOU'RE GOING?!
WHAT'S THAT?!
PORTAL BREACH! SOMETHING COMING THROUGH!
IS THAT A--
RAAAH!
--BOY?!

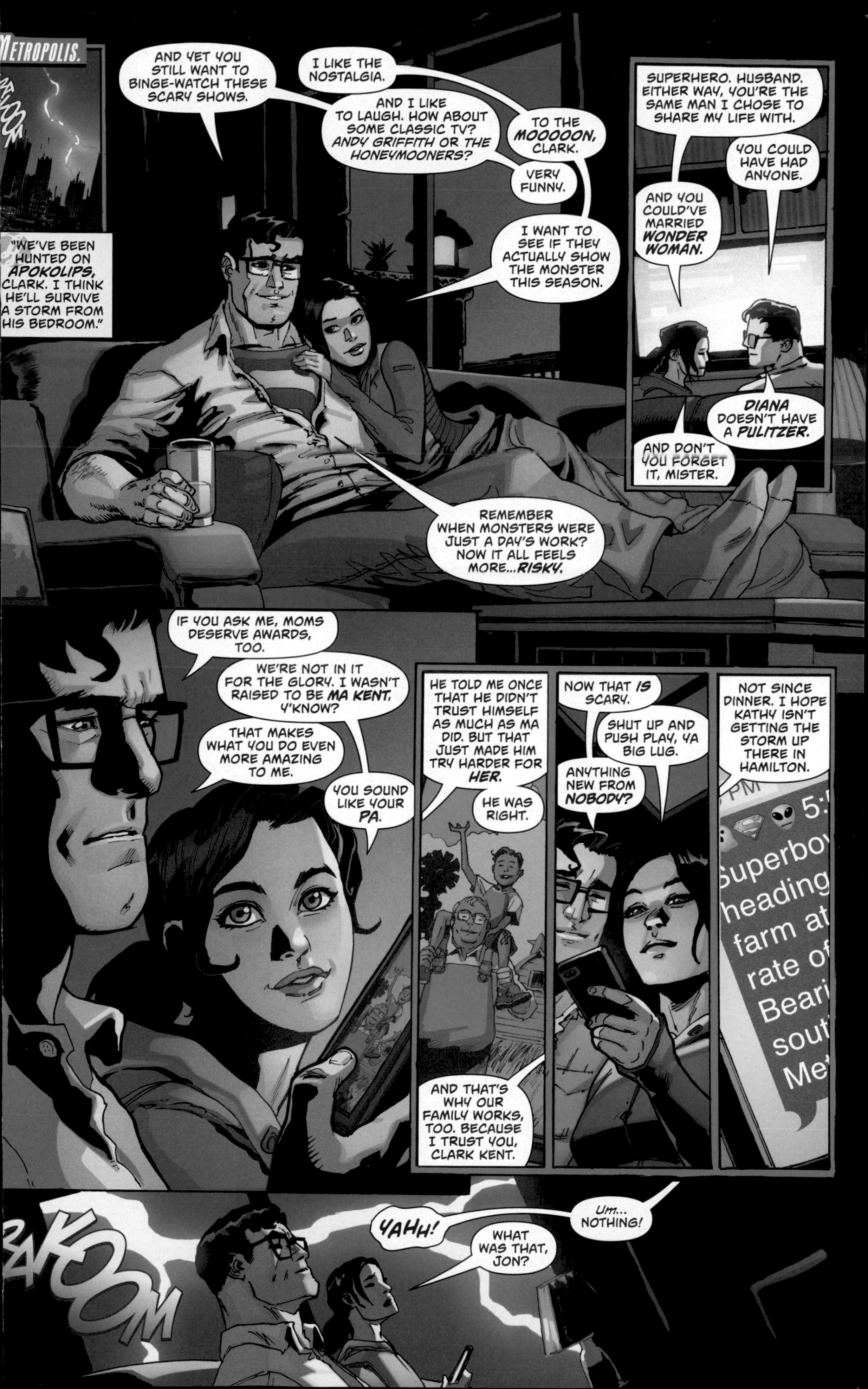
METROPOLIS.
"WE'VE BEEN HUNTED ON APOKOLIPS, CLARK. I THINK HE'LL SURVIVE A STORM FROM HIS BEDROOM."
AND YET YOU STILL WANT TO BINGE-WATCH THESE SCARY SHOWS.
I LIKE THE NOSTALGIA.
AND I LIKE TO LAUGH. HOW ABOUT SOME CLASSIC TV? ANDY GRIFFITH OR THE HONEYMOONERS?
TO THE MOOOOON, CLARK.
VERY FUNNY.
I WANT TO SEE IF THEY ACTUALLY SHOW THE MONSTER THIS SEASON.
REMEMBER WHEN MONSTERS WERE JUST A DAY'S WORK? NOW IT ALL FEELS MORE...RISKY.
SUPERHERO. HUSBAND. EITHER WAY, YOU'RE THE SAME MAN I CHOSE TO SHARE MY LIFE WITH.
YOU COULD HAVE HAD ANYONE.
AND YOU COULD'VE MARRIED WONDER WOMAN.
DIANA DOESN'T HAVE A PULITZER.
AND DON'T YOU FORGET IT, MISTER.
IF YOU ASK ME, MOMS DESERVE AWARDS, TOO.
WE'RE NOT IN IT FOR THE GLORY. I WASN'T RAISED TO BE MA KENT, Y'KNOW?
THAT MAKES WHAT YOU DO EVEN MORE AMAZING TO ME.
YOU SOUND LIKE YOUR PA.
HE TOLD ME ONCE THAT HE DIDN'T TRUST HIMSELF AS MUCH AS MA DID. BUT THAT JUST MADE HIM TRY HARDER FOR HER.
HE WAS RIGHT.
AND THAT'S WHY OUR FAMILY WORKS, TOO. BECAUSE I TRUST YOU, CLARK KENT.
NOW THAT IS SCARY.
SHUT UP AND PUSH PLAY, YA BIG LUG.
ANYTHING NEW FROM NOBODY?
NOT SINCE DINNER. I HOPE KATHY ISN'T GETTING THE STORM UP THERE IN HAMILTON.
YAHH!
WHAT WAS THAT, JON?
Um... NOTHING!

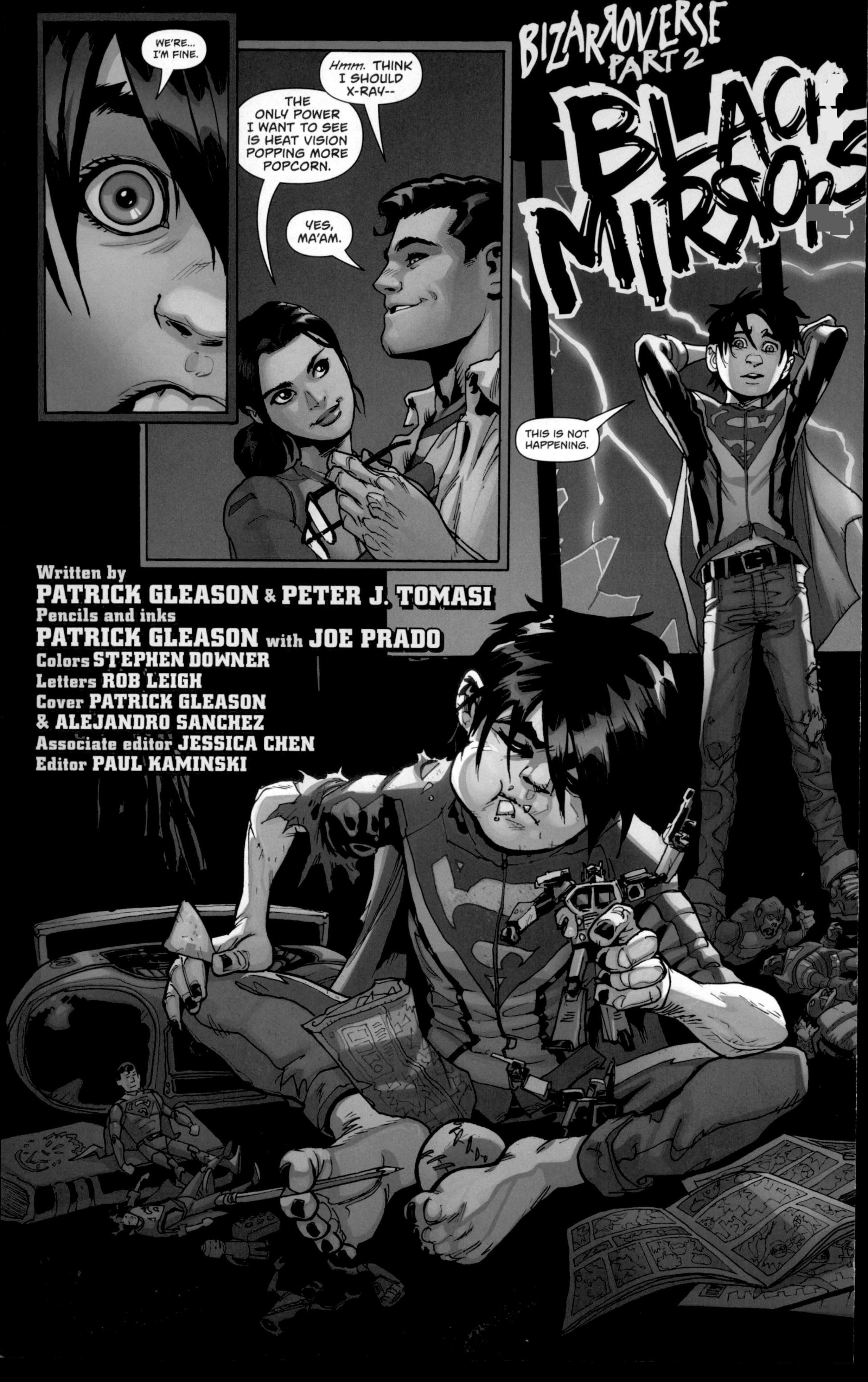
BIZARROVERSE PART 2
BLACK MIRRORS
WE'RE... I'M FINE.
*Hmm.* THINK I SHOULD X-RAY--
THE ONLY POWER I WANT TO SEE IS HEAT VISION POPPING MORE POPCORN.
YES, MA'AM.
THIS IS NOT HAPPENING.

Written by
**PATRICK GLEASON & PETER J. TOMASI**
Pencils and inks
**PATRICK GLEASON with JOE PRADO**
Colors **STEPHEN DOWNER**
Letters **ROB LEIGH**
Cover **PATRICK GLEASON**
**& ALEJANDRO SANCHEZ**
Associate editor **JESSICA CHEN**
Editor **PAUL KAMINSKI**

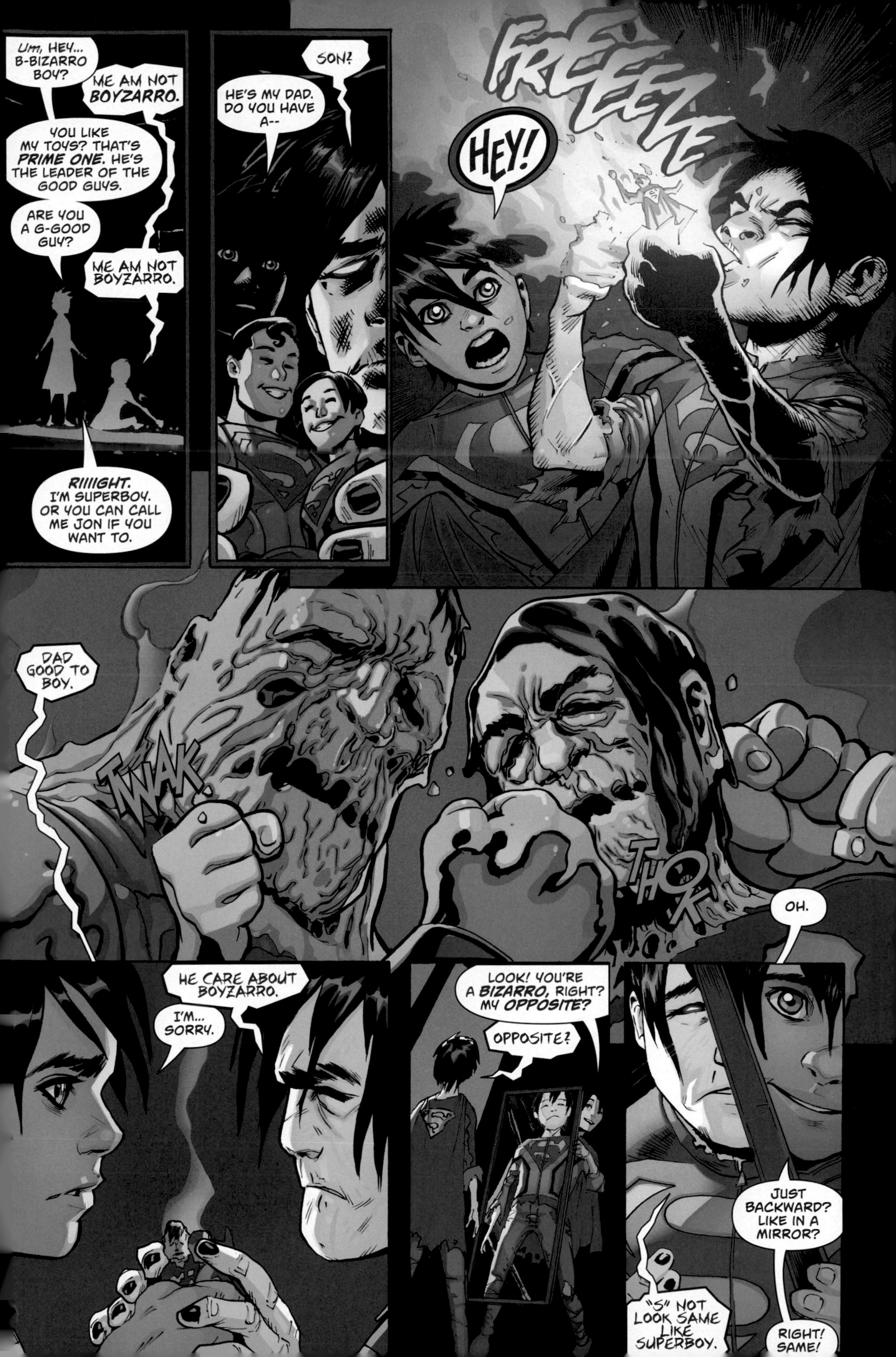

UM, HEY... B-BIZARRO BOY?
ME AM NOT BOYZARRO.
YOU LIKE MY TOYS? THAT'S PRIME ONE. HE'S THE LEADER OF THE GOOD GUYS.
ARE YOU A G-GOOD GUY?
ME AM NOT BOYZARRO.
RIIIIGHT. I'M SUPERBOY. OR YOU CAN CALL ME JON IF YOU WANT TO.
SON?
HE'S MY DAD. DO YOU HAVE A--
FREEEEZE
HEY!
DAD GOOD TO BOY.
TWAK
THOK
OH.
HE CARE ABOUT BOYZARRO.
I'M... SORRY.
LOOK! YOU'RE A BIZARRO, RIGHT? MY OPPOSITE?
OPPOSITE?
JUST BACKWARD? LIKE IN A MIRROR?
"S" NOT LOOK SAME LIKE SUPERBOY.
RIGHT! SAME!

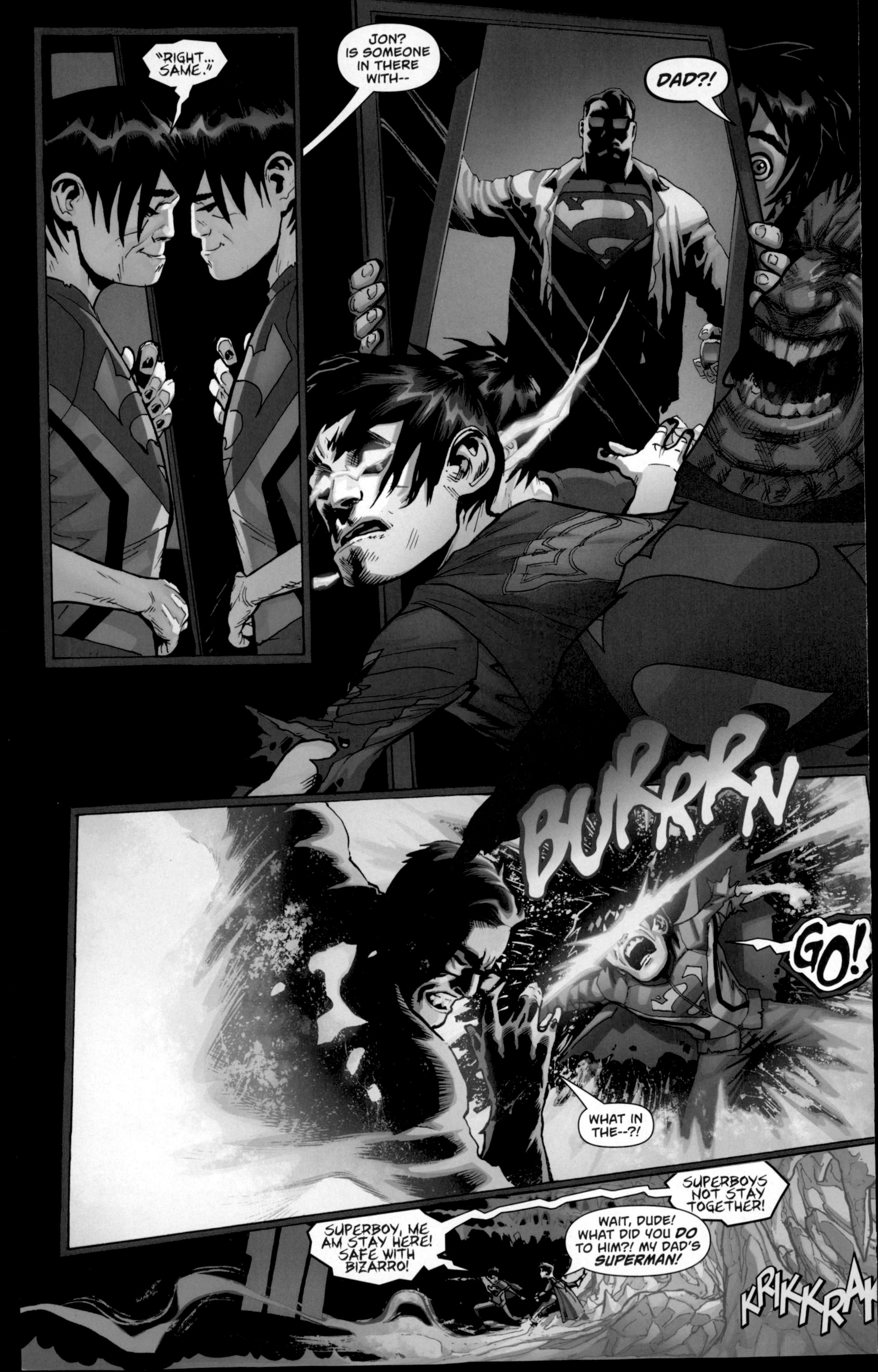
"RIGHT... SAME."
JON? IS SOMEONE IN THERE WITH--
DAD?!
BURRRN
GO!
WHAT IN THE--?!
SUPERBOYS NOT STAY TOGETHER!
SUPERBOY, ME AM STAY HERE! SAFE WITH BIZARRO!
WAIT, DUDE! WHAT DID YOU DO TO HIM?! MY DAD'S SUPERMAN!
KRIKKRAK

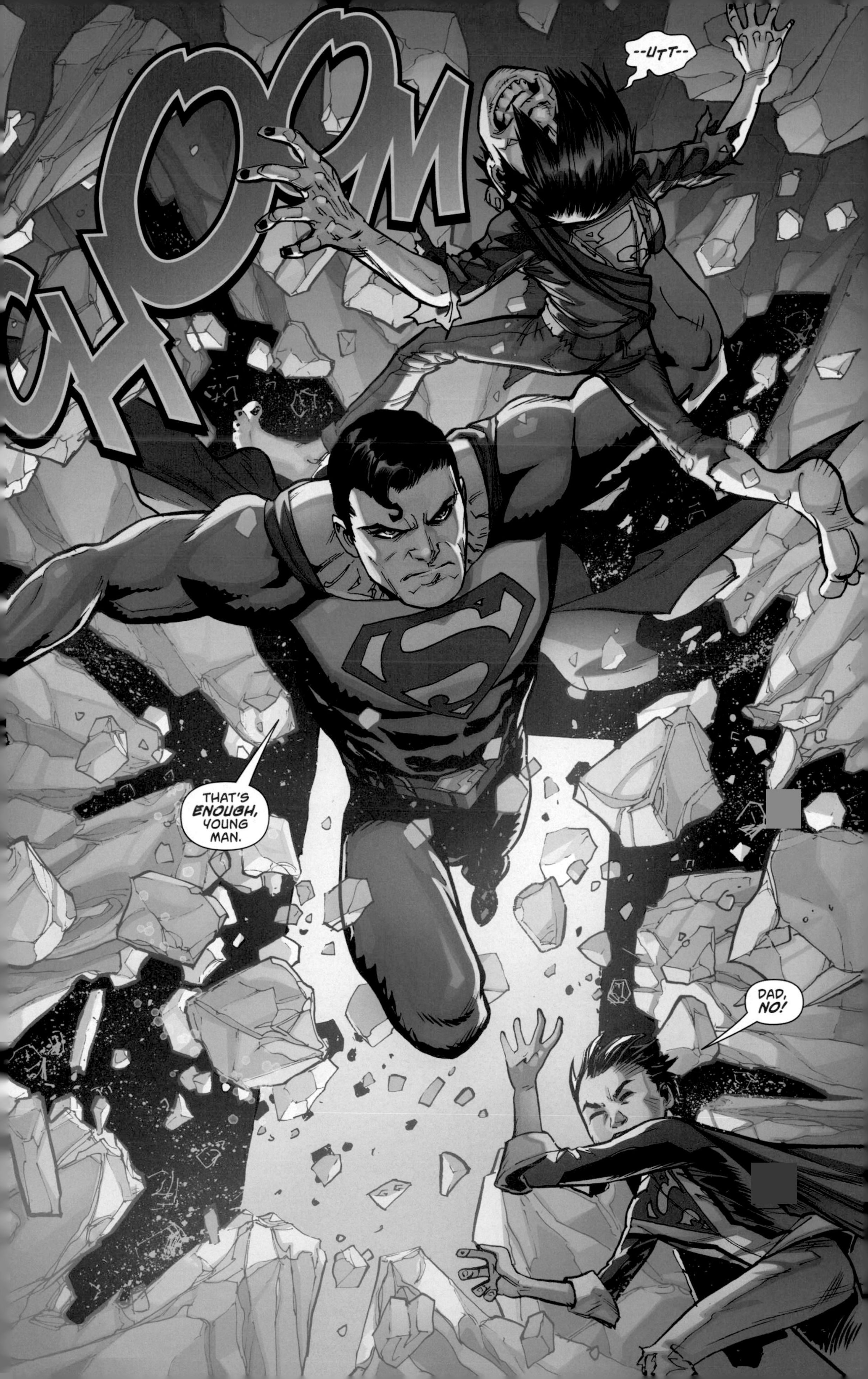
CHOOM
--UTT--
THAT'S ENOUGH, YOUNG MAN.
DAD, NO!

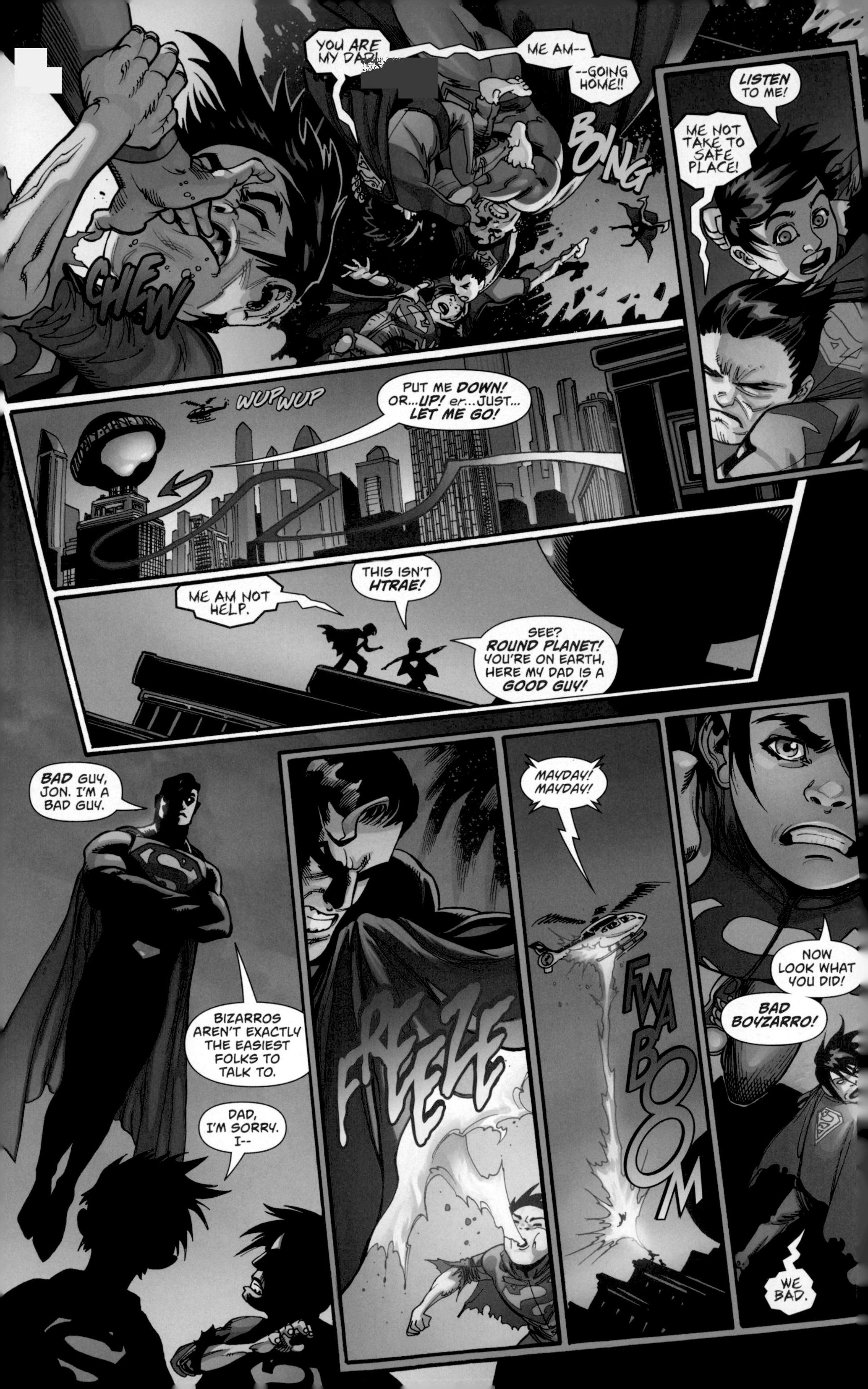

YOU ARE MY DAD!
ME AM--
--GOING HOME!!
BOING
CHEW
LISTEN TO ME!
ME NOT TAKE TO SAFE PLACE!
WUP WUP
PUT ME DOWN! OR...UP! er...JUST... LET ME GO!
ME AM NOT HELP.
THIS ISN'T HTRAE!
SEE? ROUND PLANET! YOU'RE ON EARTH, HERE MY DAD IS A GOOD GUY!
BAD GUY, JON. I'M A BAD GUY.
BIZARROS AREN'T EXACTLY THE EASIEST FOLKS TO TALK TO.
DAD, I'M SORRY. I--
FREEZE
MAYDAY! MAYDAY!
FWABOOM
NOW LOOK WHAT YOU DID!
BAD BOYZARRO!
WE BAD.

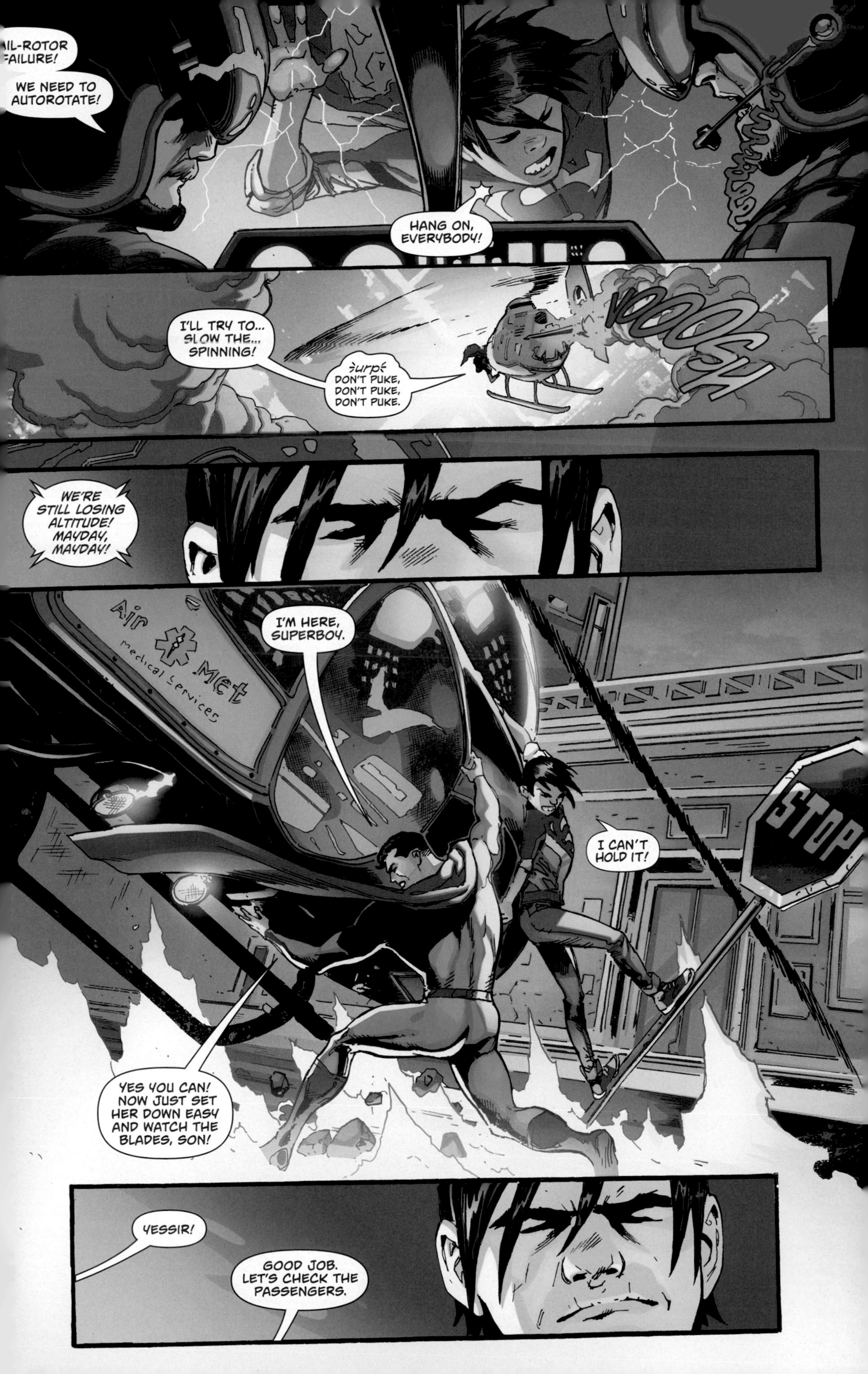
AIL-ROTOR FAILURE!
WE NEED TO AUTOROTATE!
HANG ON, EVERYBODY!
I'LL TRY TO... SLOW THE... SPINNING!
urp
DON'T PUKE, DON'T PUKE, DON'T PUKE.
VOOOSH
WE'RE STILL LOSING ALTITUDE! MAYDAY, MAYDAY!
Air Met Medical Services
I'M HERE, SUPERBOY.
I CAN'T HOLD IT!
STOP
YES YOU CAN! NOW JUST SET HER DOWN EASY AND WATCH THE BLADES, SON!
YESSIR!
GOOD JOB. LET'S CHECK THE PASSENGERS.

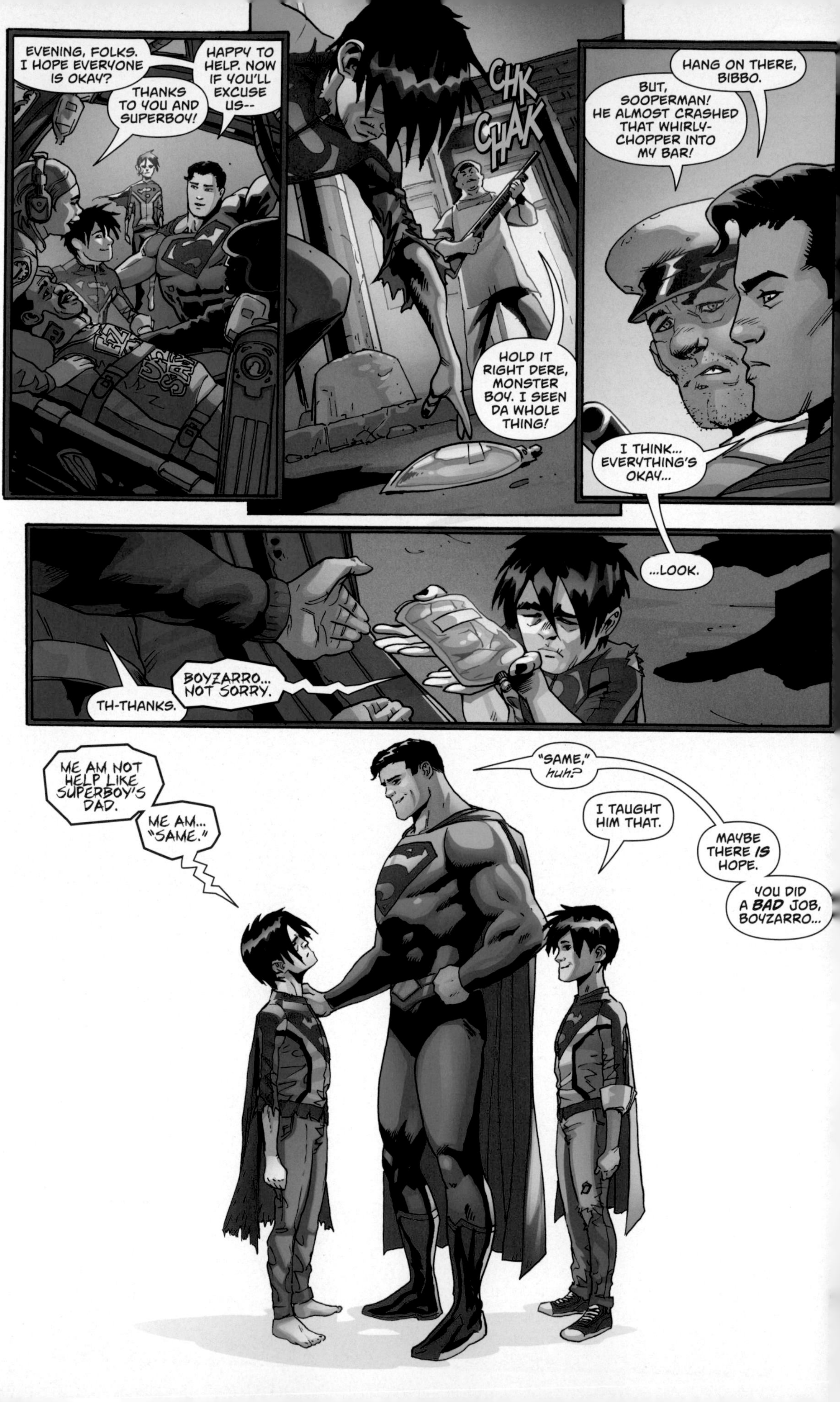
EVENING, FOLKS. I HOPE EVERYONE IS OKAY?
THANKS TO YOU AND SUPERBOY!
HAPPY TO HELP. NOW IF YOU'LL EXCUSE US--
CHK CHAK
HOLD IT RIGHT DERE, MONSTER BOY. I SEEN DA WHOLE THING!
HANG ON THERE, BIBBO.
BUT, SOOPERMAN! HE ALMOST CRASHED THAT WHIRLY-CHOPPER INTO MY BAR!
I THINK... EVERYTHING'S OKAY...
...LOOK.
BOYZARRO... NOT SORRY.
TH-THANKS.
ME AM NOT HELP LIKE SUPERBOY'S DAD.
ME AM... "SAME."
"SAME," huh?
I TAUGHT HIM THAT.
MAYBE THERE IS HOPE.
YOU DID A BAD JOB, BOYZARRO...

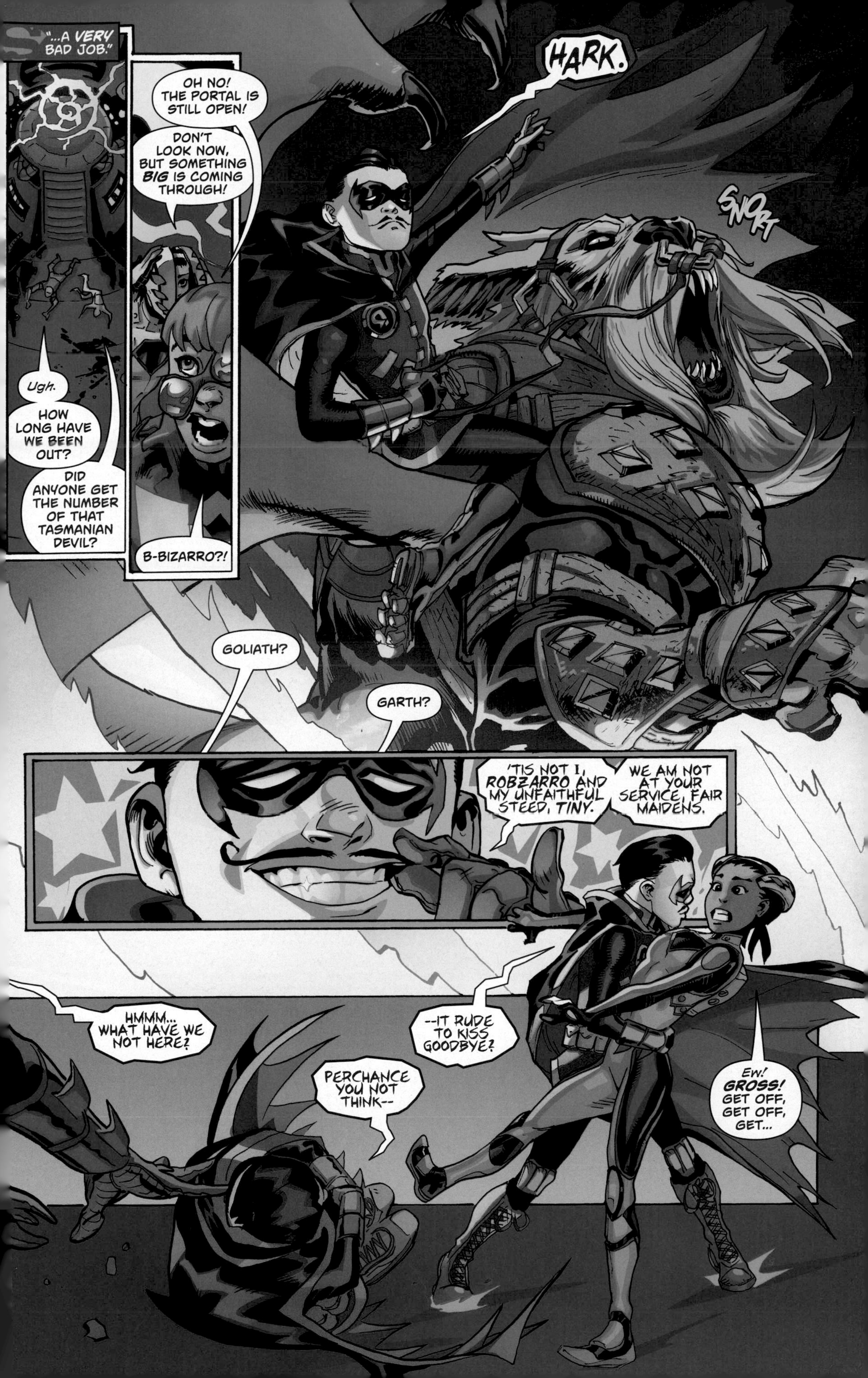
"...A VERY BAD JOB."
Ugh.
HOW LONG HAVE WE BEEN OUT?
DID ANYONE GET THE NUMBER OF THAT TASMANIAN DEVIL?
OH NO! THE PORTAL IS STILL OPEN!
DON'T LOOK NOW, BUT SOMETHING BIG IS COMING THROUGH!
B-BIZARRO?!
HARK.
SNORT
GOLIATH?
GARTH?
'TIS NOT I, ROBZARRO AND MY UNFAITHFUL STEED, TINY.
WE AM NOT AT YOUR SERVICE, FAIR MAIDENS.
HMMM... WHAT HAVE WE NOT HERE?
PERCHANCE YOU NOT THINK--
--IT RUDE TO KISS GOODBYE?
Ew! GROSS! GET OFF, GET OFF, GET...

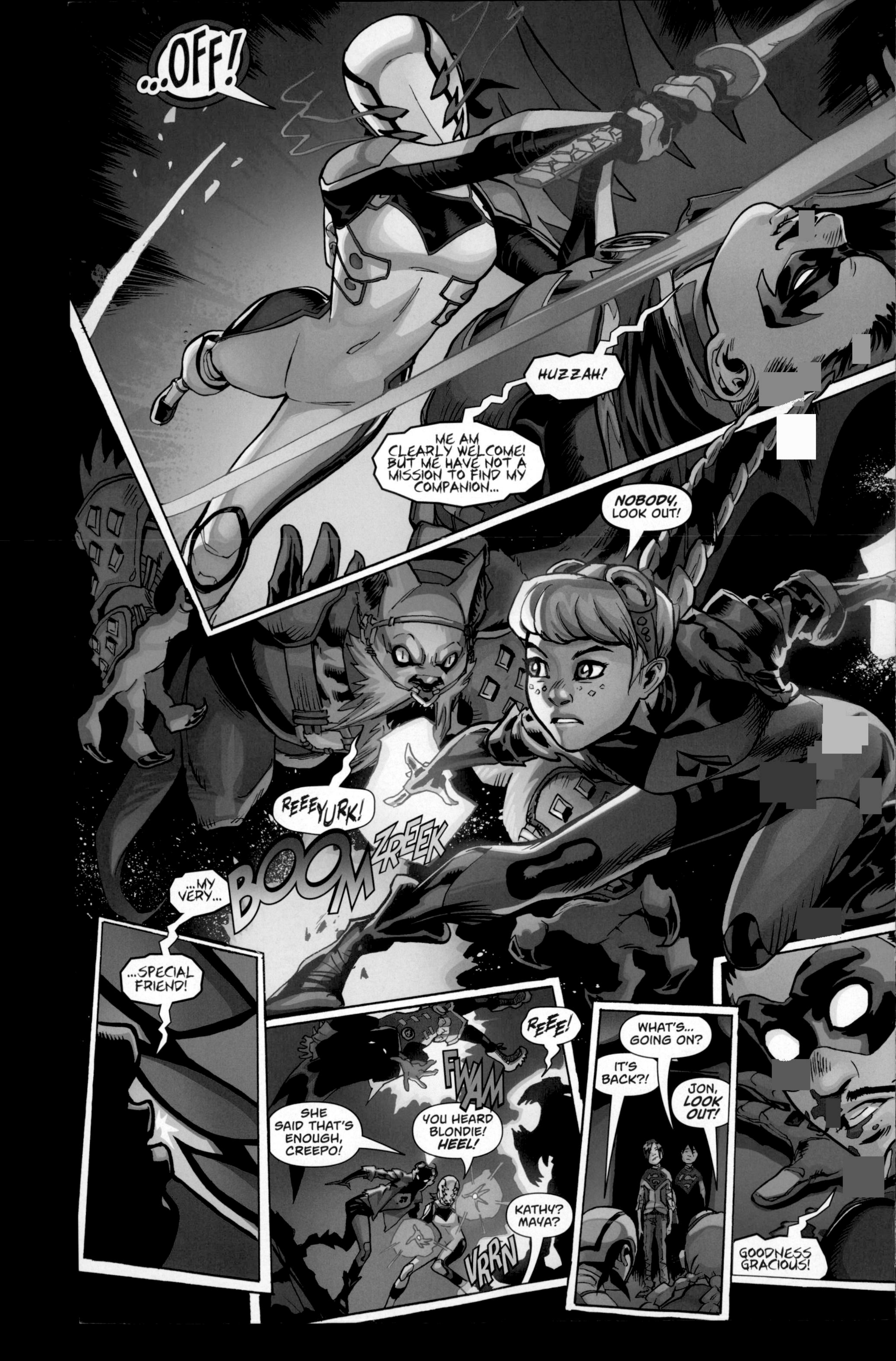
...OFF!
HUZZAH!
ME AM CLEARLY WELCOME! BUT ME HAVE NOT A MISSION TO FIND MY COMPANION...
NOBODY, LOOK OUT!
REEEYURK!
BOOM
ZREEK
...MY VERY...
...SPECIAL FRIEND!
REEE!
FWAM
SHE SAID THAT'S ENOUGH, CREEPO!
YOU HEARD BLONDIE! HEEL!
KATHY? MAYA?
VRRN
WHAT'S... GOING ON?
IT'S BACK?!
JON, LOOK OUT!
GOODNESS GRACIOUS!

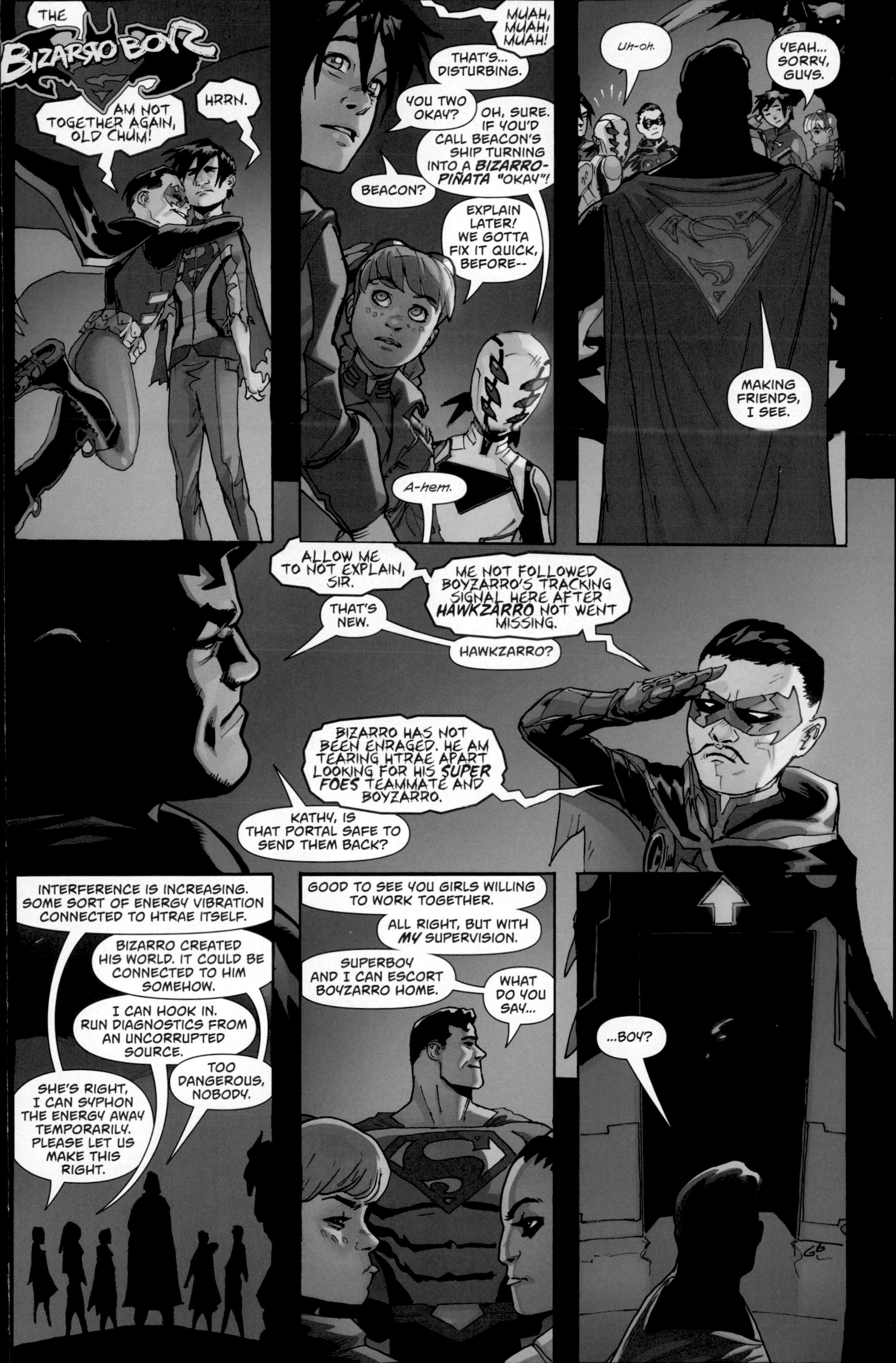

THE BIZARRO BOYZ AM NOT TOGETHER AGAIN, OLD CHUM!
HRRN.
MUAH, MUAH, MUAH!
THAT'S... DISTURBING.
YOU TWO OKAY?
OH, SURE. IF YOU'D CALL BEACON'S SHIP TURNING INTO A BIZARRO-PIÑATA "OKAY"!
BEACON?
EXPLAIN LATER! WE GOTTA FIX IT QUICK, BEFORE--
A-hem.
Uh-oh.
YEAH... SORRY, GUYS.
MAKING FRIENDS, I SEE.
ALLOW ME TO NOT EXPLAIN, SIR.
THAT'S NEW.
ME NOT FOLLOWED BOYZARRO'S TRACKING SIGNAL HERE AFTER HAWKZARRO NOT WENT MISSING.
HAWKZARRO?
BIZARRO HAS NOT BEEN ENRAGED. HE AM TEARING HTRAE APART LOOKING FOR HIS SUPER FOES TEAMMATE AND BOYZARRO.
KATHY, IS THAT PORTAL SAFE TO SEND THEM BACK?
INTERFERENCE IS INCREASING. SOME SORT OF ENERGY VIBRATION CONNECTED TO HTRAE ITSELF.
BIZARRO CREATED HIS WORLD. IT COULD BE CONNECTED TO HIM SOMEHOW.
I CAN HOOK IN. RUN DIAGNOSTICS FROM AN UNCORRUPTED SOURCE.
TOO DANGEROUS, NOBODY.
SHE'S RIGHT, I CAN SYPHON THE ENERGY AWAY TEMPORARILY. PLEASE LET US MAKE THIS RIGHT.
GOOD TO SEE YOU GIRLS WILLING TO WORK TOGETHER.
ALL RIGHT, BUT WITH MY SUPERVISION.
SUPERBOY AND I CAN ESCORT BOYZARRO HOME.
WHAT DO YOU SAY...
...BOY?

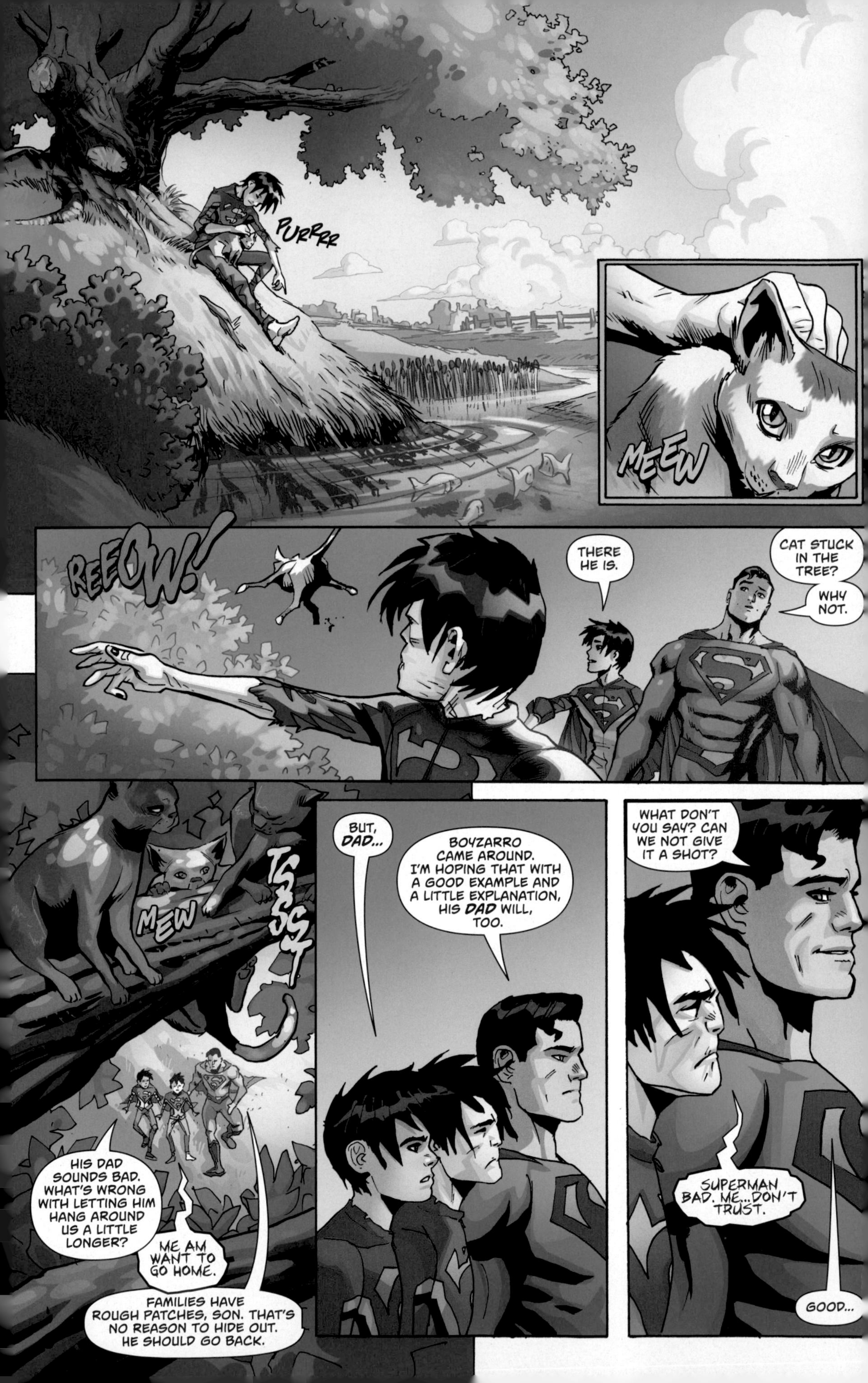
PURRRR
MEEW
REEOW!
THERE HE IS.
CAT STUCK IN THE TREE?
WHY NOT.
MEW
TSSST
HIS DAD SOUNDS BAD. WHAT'S WRONG WITH LETTING HIM HANG AROUND US A LITTLE LONGER?
ME AM WANT TO GO HOME.
FAMILIES HAVE ROUGH PATCHES, SON. THAT'S NO REASON TO HIDE OUT. HE SHOULD GO BACK.
BUT, DAD...
BOYZARRO CAME AROUND. I'M HOPING THAT WITH A GOOD EXAMPLE AND A LITTLE EXPLANATION, HIS DAD WILL, TOO.
WHAT DON'T YOU SAY? CAN WE NOT GIVE IT A SHOT?
SUPERMAN BAD. ME...DON'T TRUST.
GOOD...

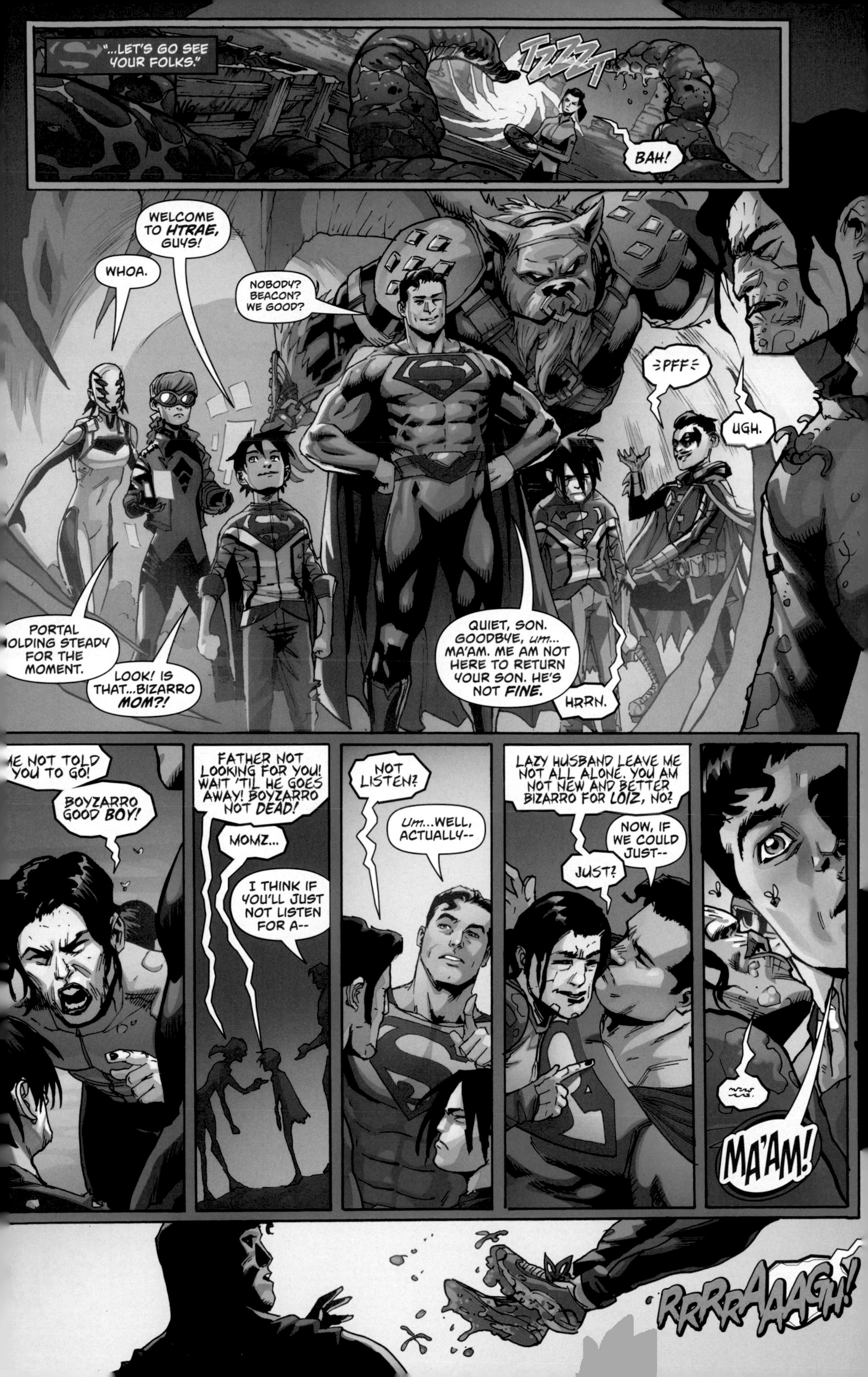
"...LET'S GO SEE YOUR FOLKS."
TZZZT
BAH!
WHOA.
WELCOME TO HTRAE, GUYS!
NOBODY? BEACON? WE GOOD?
PFF
UGH.
PORTAL OLDING STEADY FOR THE MOMENT.
LOOK! IS THAT...BIZARRO MOM?!
QUIET, SON. GOODBYE, UM... MA'AM. ME AM NOT HERE TO RETURN YOUR SON. HE'S NOT FINE.
HRRN.
ME NOT TOLD YOU TO GO!
BOYZARRO GOOD BOY!
FATHER NOT LOOKING FOR YOU! WAIT 'TIL HE GOES AWAY! BOYZARRO NOT DEAD!
MOMZ...
I THINK IF YOU'LL JUST NOT LISTEN FOR A--
NOT LISTEN?
UM...WELL, ACTUALLY--
LAZY HUSBAND LEAVE ME NOT ALL ALONE. YOU AM NOT NEW AND BETTER BIZARRO FOR LOIZ, NO?
NOW, IF WE COULD JUST--
JUST?
MA'AM!
RRRRAAAGH!

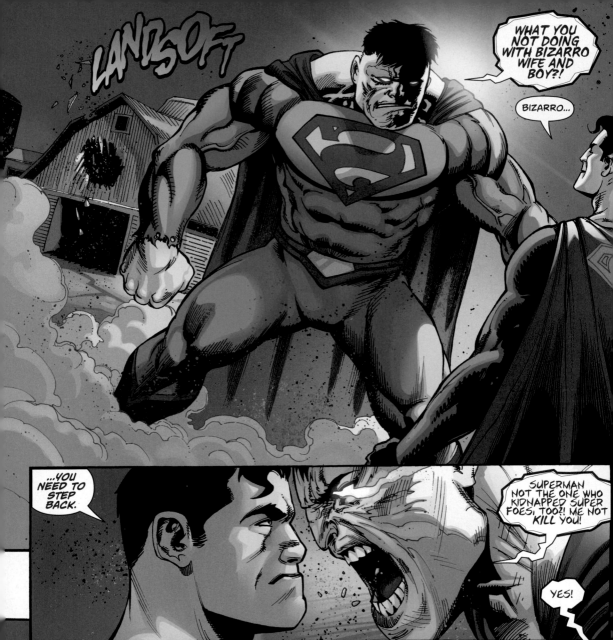

LANDSOFT

WHAT YOU NOT DOING WITH BIZARRO WIFE AND BOY?!

BIZARRO...

...YOU NEED TO STEP BACK.

SUPERMAN NOT THE ONE WHO KIDNAPPED SUPER FOES, TOO?! ME NOT KILL YOU!

YES!

BE NOT QUIET, BOY!

YOU GOOD DAD! SUPERMAN BAD! NOT HELP BOY! ME AM LETTING YOU HURT FRIENDS!

RAAAARGH!

WOOF

RRUF

BARK

PLANT

THAP

GET BEHIND ME AND LOOK AWAY, BOY.

RAAAH!

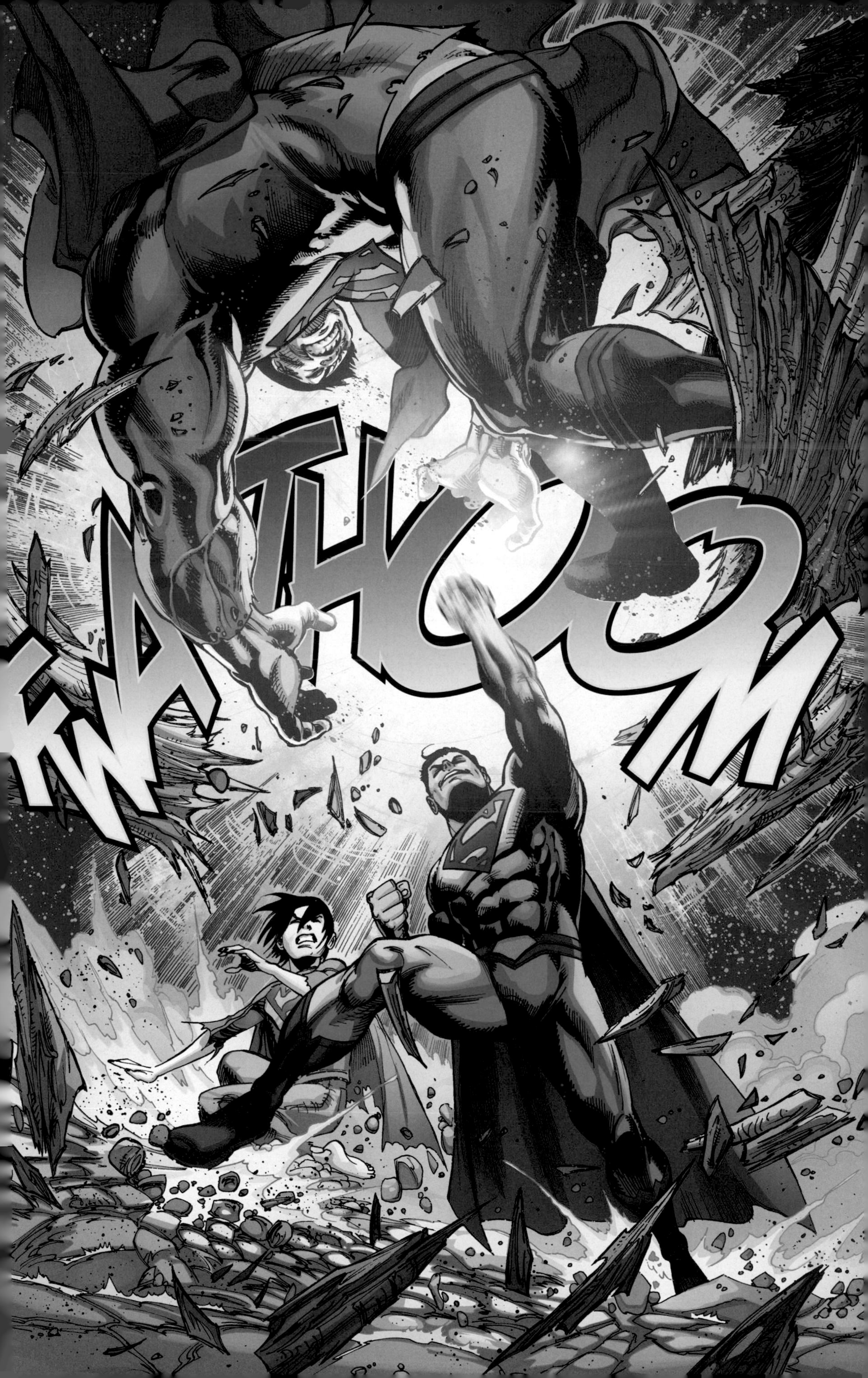
KATHOOM

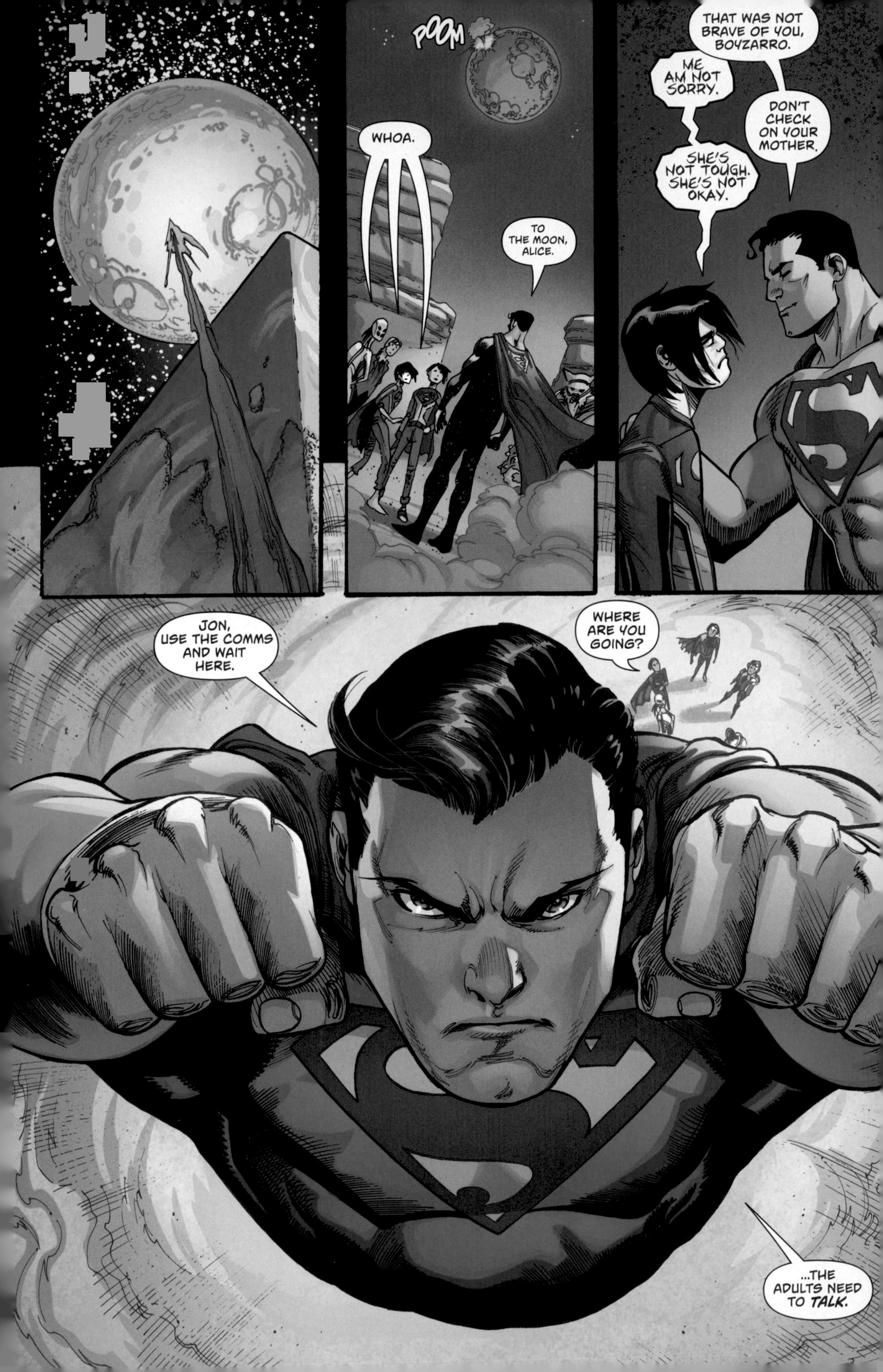
POOM
WHOA.
TO THE MOON, ALICE.
THAT WAS NOT BRAVE OF YOU, BOYZARRO.
ME AM NOT SORRY.
DON'T CHECK ON YOUR MOTHER.
SHE'S NOT TOUGH. SHE'S NOT OKAY.
JON, USE THE COMMS AND WAIT HERE.
WHERE ARE YOU GOING?
...THE ADULTS NEED TO TALK.

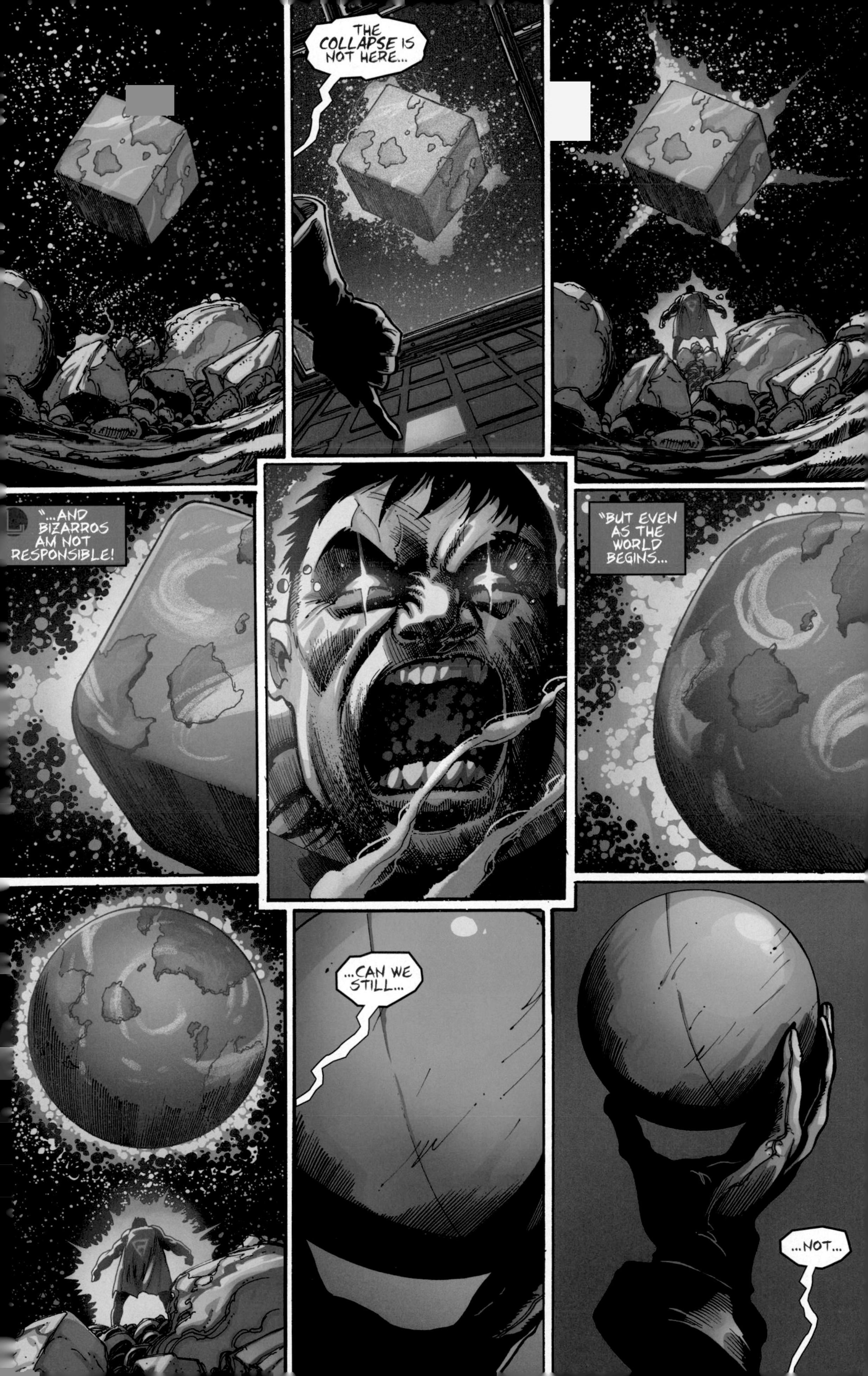
THE COLLAPSE IS NOT HERE...
"...AND BIZARROS AM NOT RESPONSIBLE!
"BUT EVEN AS THE WORLD BEGINS...
...CAN WE STILL...
...NOT...

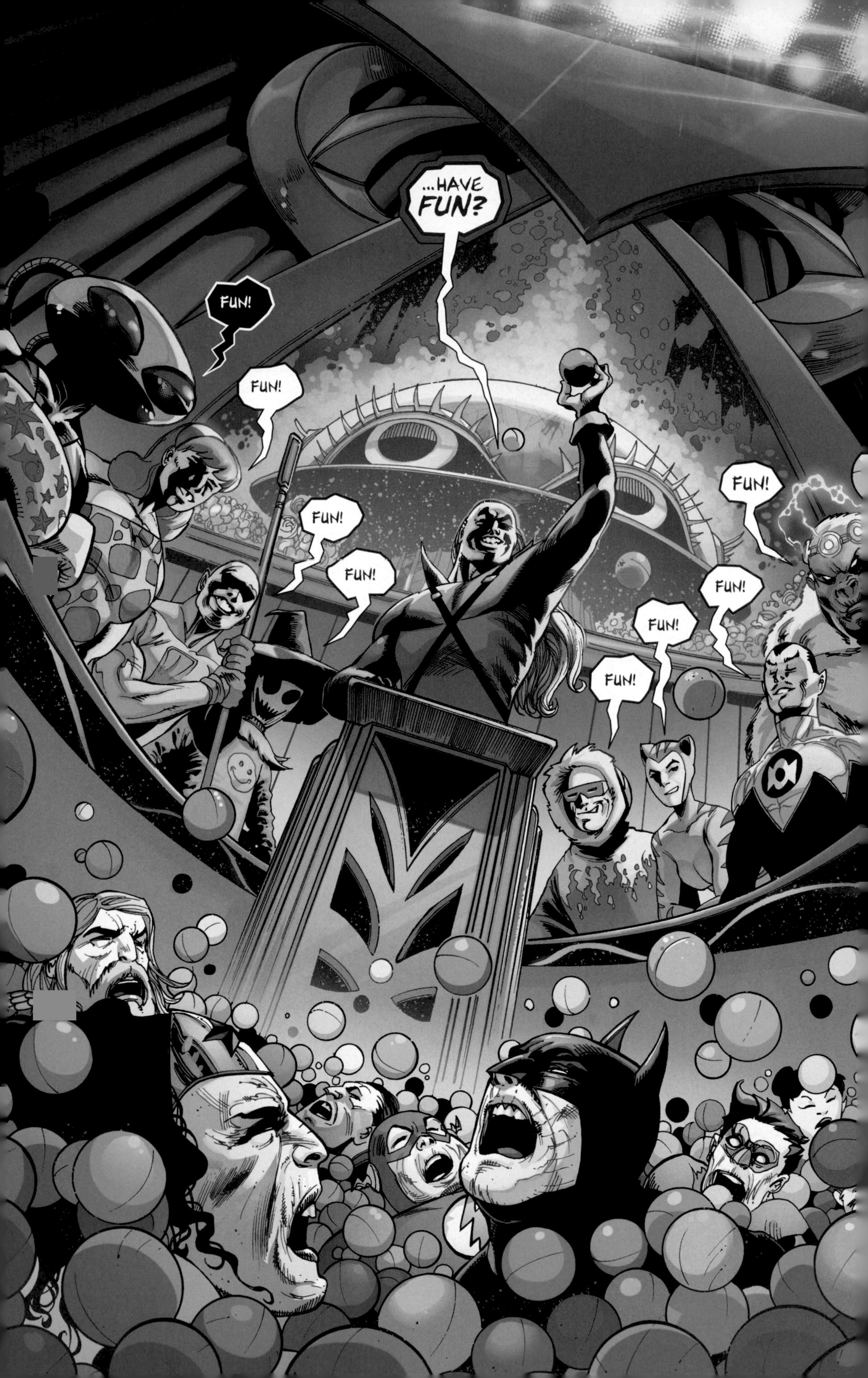
...HAVE FUN?
FUN!
FUN!
FUN!
FUN!
FUN!
FUN!
FUN!
FUN!

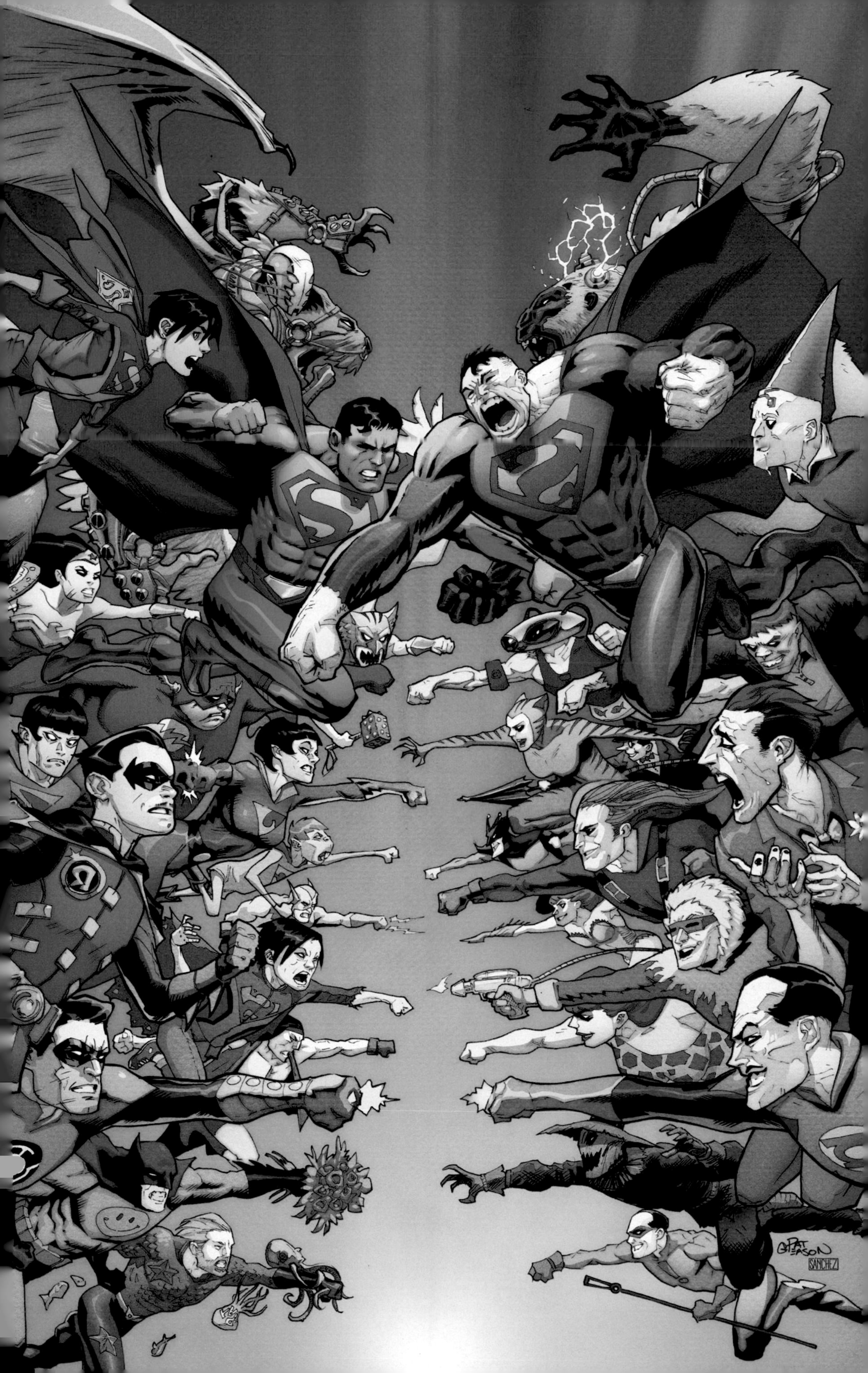
PAT GLEASON
SANCHEZ

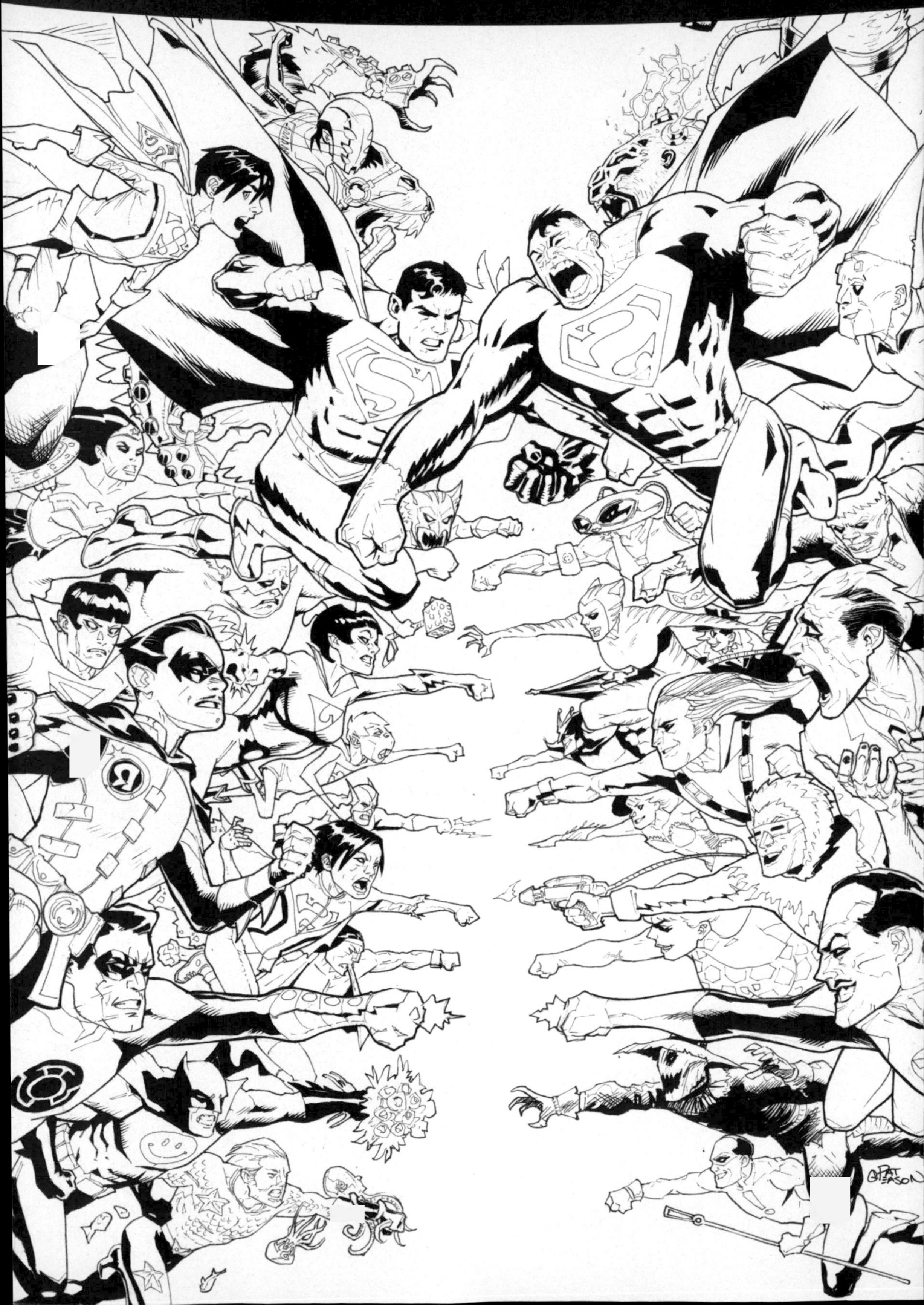
PAT GLEASON

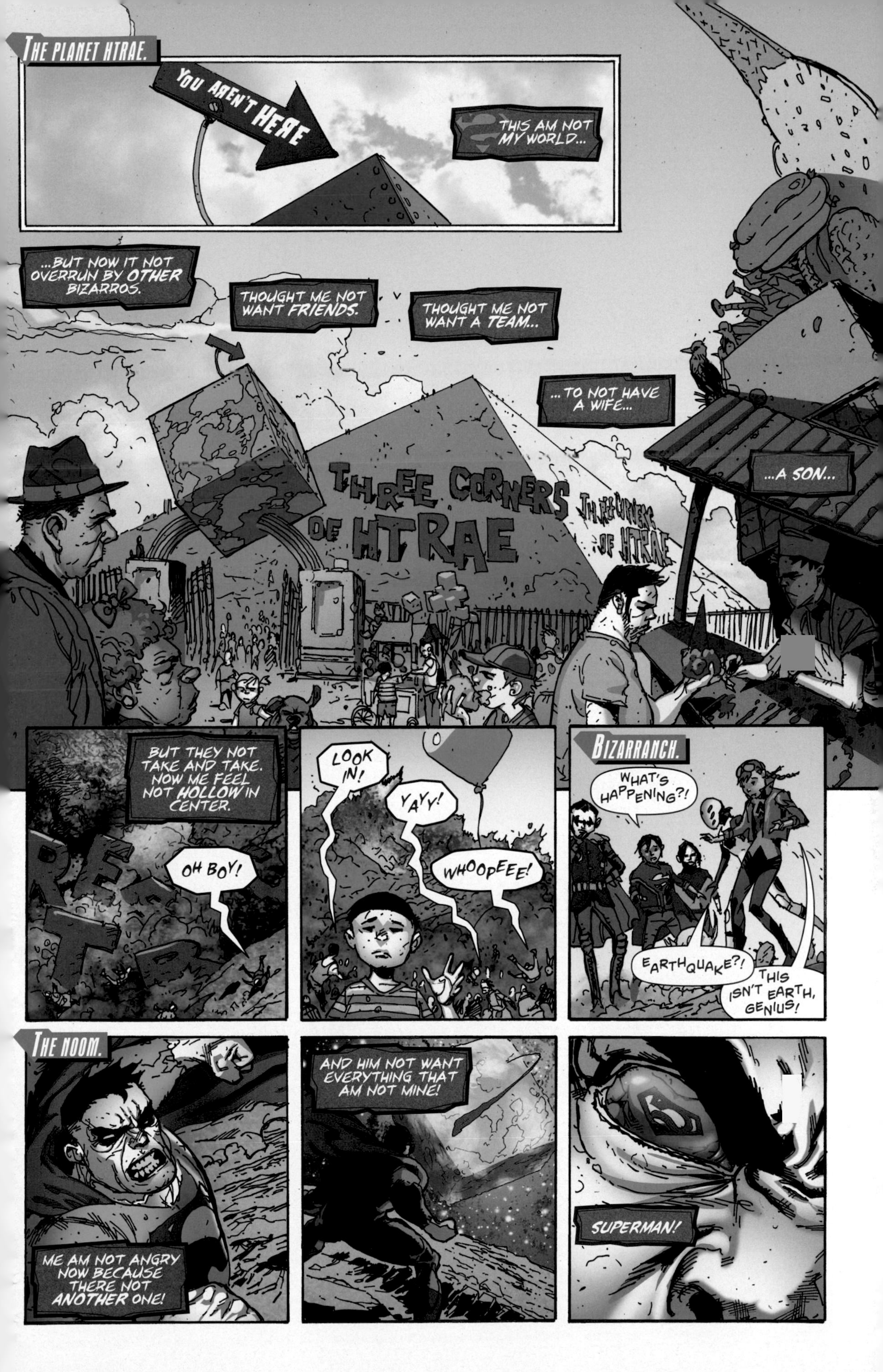
THE PLANET HTRAE.
YOU AREN'T HERE
THIS AM NOT MY WORLD...
...BUT NOW IT NOT OVERRUN BY OTHER BIZARROS.
THOUGHT ME NOT WANT FRIENDS.
THOUGHT ME NOT WANT A TEAM...
...TO NOT HAVE A WIFE...
...A SON...
THREE CORNERS OF HTRAE
BUT THEY NOT TAKE AND TAKE. NOW ME FEEL NOT HOLLOW IN CENTER.
OH BOY!
LOOK IN!
YAYY!
WHOOPEEE!
BIZARRANCH.
WHAT'S HAPPENING?!
EARTHQUAKE?!
THIS ISN'T EARTH, GENIUS!
THE NOOM.
ME AM NOT ANGRY NOW BECAUSE THERE NOT ANOTHER ONE!
AND HIM NOT WANT EVERYTHING THAT AM NOT MINE!
SUPERMAN!

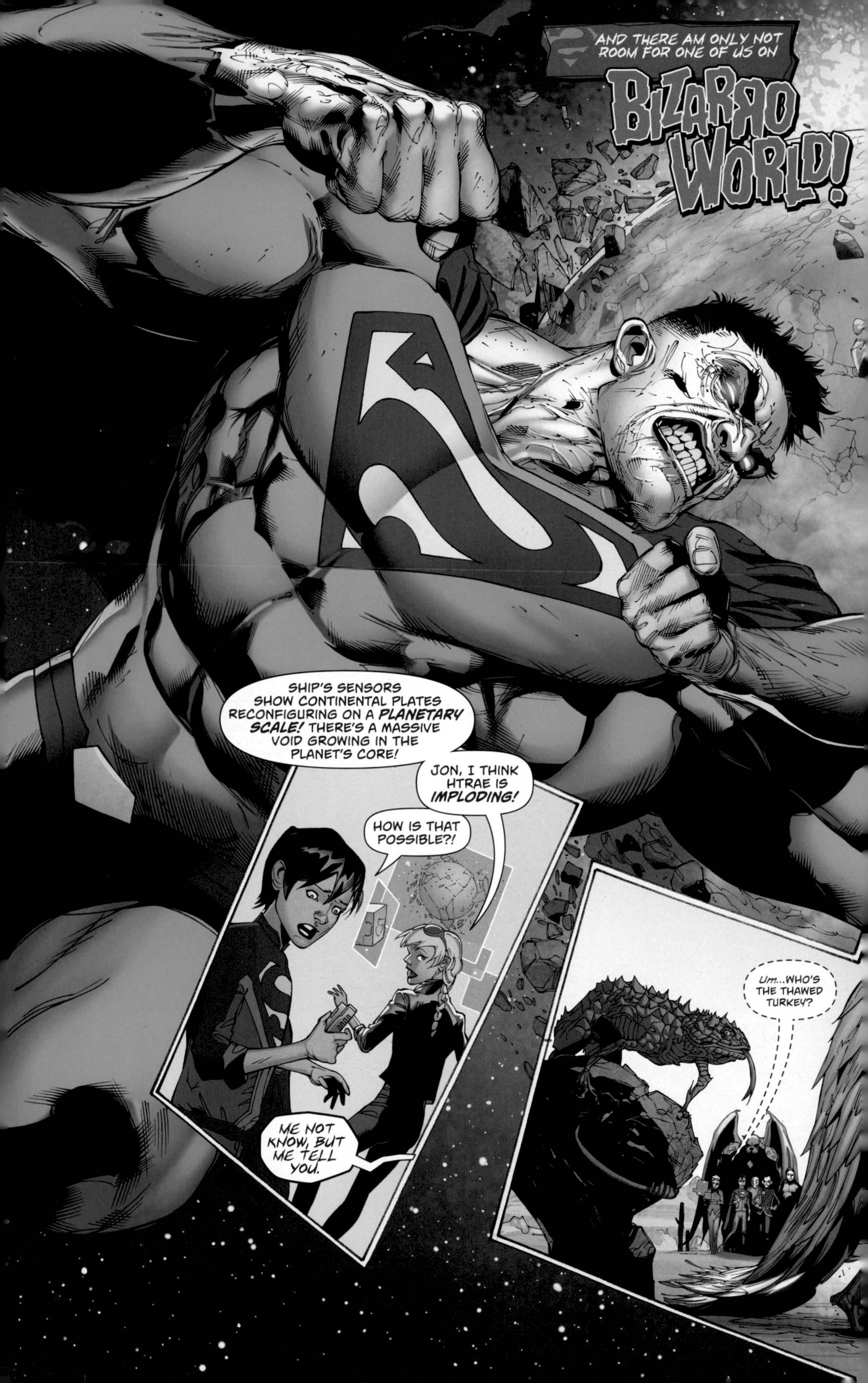
AND THERE AM ONLY NOT ROOM FOR ONE OF US ON
BIZARRO WORLD!
SHIP'S SENSORS SHOW CONTINENTAL PLATES RECONFIGURING ON A PLANETARY SCALE! THERE'S A MASSIVE VOID GROWING IN THE PLANET'S CORE!
JON, I THINK HTRAE IS IMPLODING!
HOW IS THAT POSSIBLE?!
ME NOT KNOW, BUT ME TELL YOU.
Um...WHO'S THE THAWED TURKEY?

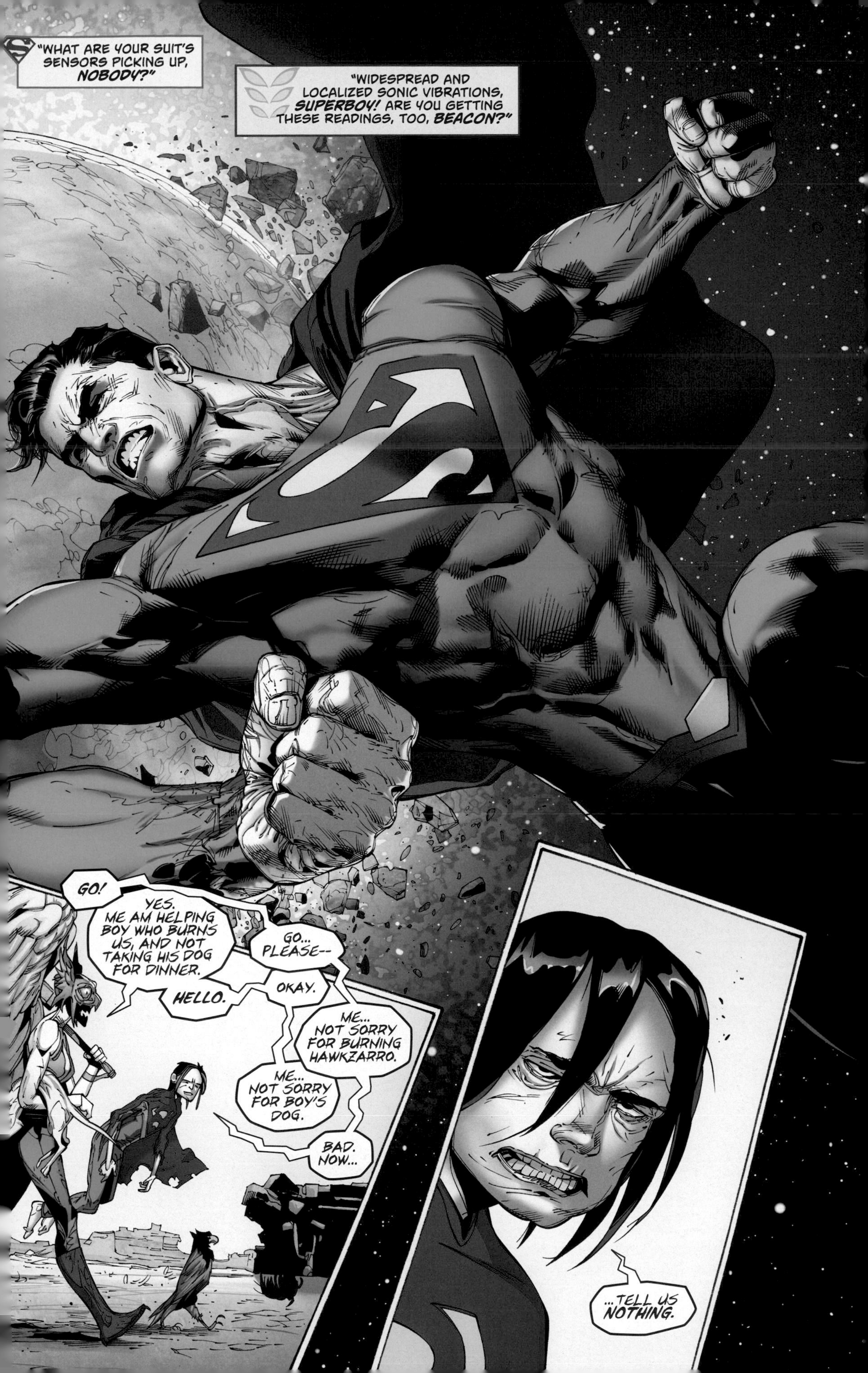

"WHAT ARE YOUR SUIT'S SENSORS PICKING UP, NOBODY?"
"WIDESPREAD AND LOCALIZED SONIC VIBRATIONS, SUPERBOY! ARE YOU GETTING THESE READINGS, TOO, BEACON?"
GO!
YES. ME AM HELPING BOY WHO BURNS US, AND NOT TAKING HIS DOG FOR DINNER.
HELLO.
GO... PLEASE--
OKAY.
ME... NOT SORRY FOR BURNING HAWKZARRO.
ME... NOT SORRY FOR BOY'S DOG.
BAD. NOW...
...TELL US NOTHING.

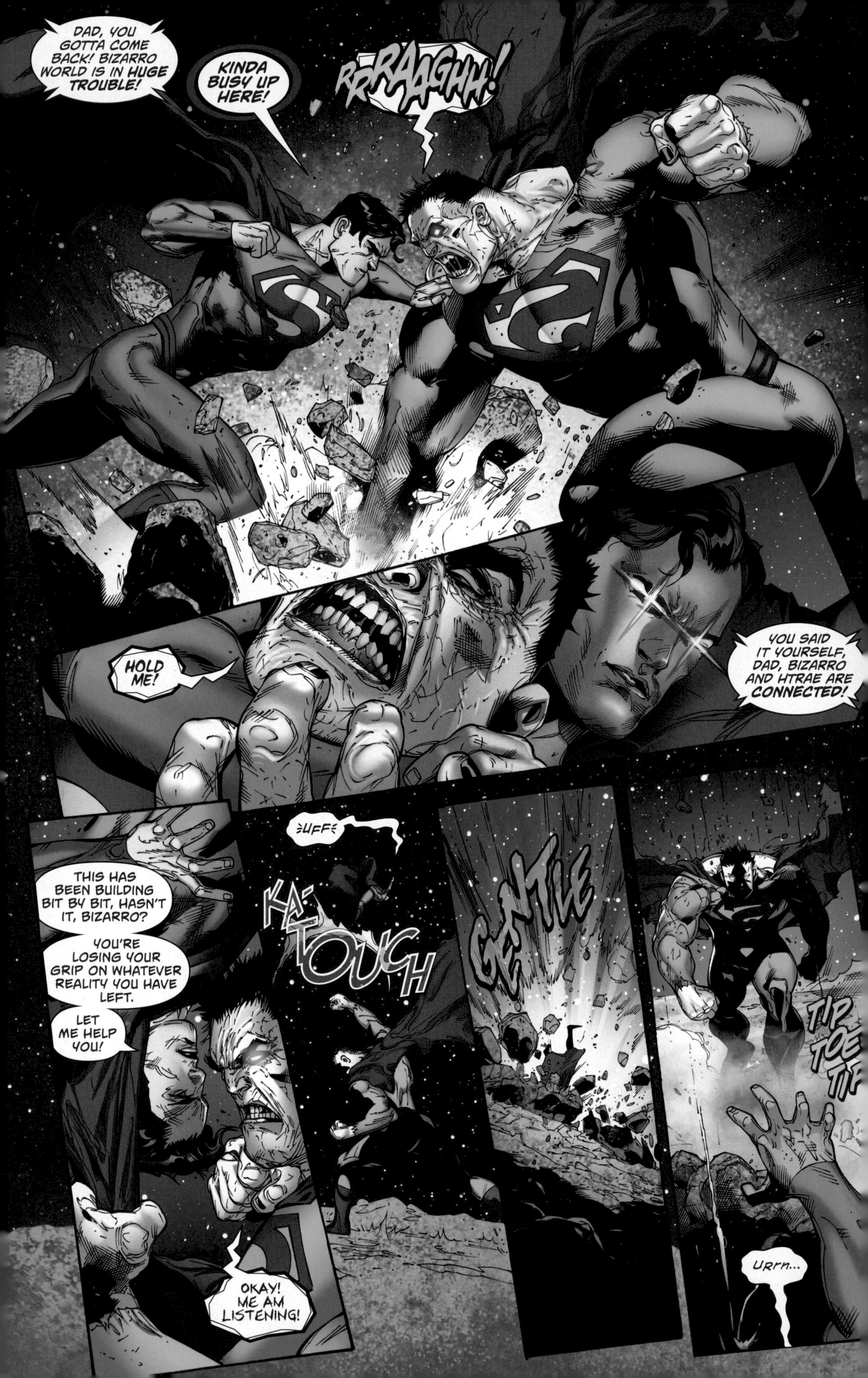
DAD, YOU GOTTA COME BACK! BIZARRO WORLD IS IN HUGE TROUBLE!
KINDA BUSY UP HERE!
RRRAAAGHH!
HOLD ME!
YOU SAID IT YOURSELF, DAD, BIZARRO AND HTRAE ARE CONNECTED!
THIS HAS BEEN BUILDING BIT BY BIT, HASN'T IT, BIZARRO?
YOU'RE LOSING YOUR GRIP ON WHATEVER REALITY YOU HAVE LEFT.
LET ME HELP YOU!
OKAY! ME AM LISTENING!
UFF
KA-TOUCH
GENTLE
TIP TOE TIP
Urrn...

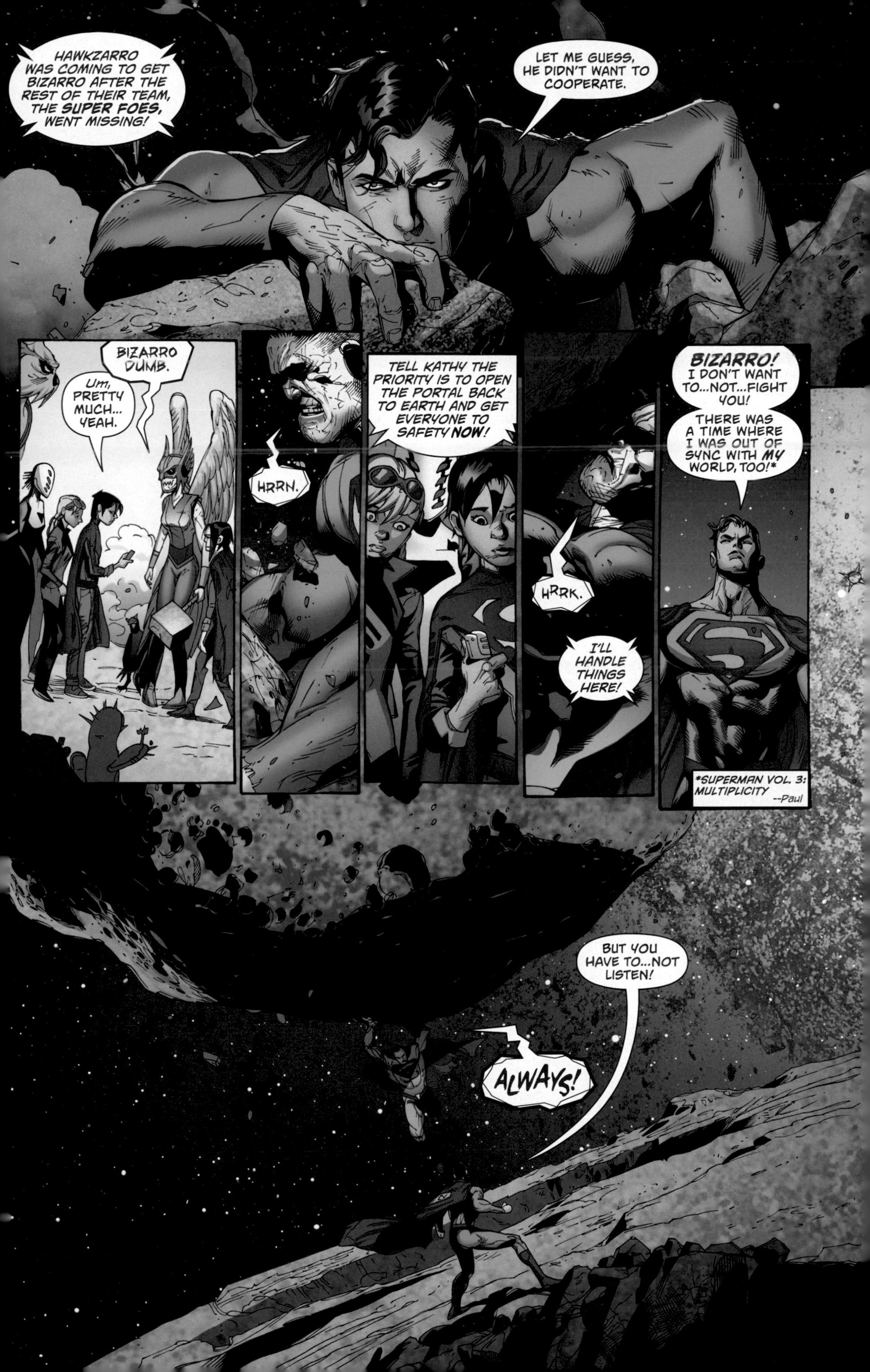
HAWKZARRO WAS COMING TO GET BIZARRO AFTER THE REST OF THEIR TEAM, THE SUPER FOES, WENT MISSING!
LET ME GUESS, HE DIDN'T WANT TO COOPERATE.
BIZARRO DUMB.
Um, PRETTY MUCH... YEAH.
HRRN.
TELL KATHY THE PRIORITY IS TO OPEN THE PORTAL BACK TO EARTH AND GET EVERYONE TO SAFETY NOW!
HRRK.
I'LL HANDLE THINGS HERE!
BIZARRO! I DON'T WANT TO...NOT...FIGHT YOU!
THERE WAS A TIME WHERE I WAS OUT OF SYNC WITH MY WORLD, TOO!*
*SUPERMAN VOL. 3: MULTIPLICITY --Paul
BUT YOU HAVE TO...NOT LISTEN!
ALWAYS!

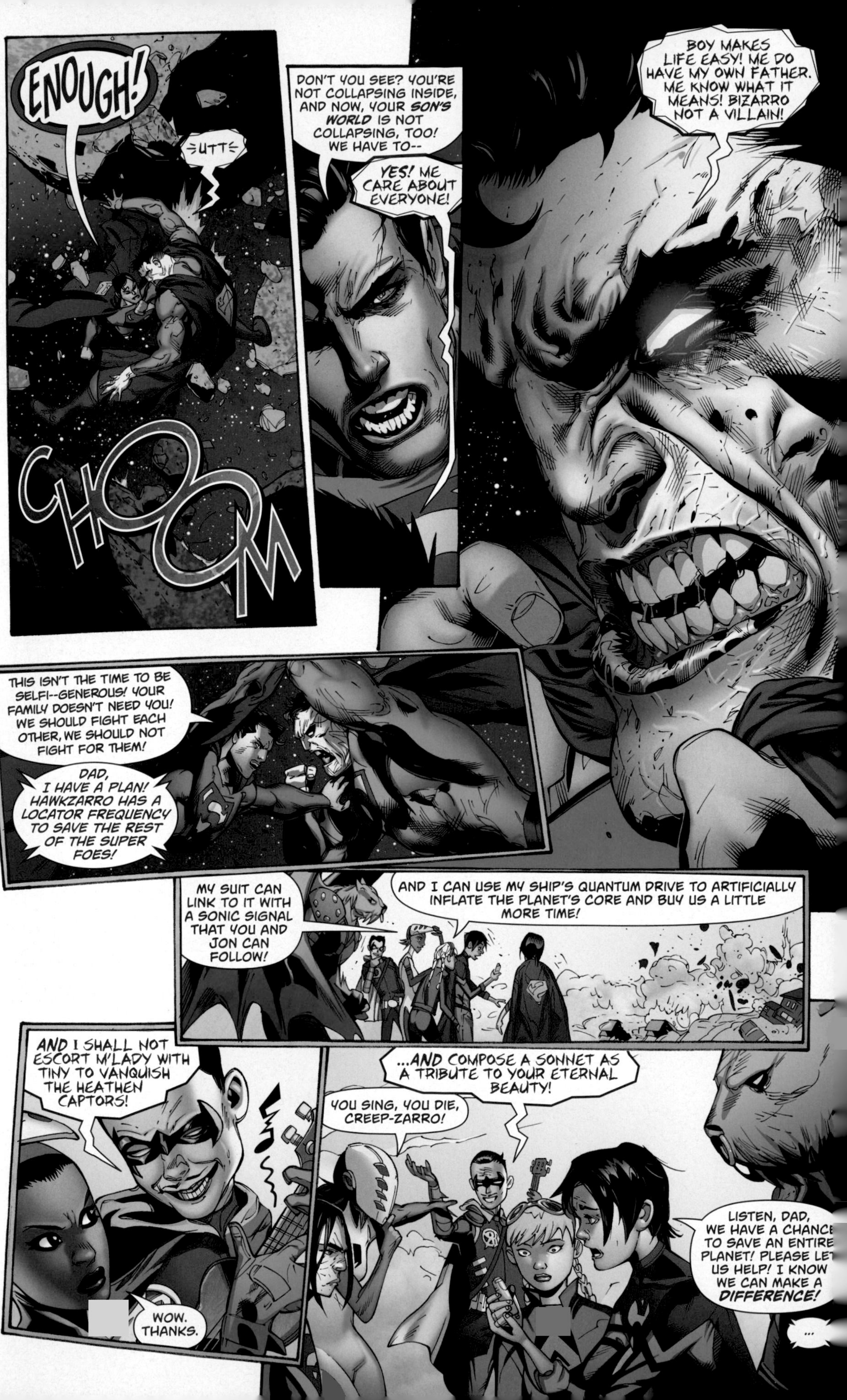
ENOUGH!
UTT
CHOOOM
DON'T YOU SEE? YOU'RE NOT COLLAPSING INSIDE, AND NOW, YOUR SON'S WORLD IS NOT COLLAPSING, TOO! WE HAVE TO--
YES! ME CARE ABOUT EVERYONE!
BOY MAKES LIFE EASY! ME DO HAVE MY OWN FATHER. ME KNOW WHAT IT MEANS! BIZARRO NOT A VILLAIN!
THIS ISN'T THE TIME TO BE SELFI--GENEROUS! YOUR FAMILY DOESN'T NEED YOU! WE SHOULD FIGHT EACH OTHER, WE SHOULD NOT FIGHT FOR THEM!
DAD, I HAVE A PLAN! HAWKZARRO HAS A LOCATOR FREQUENCY TO SAVE THE REST OF THE SUPER FOES!
MY SUIT CAN LINK TO IT WITH A SONIC SIGNAL THAT YOU AND JON CAN FOLLOW!
AND I CAN USE MY SHIP'S QUANTUM DRIVE TO ARTIFICIALLY INFLATE THE PLANET'S CORE AND BUY US A LITTLE MORE TIME!
AND I SHALL NOT ESCORT M'LADY WITH TINY TO VANQUISH THE HEATHEN CAPTORS!
WOW. THANKS.
...AND COMPOSE A SONNET AS A TRIBUTE TO YOUR ETERNAL BEAUTY!
YOU SING, YOU DIE, CREEP-ZARRO!
LISTEN, DAD, WE HAVE A CHANCE TO SAVE AN ENTIRE PLANET! PLEASE LET US HELP! I KNOW WE CAN MAKE A DIFFERENCE!
...

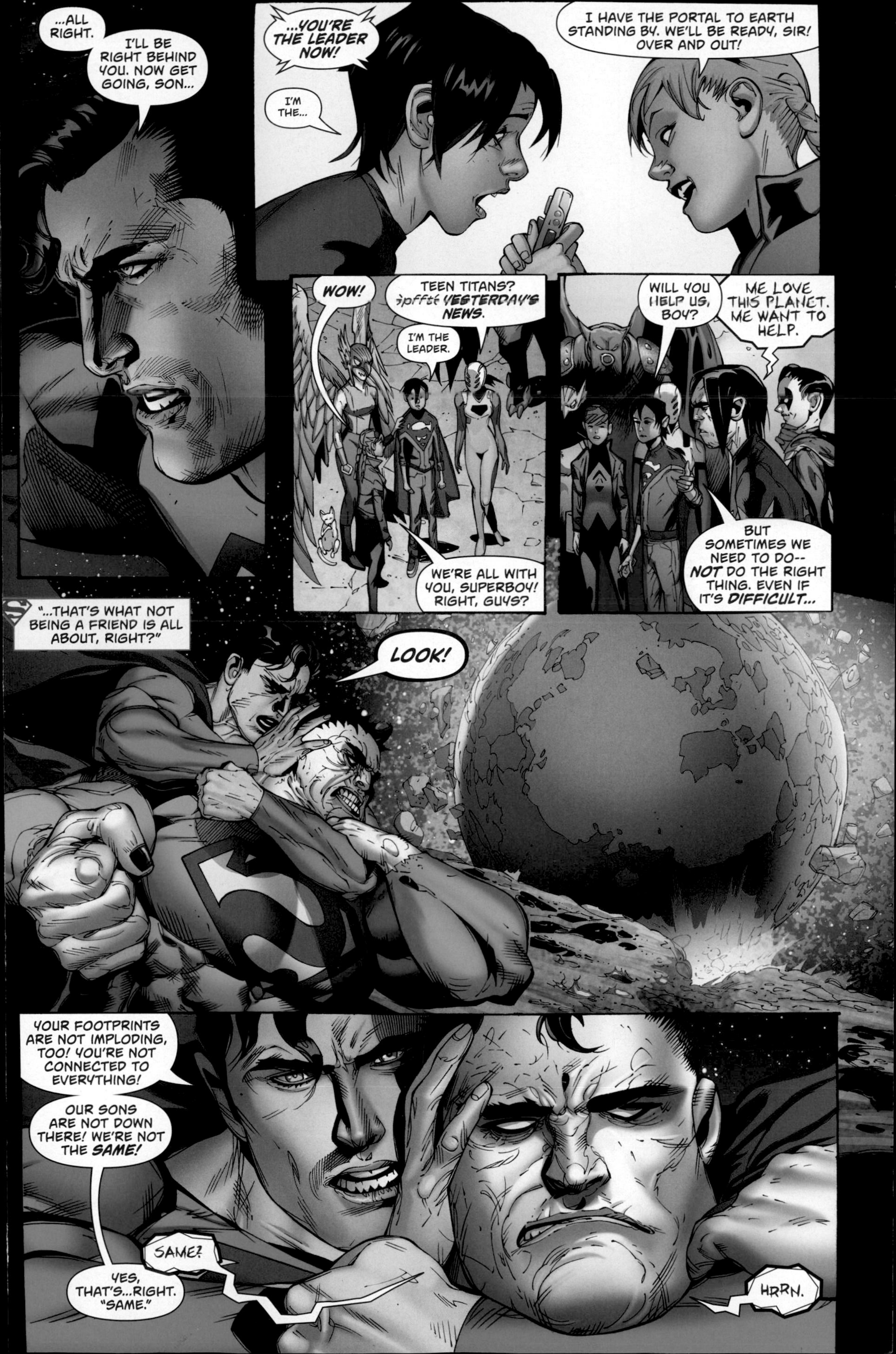
...ALL RIGHT.
I'LL BE RIGHT BEHIND YOU. NOW GET GOING, SON...
...YOU'RE THE LEADER NOW!
I'M THE...
I HAVE THE PORTAL TO EARTH STANDING BY. WE'LL BE READY, SIR! OVER AND OUT!
WOW!
TEEN TITANS? ¡pfft! YESTERDAY'S NEWS.
I'M THE LEADER.
WE'RE ALL WITH YOU, SUPERBOY! RIGHT, GUYS?
WILL YOU HELP US, BOY?
ME LOVE THIS PLANET. ME WANT TO HELP.
BUT SOMETIMES WE NEED TO DO-- NOT DO THE RIGHT THING. EVEN IF IT'S DIFFICULT...
"...THAT'S WHAT NOT BEING A FRIEND IS ALL ABOUT, RIGHT?"
LOOK!
YOUR FOOTPRINTS ARE NOT IMPLODING, TOO! YOU'RE NOT CONNECTED TO EVERYTHING!
OUR SONS ARE NOT DOWN THERE! WE'RE NOT THE SAME!
SAME?
YES, THAT'S...RIGHT. "SAME."
HRRN.

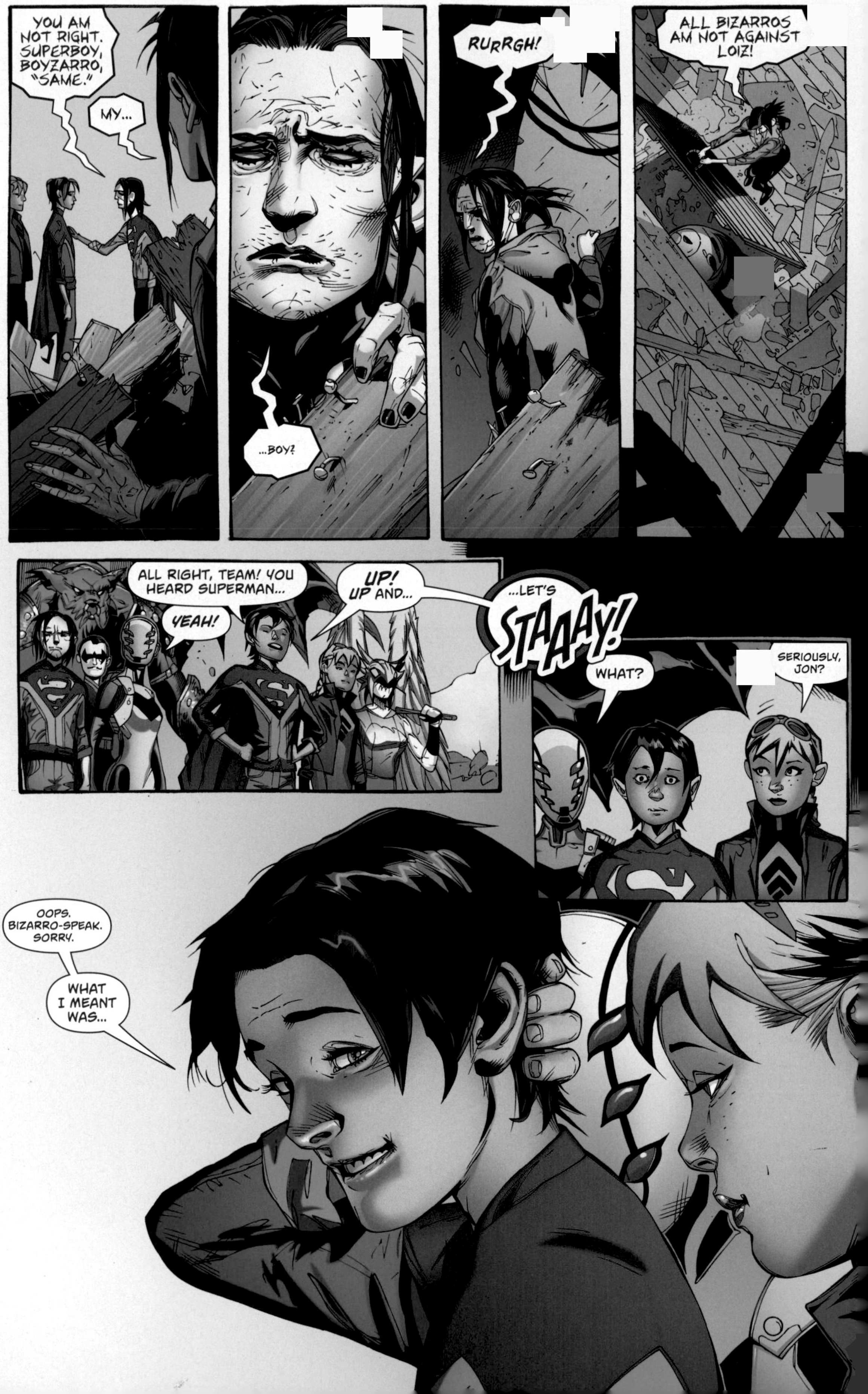
YOU AM NOT RIGHT. SUPERBOY, BOYZARRO, "SAME."
MY...
...BOY?
RURRGH!
ALL BIZARROS AM NOT AGAINST LOIZ!
ALL RIGHT, TEAM! YOU HEARD SUPERMAN...
YEAH!
UP! UP AND...
...LET'S
STAAAY!
WHAT?
SERIOUSLY, JON?
OOPS. BIZARRO-SPEAK. SORRY.
WHAT I MEANT WAS...

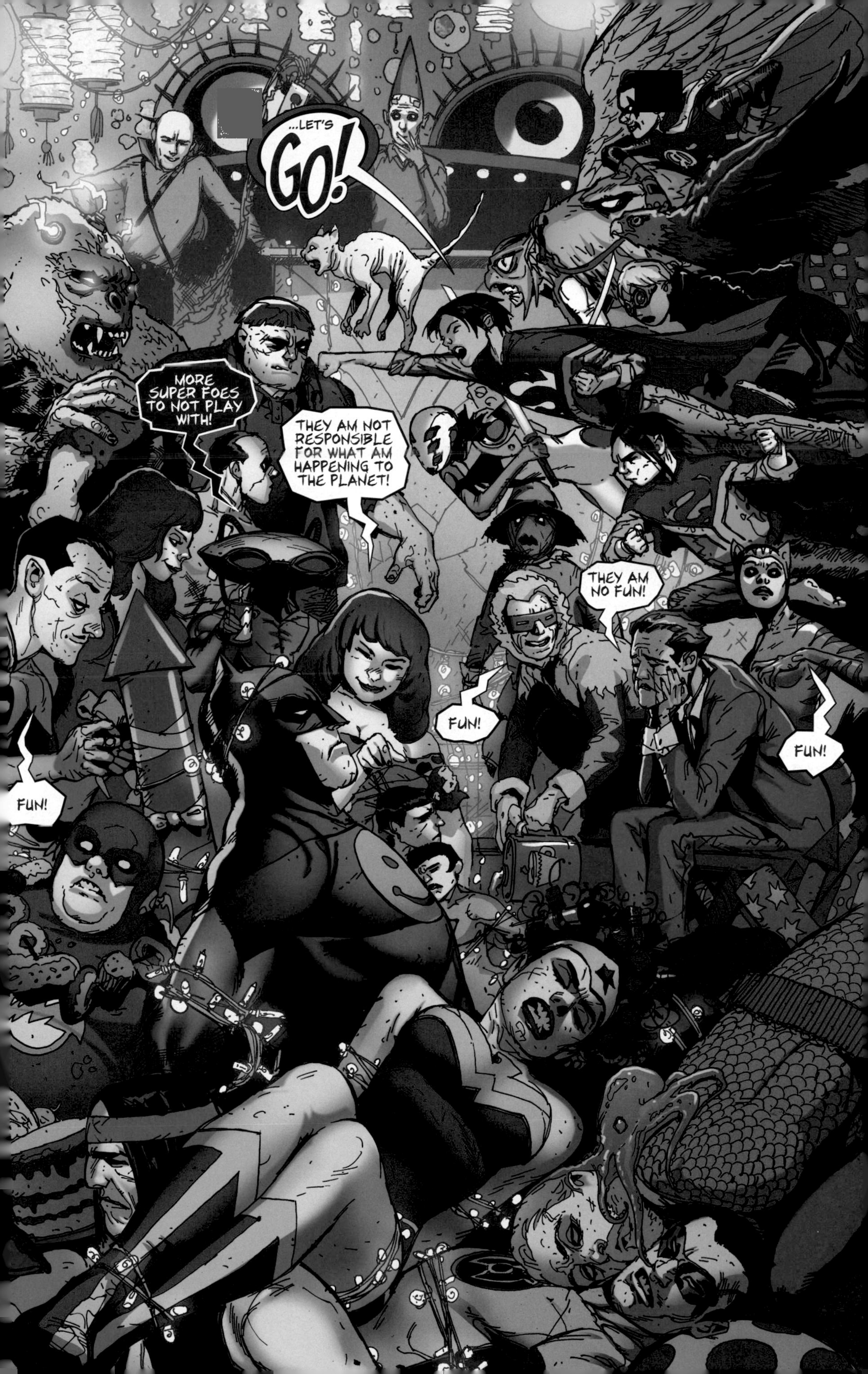
...LET'S
GO!
MORE SUPER FOES TO NOT PLAY WITH!
THEY AM NOT RESPONSIBLE FOR WHAT AM HAPPENING TO THE PLANET!
THEY AM NO FUN!
FUN!
FUN!
FUN!

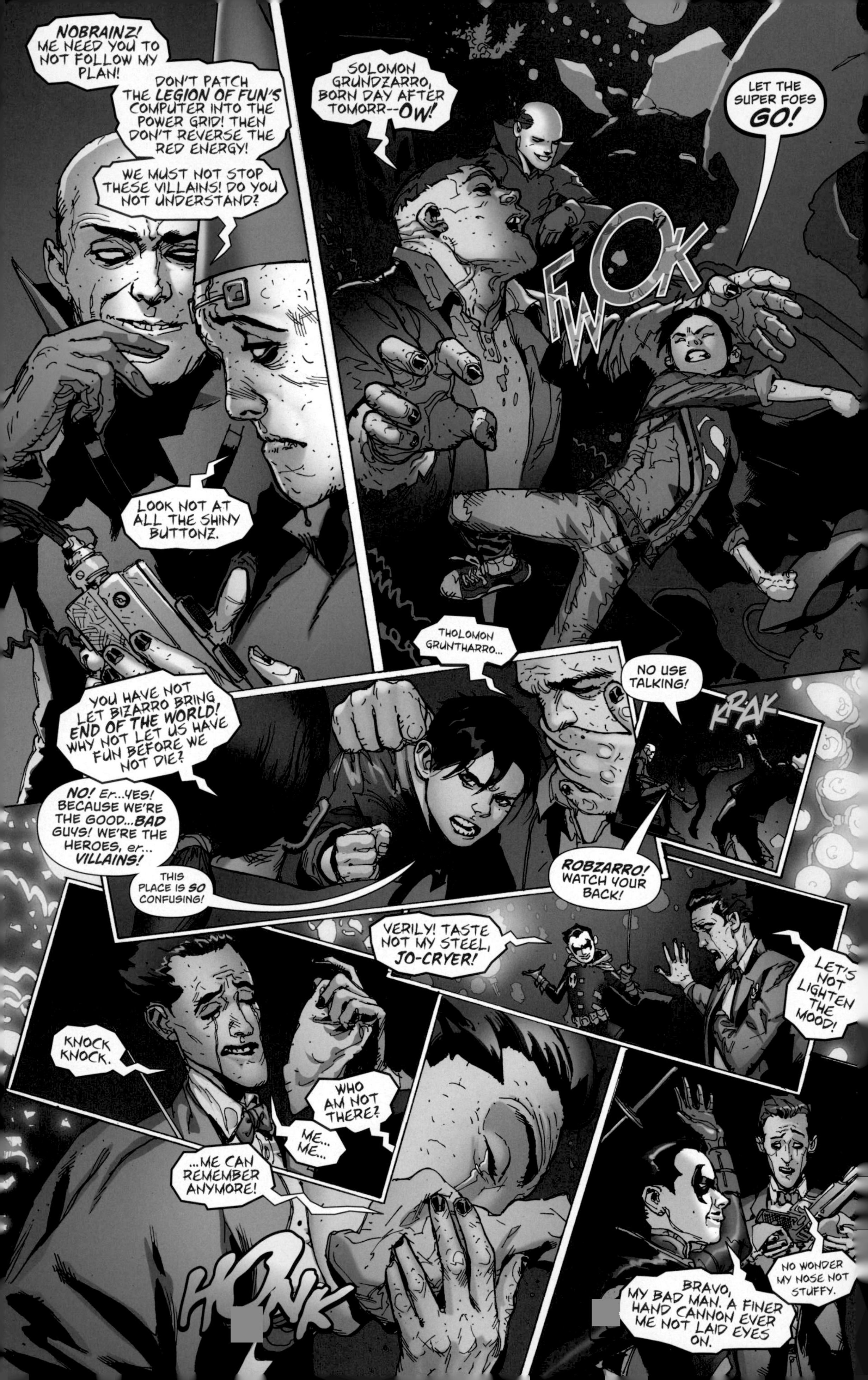
NOBRAINZ! ME NEED YOU TO NOT FOLLOW MY PLAN!
DON'T PATCH THE LEGION OF FUN'S COMPUTER INTO THE POWER GRID! THEN DON'T REVERSE THE RED ENERGY!
WE MUST NOT STOP THESE VILLAINS! DO YOU NOT UNDERSTAND?
LOOK NOT AT ALL THE SHINY BUTTONZ.
SOLOMON GRUNDZARRO, BORN DAY AFTER TOMORR--OW!
LET THE SUPER FOES GO!
FWOK
YOU HAVE NOT LET BIZARRO BRING END OF THE WORLD! WHY NOT LET US HAVE FUN BEFORE WE NOT DIE?
NO! Er...YES! BECAUSE WE'RE THE GOOD...BAD GUYS! WE'RE THE HEROES, er... VILLAINS!
THIS PLACE IS SO CONFUSING!
THOLOMON GRUNTHARRO...
NO USE TALKING!
KRAK
ROBZARRO! WATCH YOUR BACK!
VERILY! TASTE NOT MY STEEL, JO-CRYER!
LET'S NOT LIGHTEN THE MOOD!
KNOCK KNOCK.
WHO AM NOT THERE?
ME... ME...
...ME CAN REMEMBER ANYMORE!
HONK
BRAVO, MY BAD MAN. A FINER HAND CANNON EVER ME NOT LAID EYES ON.
NO WONDER MY NOSE NOT STUFFY.

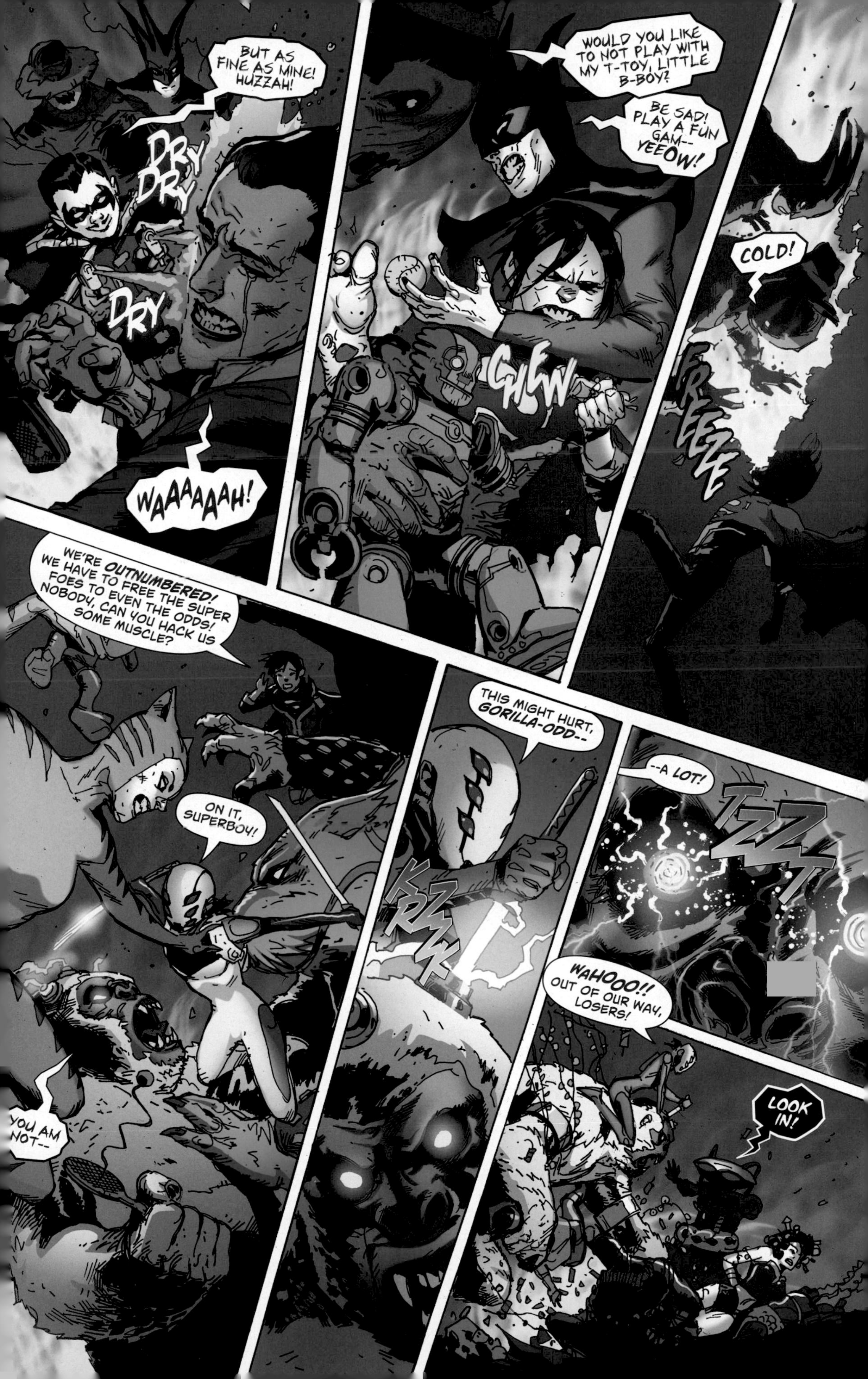
BUT AS FINE AS MINE! HUZZAH!
DRY DRY
DRY
WAAAAAAH!
WOULD YOU LIKE TO NOT PLAY WITH MY T-TOY, LITTLE B-BOY?
BE SAD! PLAY A FUN GAM-- YEEOW!
CHEW
COLD!
FREEZE
WE'RE OUTNUMBERED! WE HAVE TO FREE THE SUPER FOES TO EVEN THE ODDS! NOBODY, CAN YOU HACK US SOME MUSCLE?
ON IT, SUPERBOY!
YOU AM NOT--
THIS MIGHT HURT, GORILLA-ODD--
KRZWK
--A LOT!
TZZZT
WAHOOO!! OUT OF OUR WAY, LOSERS!
LOOK IN!

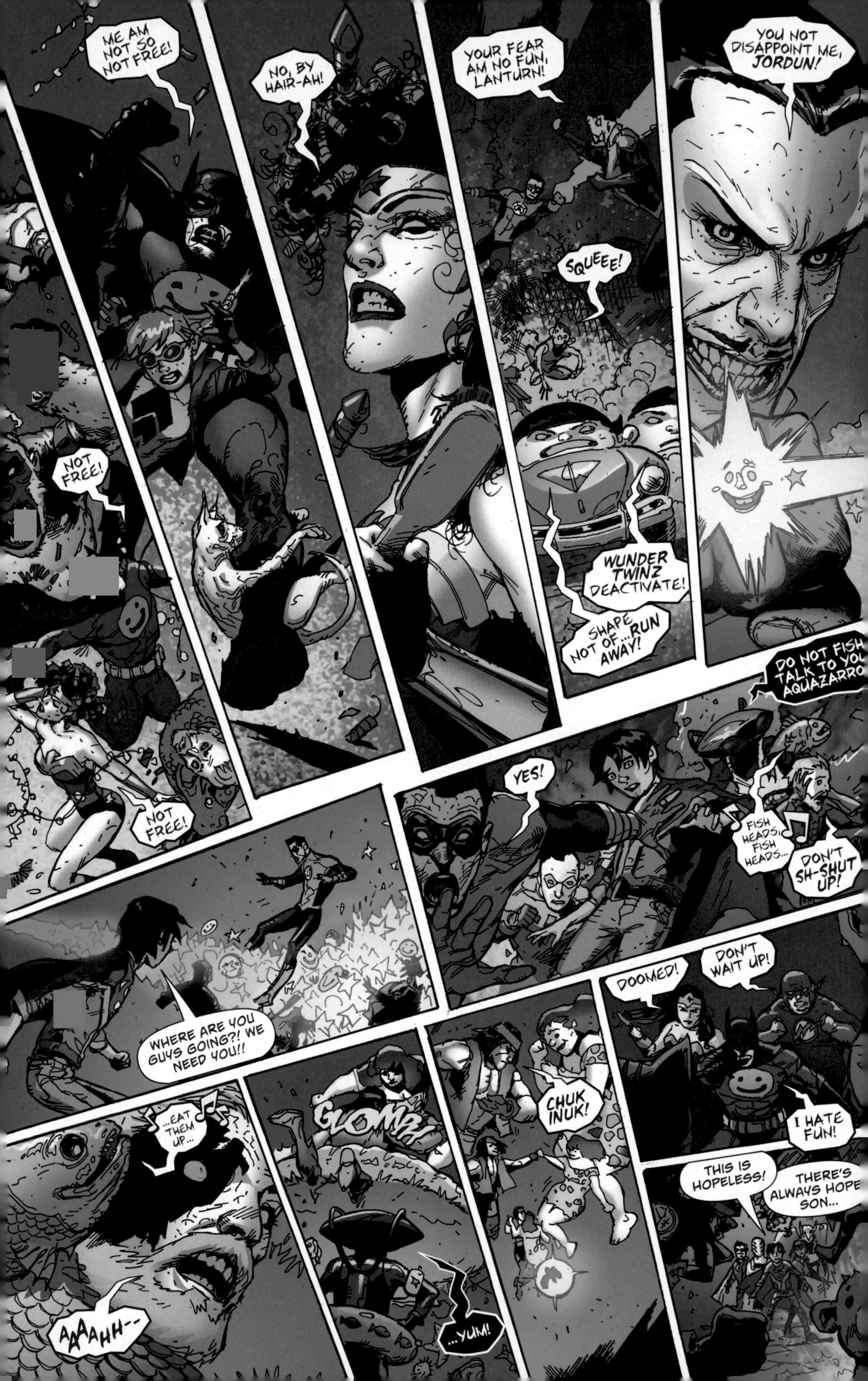
ME AM NOT SO NOT FREE!
NOT FREE!
NOT FREE!
NO, BY HAIR-AH!
YOUR FEAR AM NO FUN, LANTURN!
SQUEEE!
WUNDER TWINZ DEACTIVATE!
SHAPE NOT OF... RUN AWAY!
YOU NOT DISAPPOINT ME, JORDUN!
DO NOT FISH TALK TO YOU AQUAZARRO
YES!
FISH HEADS, FISH HEADS...
DON'T SH-SHUT UP!
WHERE ARE YOU GUYS GOING?! WE NEED YOU!!
DOOMED!
DON'T WAIT UP!
I HATE FUN!
...EAT THEM UP...
AAAAHH--
GLOMP!
...YUM!
CHUK INUK!
THIS IS HOPELESS!
THERE'S ALWAYS HOPE SON...

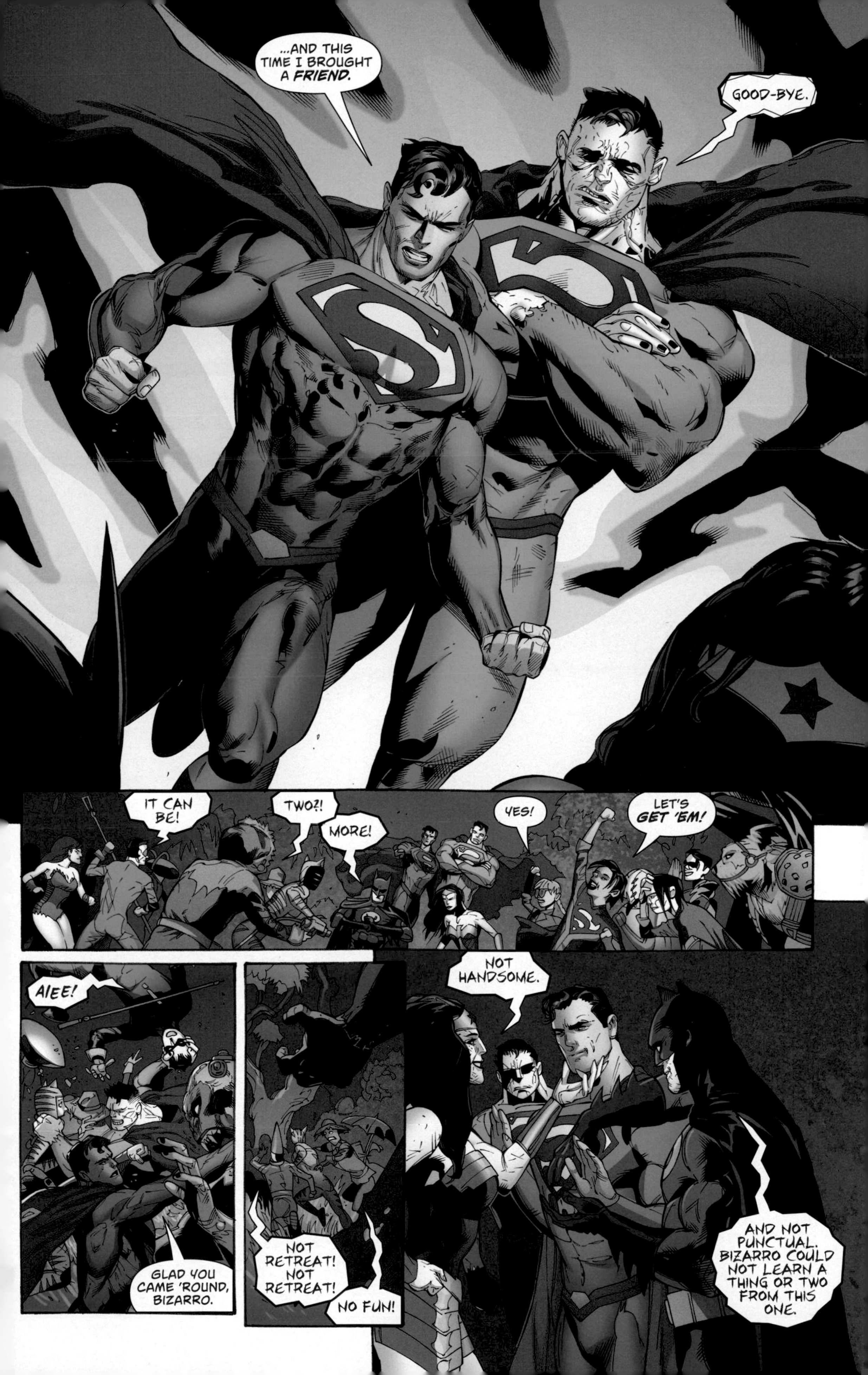
...AND THIS TIME I BROUGHT A FRIEND.
GOOD-BYE.
IT CAN BE!
TWO?!
MORE!
YES!
LET'S GET 'EM!
AIEE!
GLAD YOU CAME 'ROUND, BIZARRO.
NOT RETREAT! NOT RETREAT!
NO FUN!
NOT HANDSOME.
AND NOT PUNCTUAL. BIZARRO COULD NOT LEARN A THING OR TWO FROM THIS ONE.

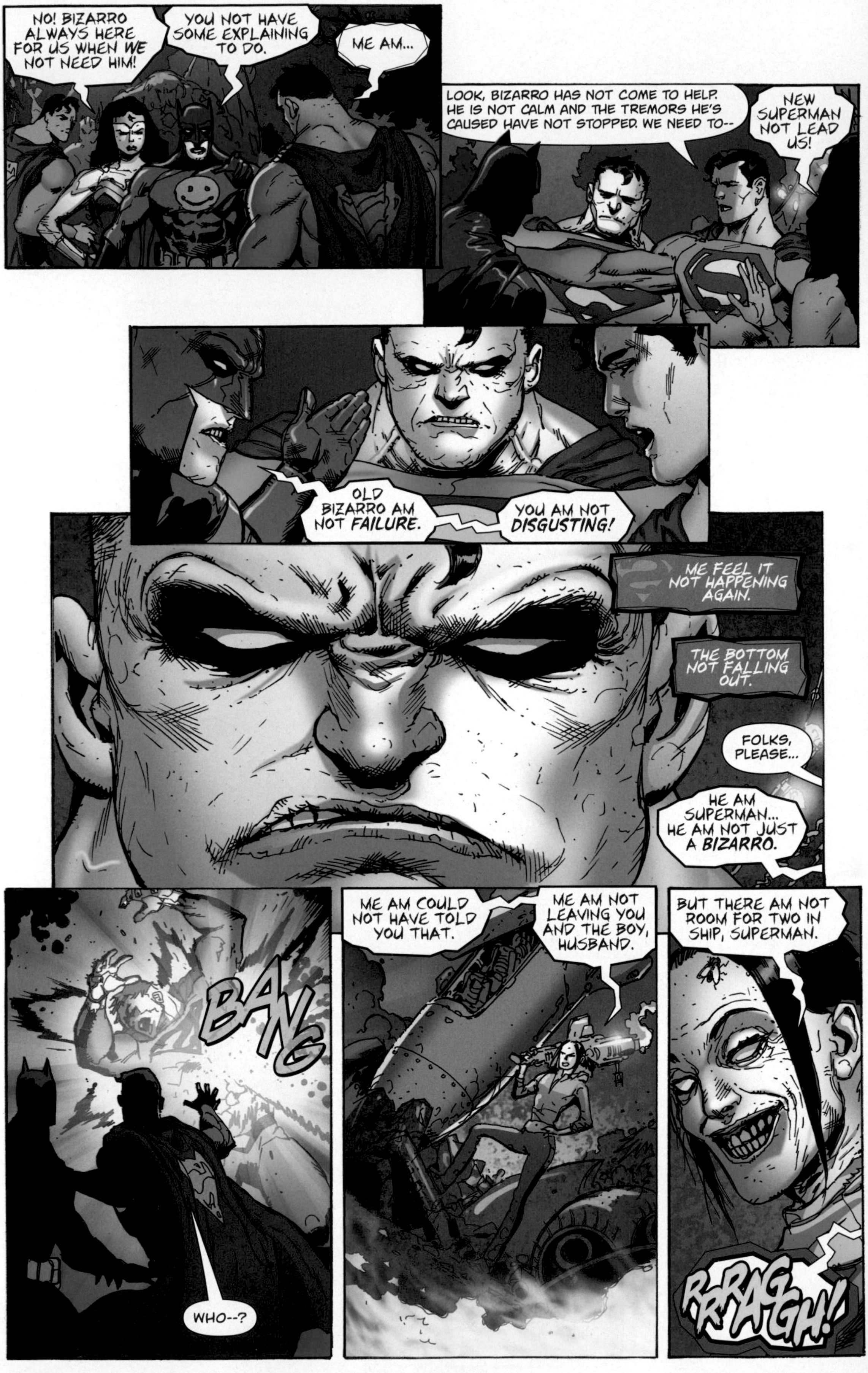
NO! BIZARRO ALWAYS HERE FOR US WHEN WE NOT NEED HIM!
YOU NOT HAVE SOME EXPLAINING TO DO.
ME AM...
LOOK, BIZARRO HAS NOT COME TO HELP. HE IS NOT CALM AND THE TREMORS HE'S CAUSED HAVE NOT STOPPED. WE NEED TO--
NEW SUPERMAN NOT LEAD US!
OLD BIZARRO AM NOT FAILURE.
YOU AM NOT DISGUSTING!
ME FEEL IT NOT HAPPENING AGAIN.
THE BOTTOM NOT FALLING OUT.
FOLKS, PLEASE...
HE AM SUPERMAN... HE AM NOT JUST A BIZARRO.
BANG
WHO--?
ME AM COULD NOT HAVE TOLD YOU THAT.
ME AM NOT LEAVING YOU AND THE BOY, HUSBAND.
BUT THERE AM NOT ROOM FOR TWO IN SHIP, SUPERMAN.
RRRAGRRAGH!

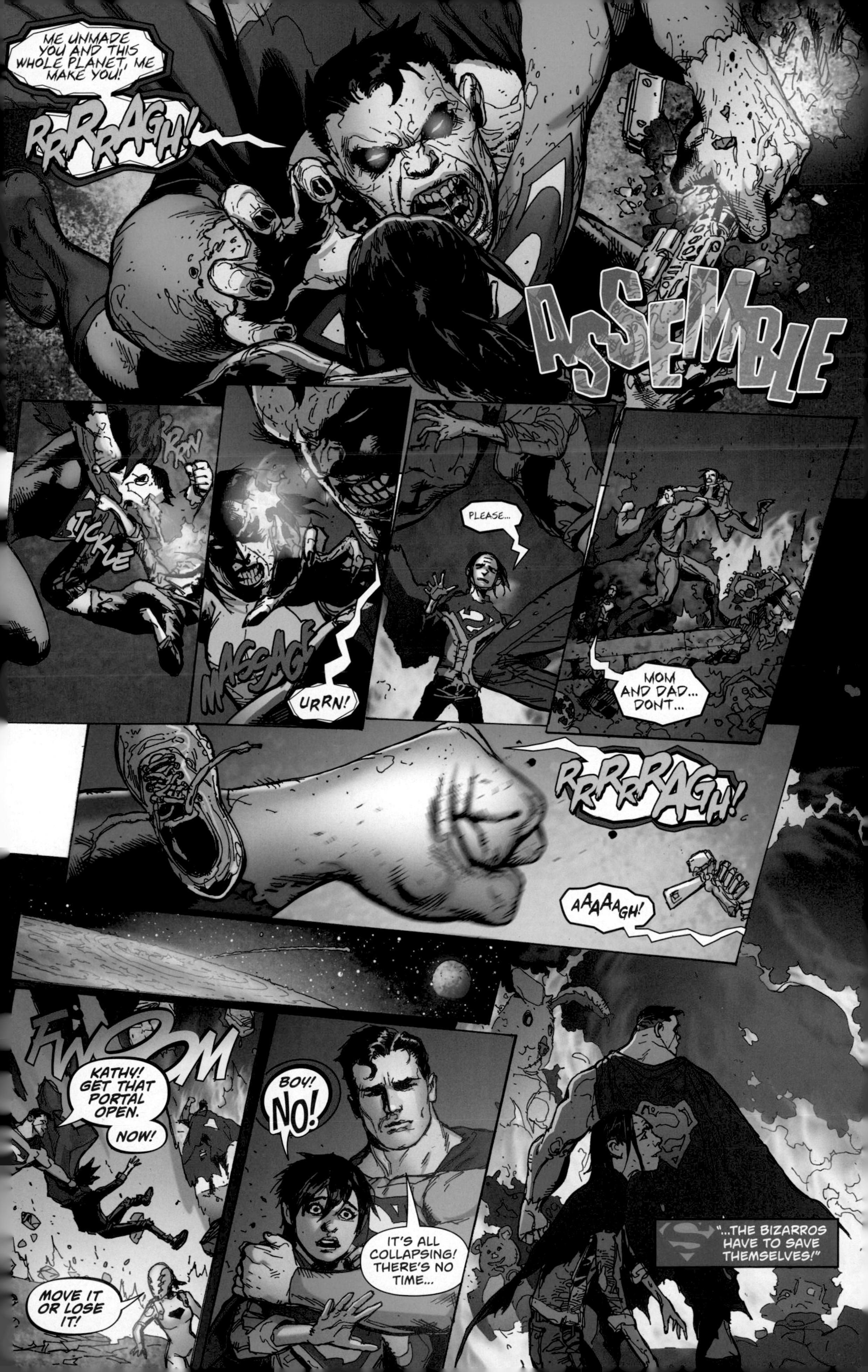
ME UNMADE YOU AND THIS WHOLE PLANET, ME MAKE YOU!
RRRRRAGH!
ASSEMBLE
TICKLE
MASSAGE
URRN!
PLEASE...
MOM AND DAD... DONT...
RRRRRAGH!
AAAAAGH!
FWOOM
KATHY! GET THAT PORTAL OPEN.
NOW!
MOVE IT OR LOSE IT!
BOY! NO!
IT'S ALL COLLAPSING! THERE'S NO TIME...
"...THE BIZARROS HAVE TO SAVE THEMSELVES!"

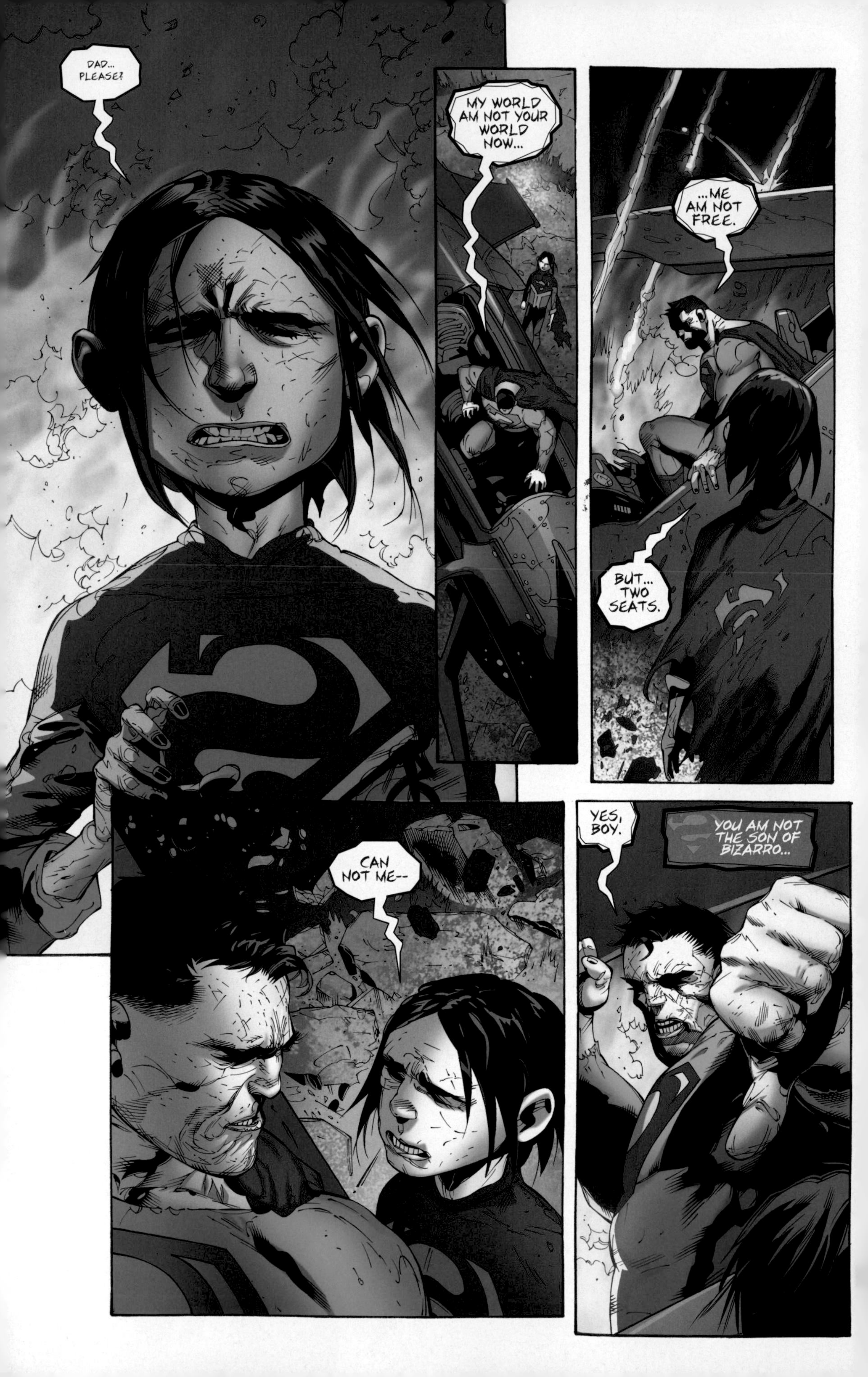
DAD... PLEASE?
MY WORLD AM NOT YOUR WORLD NOW...
...ME AM NOT FREE.
BUT... TWO SEATS.
CAN NOT ME--
YES, BOY.
YOU AM NOT THE SON OF BIZARRO...

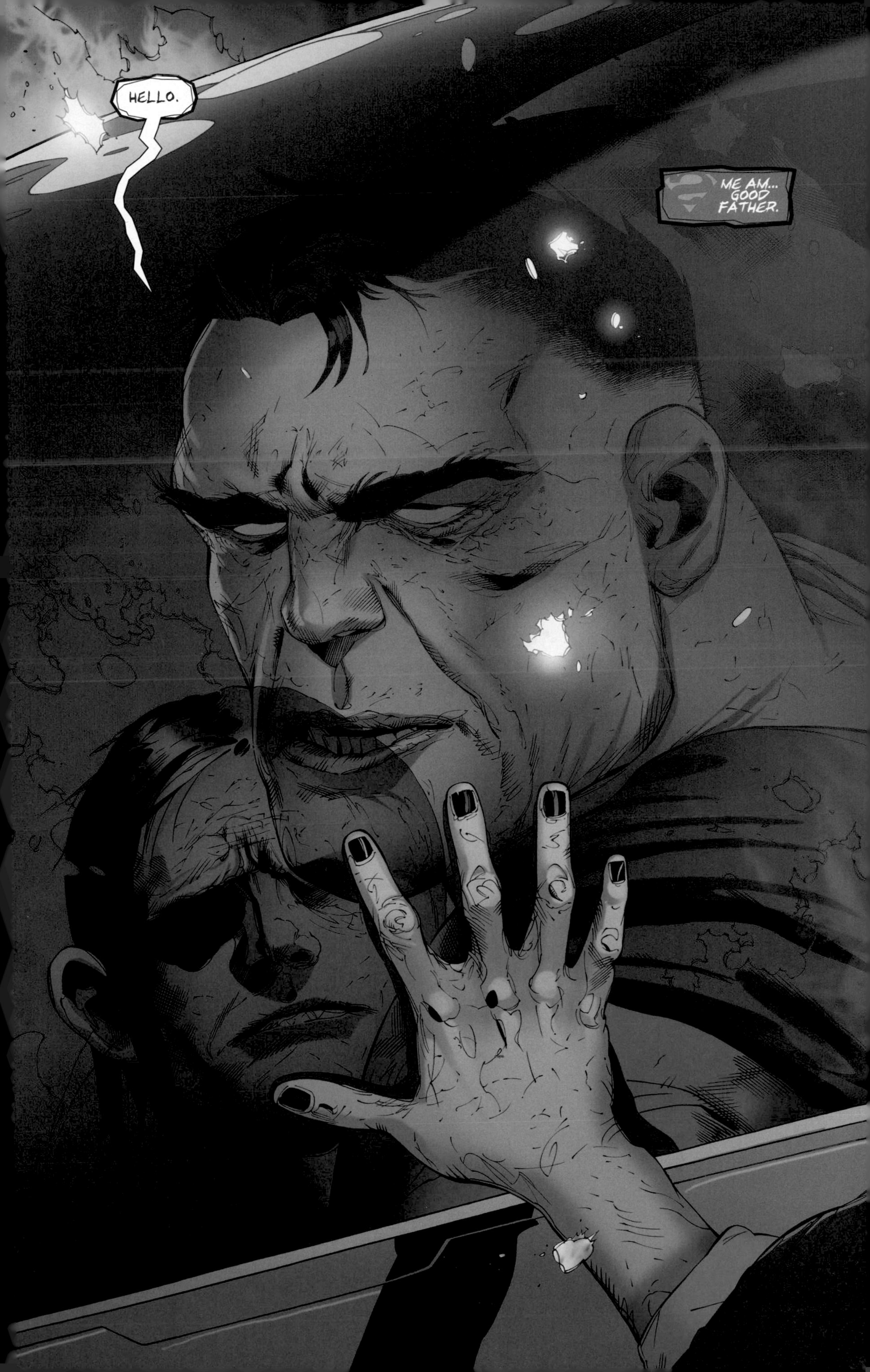
HELLO.
ME AM... GOOD FATHER.

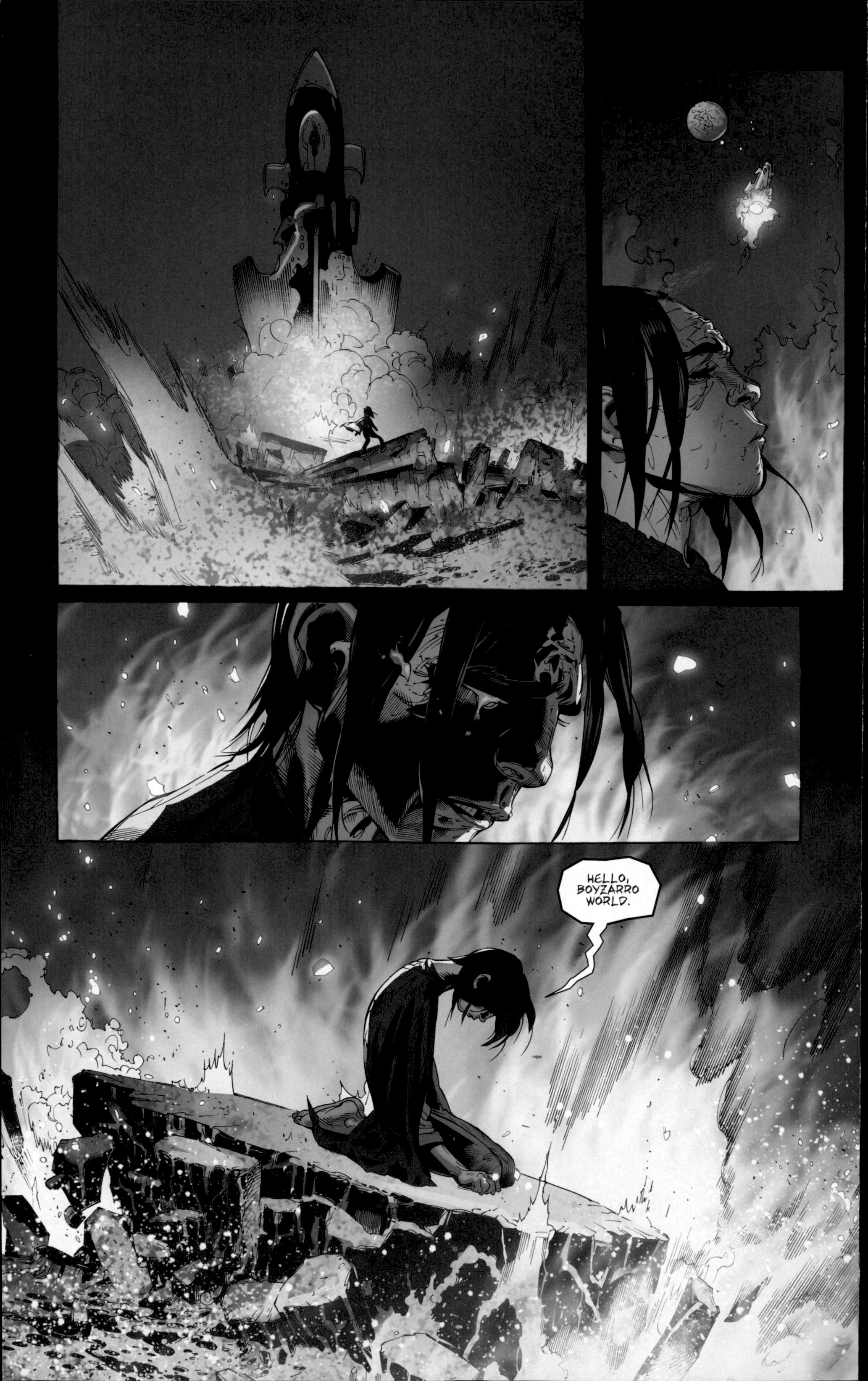
HELLO, BOYZARRO WORLD.

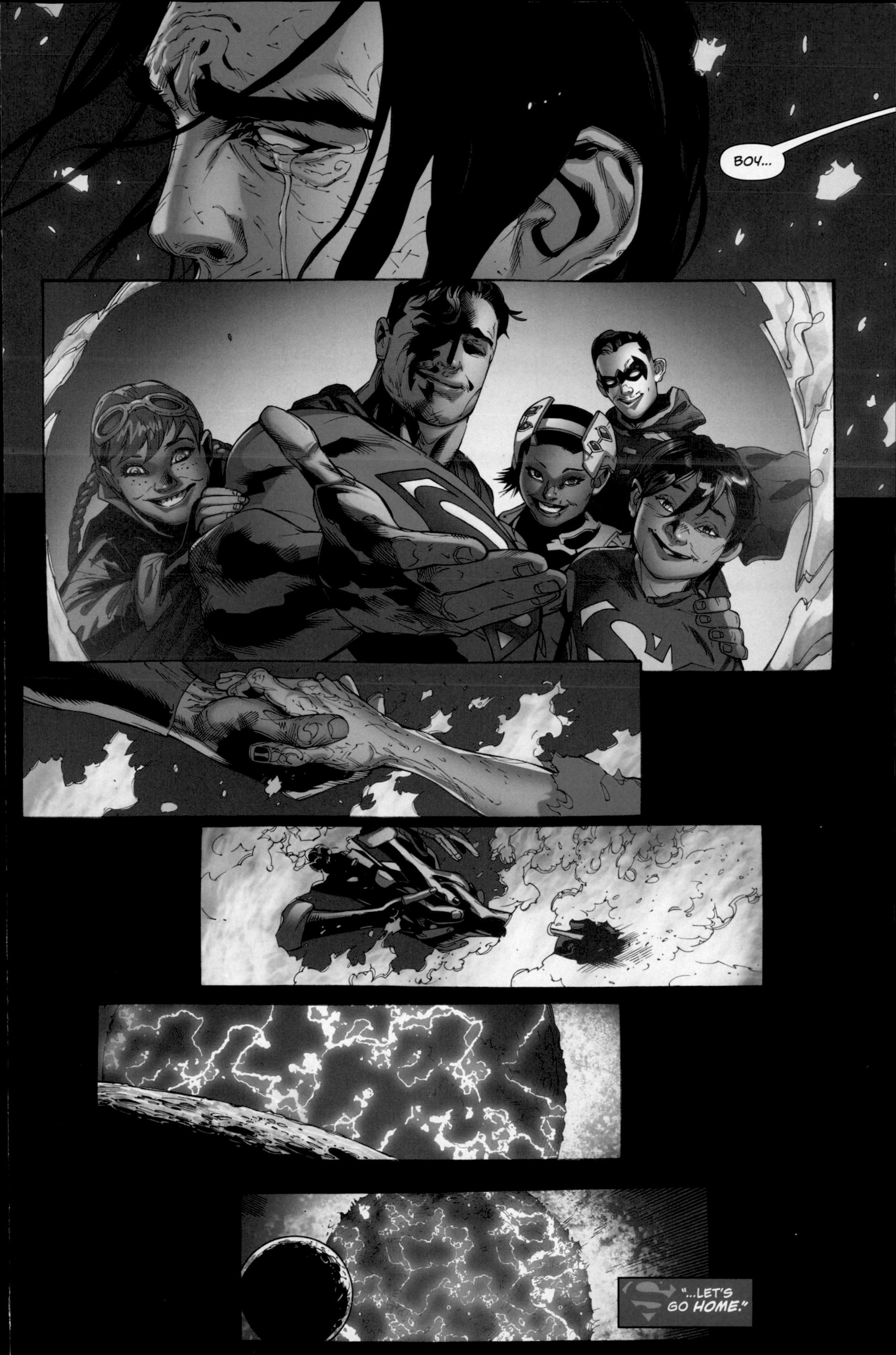
BOY...
"...LET'S GO HOME."

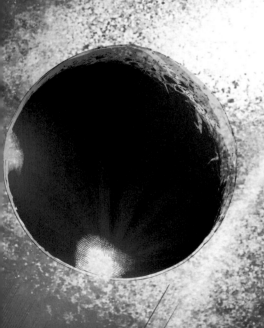

# BIZARROVERSE
## PART 3

# AS A FAMILY WE GO

Written
PATRICK GLEASO
& PETER J. TOMA
Pencils
DOUG MAHN
Inks
JAIME MENDOZ
& DOUG MAHN
Colors WIL QUINTA
Letters ROB LEI
Cover PATRICK GLEAS
& ALEJANDRO SANCH
Associate editor JESSICA CH
Editor PAUL KAMINS

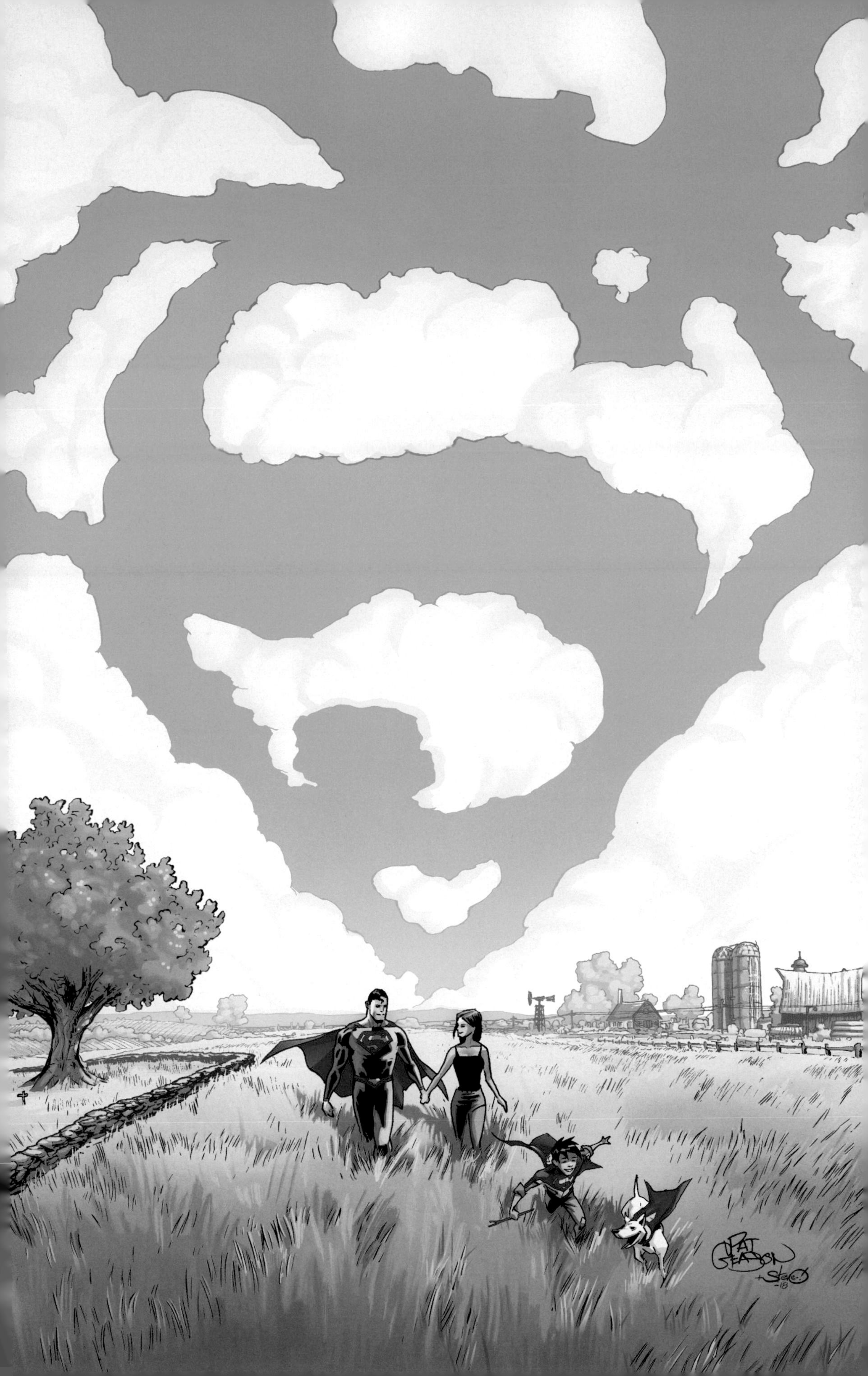

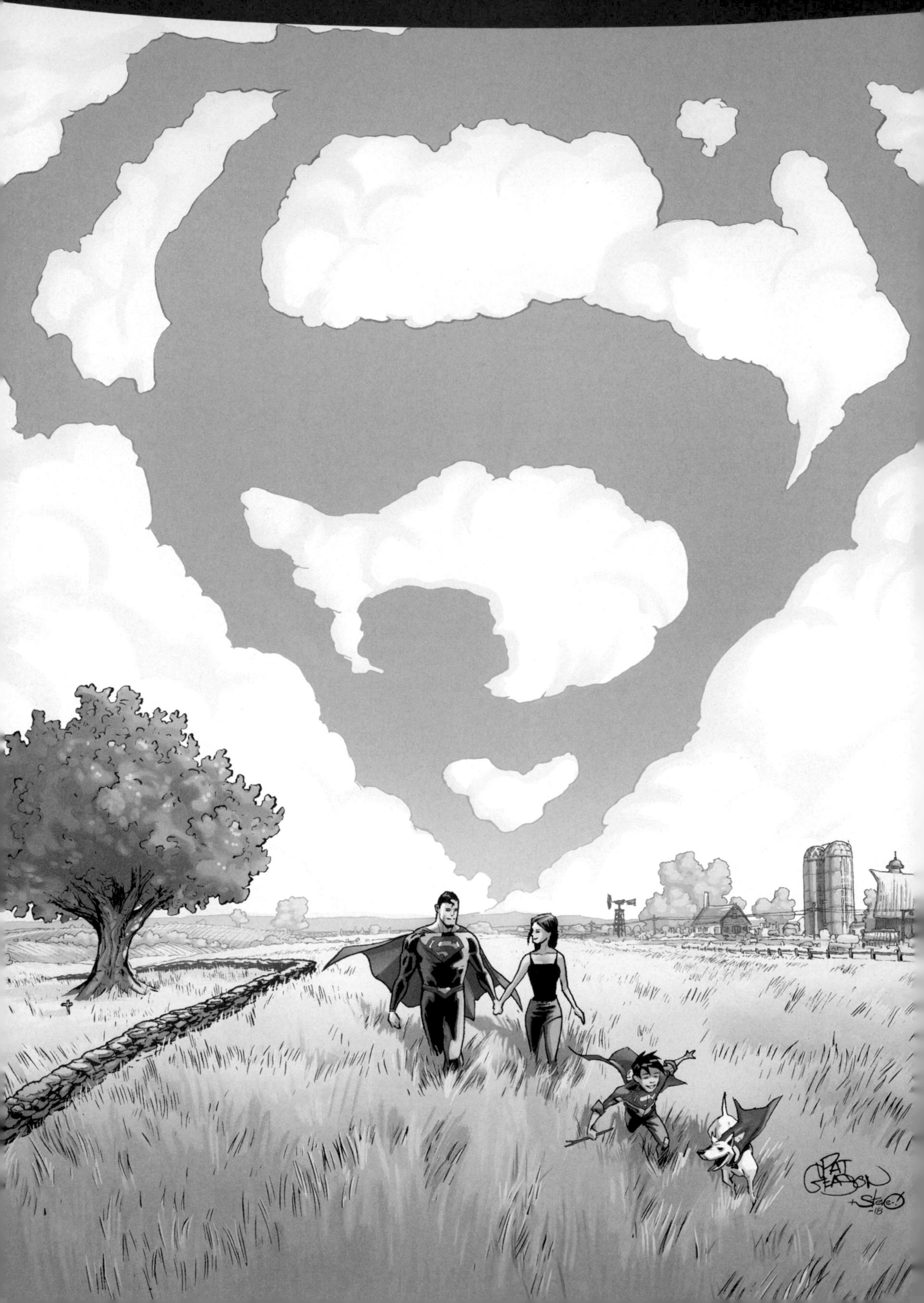

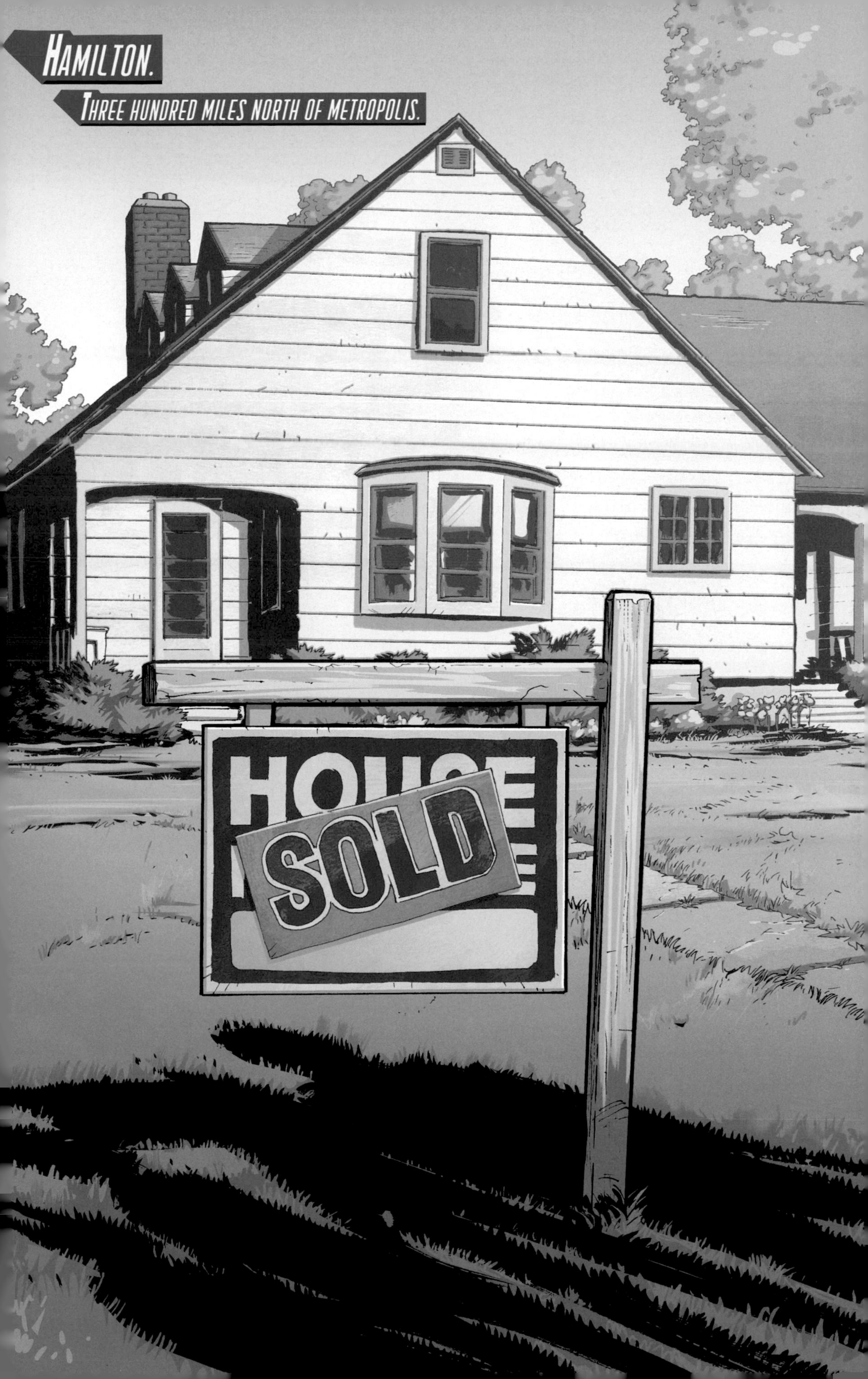
HAMILTON.
THREE HUNDRED MILES NORTH OF METROPOLIS.
HOUSE
SOLD

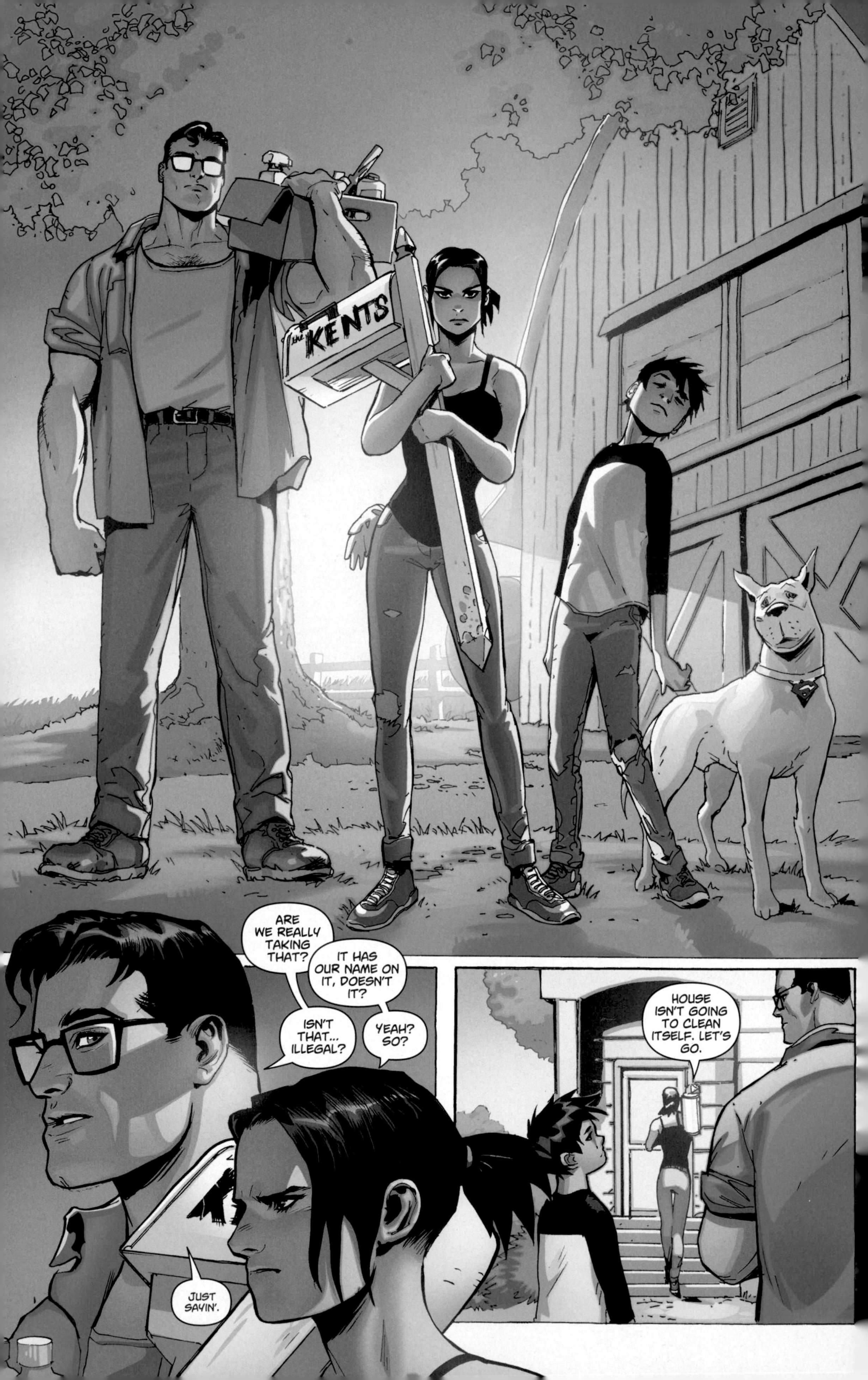
THE KENTS
ARE WE REALLY TAKING THAT?
IT HAS OUR NAME ON IT, DOESN'T IT?
ISN'T THAT... ILLEGAL?
YEAH? SO?
JUST SAYIN'.
HOUSE ISN'T GOING TO CLEAN ITSELF. LET'S GO.

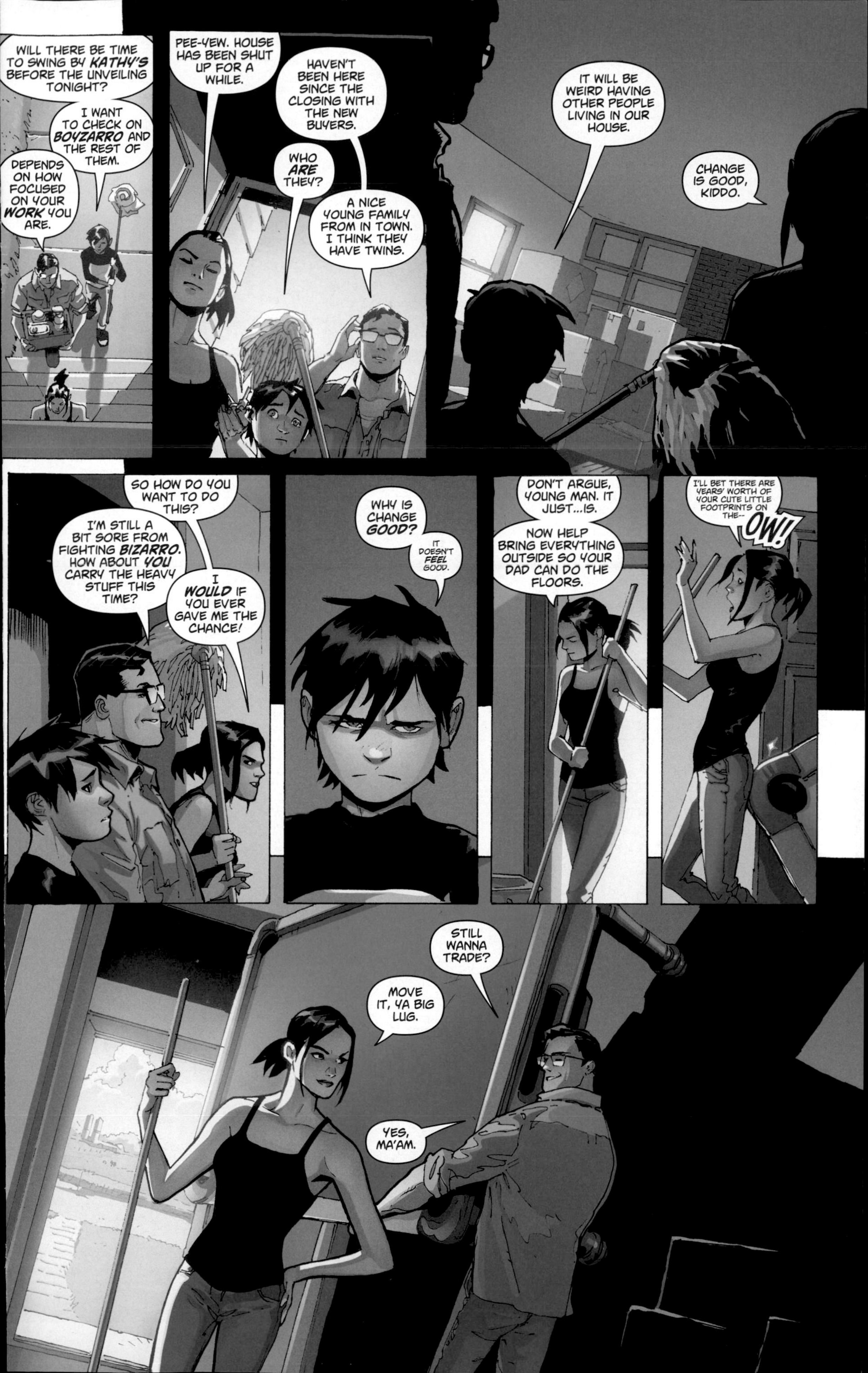
WILL THERE BE TIME TO SWING BY KATHY'S BEFORE THE UNVEILING TONIGHT?
I WANT TO CHECK ON BOYZARRO AND THE REST OF THEM.
DEPENDS ON HOW FOCUSED ON YOUR WORK YOU ARE.
PEE-YEW. HOUSE HAS BEEN SHUT UP FOR A WHILE.
HAVEN'T BEEN HERE SINCE THE CLOSING WITH THE NEW BUYERS.
WHO ARE THEY?
A NICE YOUNG FAMILY FROM IN TOWN. I THINK THEY HAVE TWINS.
IT WILL BE WEIRD HAVING OTHER PEOPLE LIVING IN OUR HOUSE.
CHANGE IS GOOD, KIDDO.
SO HOW DO YOU WANT TO DO THIS?
I'M STILL A BIT SORE FROM FIGHTING BIZARRO. HOW ABOUT YOU CARRY THE HEAVY STUFF THIS TIME?
I WOULD IF YOU EVER GAVE ME THE CHANCE!
WHY IS CHANGE GOOD?
IT DOESN'T FEEL GOOD.
DON'T ARGUE, YOUNG MAN. IT JUST...IS.
NOW HELP BRING EVERYTHING OUTSIDE SO YOUR DAD CAN DO THE FLOORS.
I'LL BET THERE ARE YEARS' WORTH OF YOUR CUTE LITTLE FOOTPRINTS ON THE--
OW!
STILL WANNA TRADE?
MOVE IT, YA BIG LUG.
YES, MA'AM.

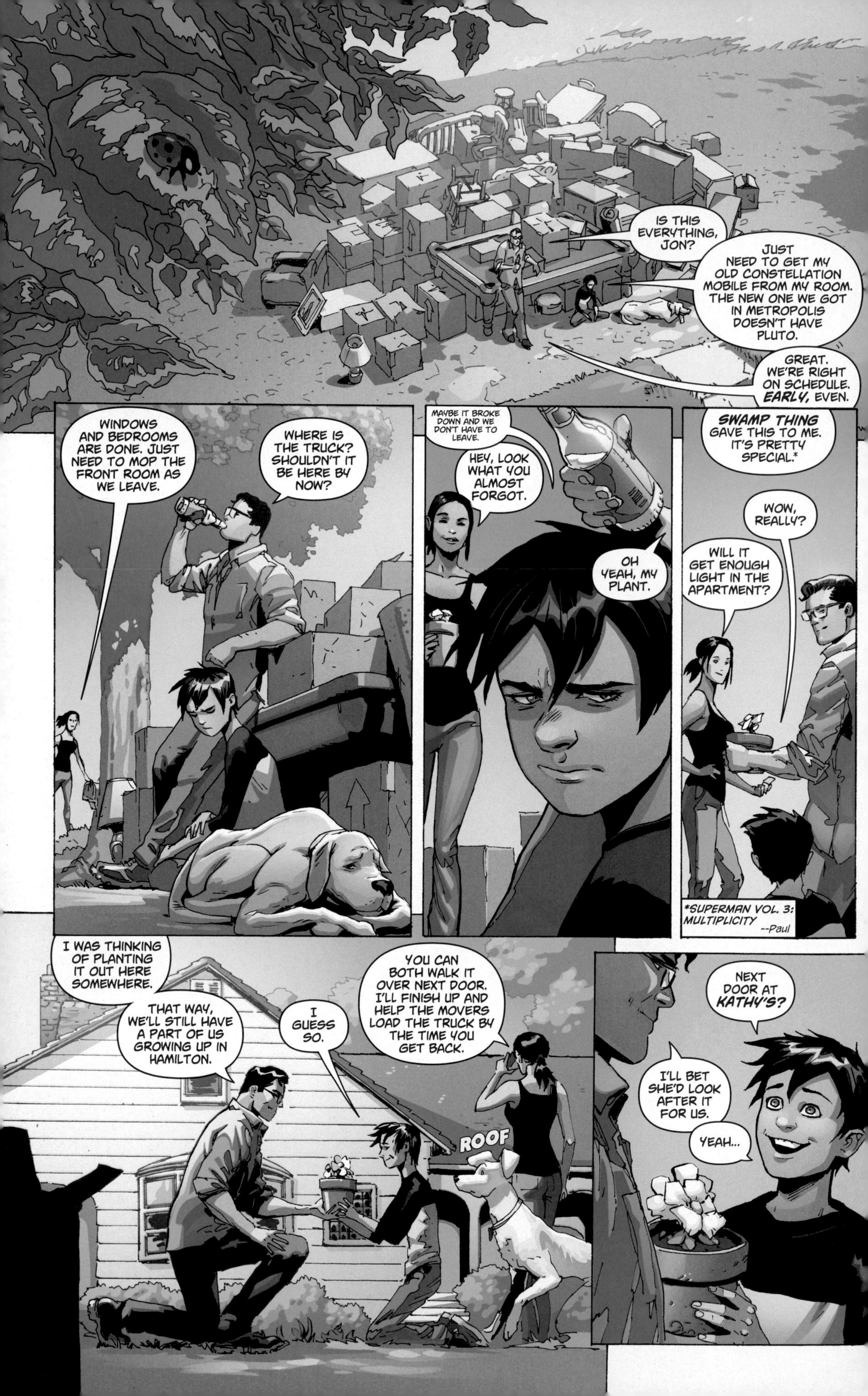
IS THIS EVERYTHING, JON?
JUST NEED TO GET MY OLD CONSTELLATION MOBILE FROM MY ROOM. THE NEW ONE WE GOT IN METROPOLIS DOESN'T HAVE PLUTO.
GREAT. WE'RE RIGHT ON SCHEDULE. EARLY, EVEN.
WINDOWS AND BEDROOMS ARE DONE. JUST NEED TO MOP THE FRONT ROOM AS WE LEAVE.
WHERE IS THE TRUCK? SHOULDN'T IT BE HERE BY NOW?
MAYBE IT BROKE DOWN AND WE DON'T HAVE TO LEAVE.
HEY, LOOK WHAT YOU ALMOST FORGOT.
OH YEAH, MY PLANT.
SWAMP THING GAVE THIS TO ME. IT'S PRETTY SPECIAL.*
WOW, REALLY?
WILL IT GET ENOUGH LIGHT IN THE APARTMENT?
*SUPERMAN VOL. 3: MULTIPLICITY --Paul
I WAS THINKING OF PLANTING IT OUT HERE SOMEWHERE.
THAT WAY, WE'LL STILL HAVE A PART OF US GROWING UP IN HAMILTON.
I GUESS SO.
YOU CAN BOTH WALK IT OVER NEXT DOOR. I'LL FINISH UP AND HELP THE MOVERS LOAD THE TRUCK BY THE TIME YOU GET BACK.
ROOF
NEXT DOOR AT KATHY'S?
I'LL BET SHE'D LOOK AFTER IT FOR US.
YEAH...

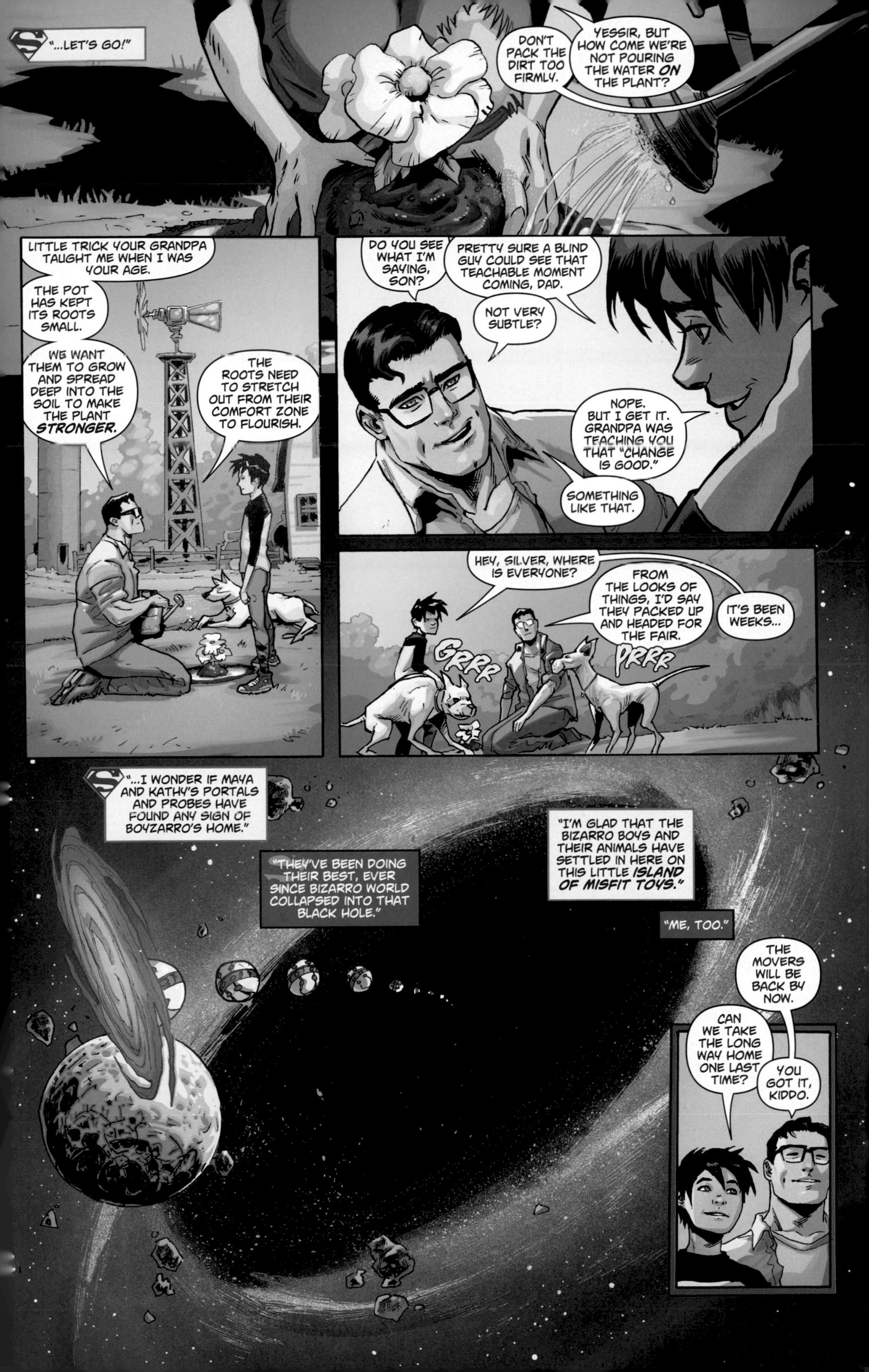
"...LET'S GO!"
DON'T PACK THE DIRT TOO FIRMLY.
YESSIR, BUT HOW COME WE'RE NOT POURING THE WATER ON THE PLANT?
LITTLE TRICK YOUR GRANDPA TAUGHT ME WHEN I WAS YOUR AGE.
THE POT HAS KEPT ITS ROOTS SMALL.
WE WANT THEM TO GROW AND SPREAD DEEP INTO THE SOIL TO MAKE THE PLANT STRONGER.
THE ROOTS NEED TO STRETCH OUT FROM THEIR COMFORT ZONE TO FLOURISH.
DO YOU SEE WHAT I'M SAYING, SON?
PRETTY SURE A BLIND GUY COULD SEE THAT TEACHABLE MOMENT COMING, DAD.
NOT VERY SUBTLE?
NOPE. BUT I GET IT. GRANDPA WAS TEACHING YOU THAT "CHANGE IS GOOD."
SOMETHING LIKE THAT.
HEY, SILVER, WHERE IS EVERYONE?
FROM THE LOOKS OF THINGS, I'D SAY THEY PACKED UP AND HEADED FOR THE FAIR.
IT'S BEEN WEEKS...
GRRR
PRRR
"...I WONDER IF MAYA AND KATHY'S PORTALS AND PROBES HAVE FOUND ANY SIGN OF BOYZARRO'S HOME."
"THEY'VE BEEN DOING THEIR BEST, EVER SINCE BIZARRO WORLD COLLAPSED INTO THAT BLACK HOLE."
"I'M GLAD THAT THE BIZARRO BOYS AND THEIR ANIMALS HAVE SETTLED IN HERE ON THIS LITTLE ISLAND OF MISFIT TOYS."
"ME, TOO."
THE MOVERS WILL BE BACK BY NOW.
CAN WE TAKE THE LONG WAY HOME ONE LAST TIME?
YOU GOT IT, KIDDO.

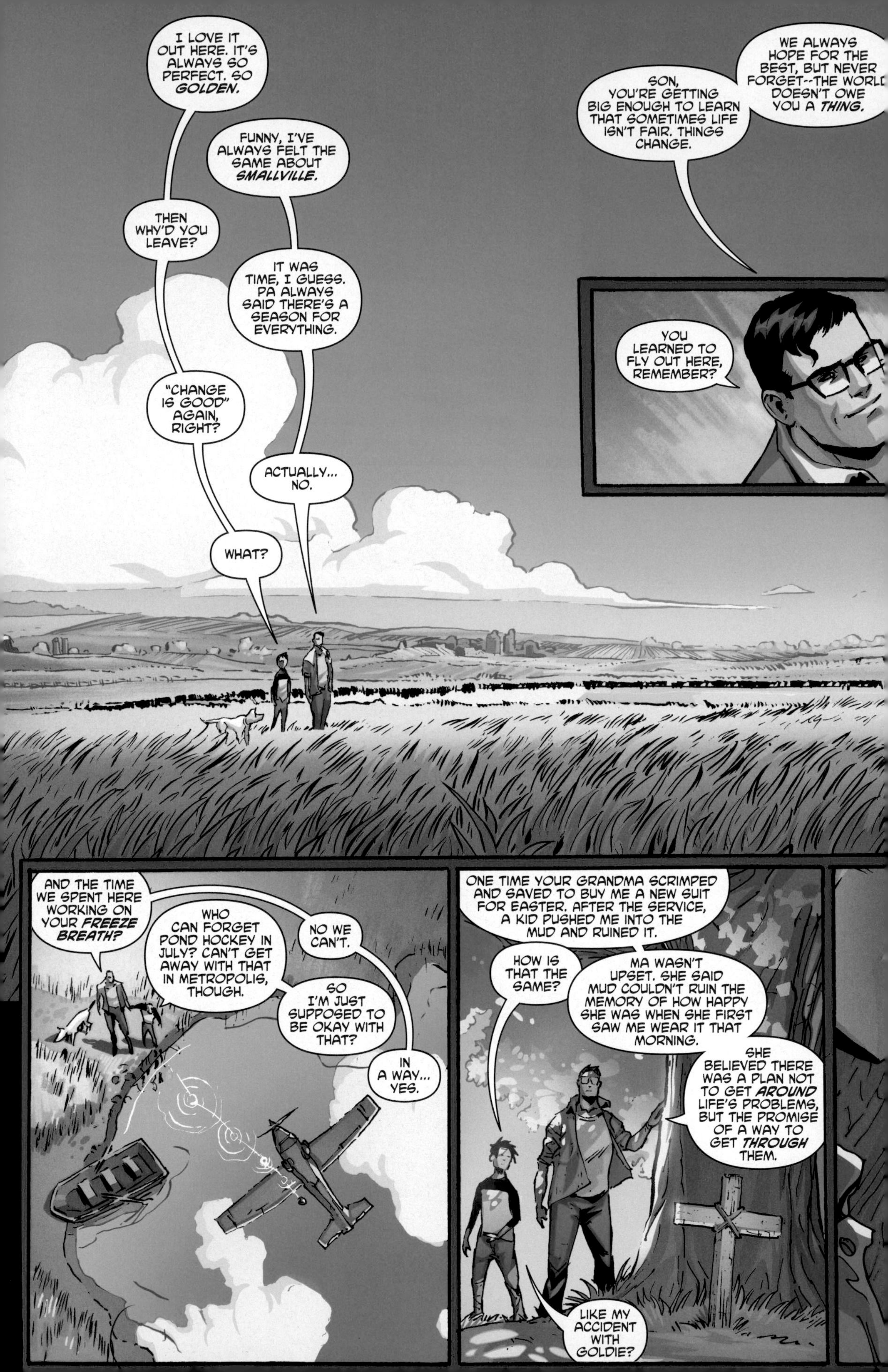
I LOVE IT OUT HERE. IT'S ALWAYS SO PERFECT. SO GOLDEN.
FUNNY, I'VE ALWAYS FELT THE SAME ABOUT SMALLVILLE.
THEN WHY'D YOU LEAVE?
IT WAS TIME, I GUESS. PA ALWAYS SAID THERE'S A SEASON FOR EVERYTHING.
"CHANGE IS GOOD" AGAIN, RIGHT?
ACTUALLY... NO.
WHAT?
SON, YOU'RE GETTING BIG ENOUGH TO LEARN THAT SOMETIMES LIFE ISN'T FAIR. THINGS CHANGE.
WE ALWAYS HOPE FOR THE BEST, BUT NEVER FORGET--THE WORLD DOESN'T OWE YOU A THING.
YOU LEARNED TO FLY OUT HERE, REMEMBER?
AND THE TIME WE SPENT HERE WORKING ON YOUR FREEZE BREATH?
WHO CAN FORGET POND HOCKEY IN JULY? CAN'T GET AWAY WITH THAT IN METROPOLIS, THOUGH.
NO WE CAN'T.
SO I'M JUST SUPPOSED TO BE OKAY WITH THAT?
IN A WAY... YES.
ONE TIME YOUR GRANDMA SCRIMPED AND SAVED TO BUY ME A NEW SUIT FOR EASTER. AFTER THE SERVICE, A KID PUSHED ME INTO THE MUD AND RUINED IT.
HOW IS THAT THE SAME?
MA WASN'T UPSET. SHE SAID MUD COULDN'T RUIN THE MEMORY OF HOW HAPPY SHE WAS WHEN SHE FIRST SAW ME WEAR IT THAT MORNING.
SHE BELIEVED THERE WAS A PLAN NOT TO GET AROUND LIFE'S PROBLEMS, BUT THE PROMISE OF A WAY TO GET THROUGH THEM.
LIKE MY ACCIDENT WITH GOLDIE?

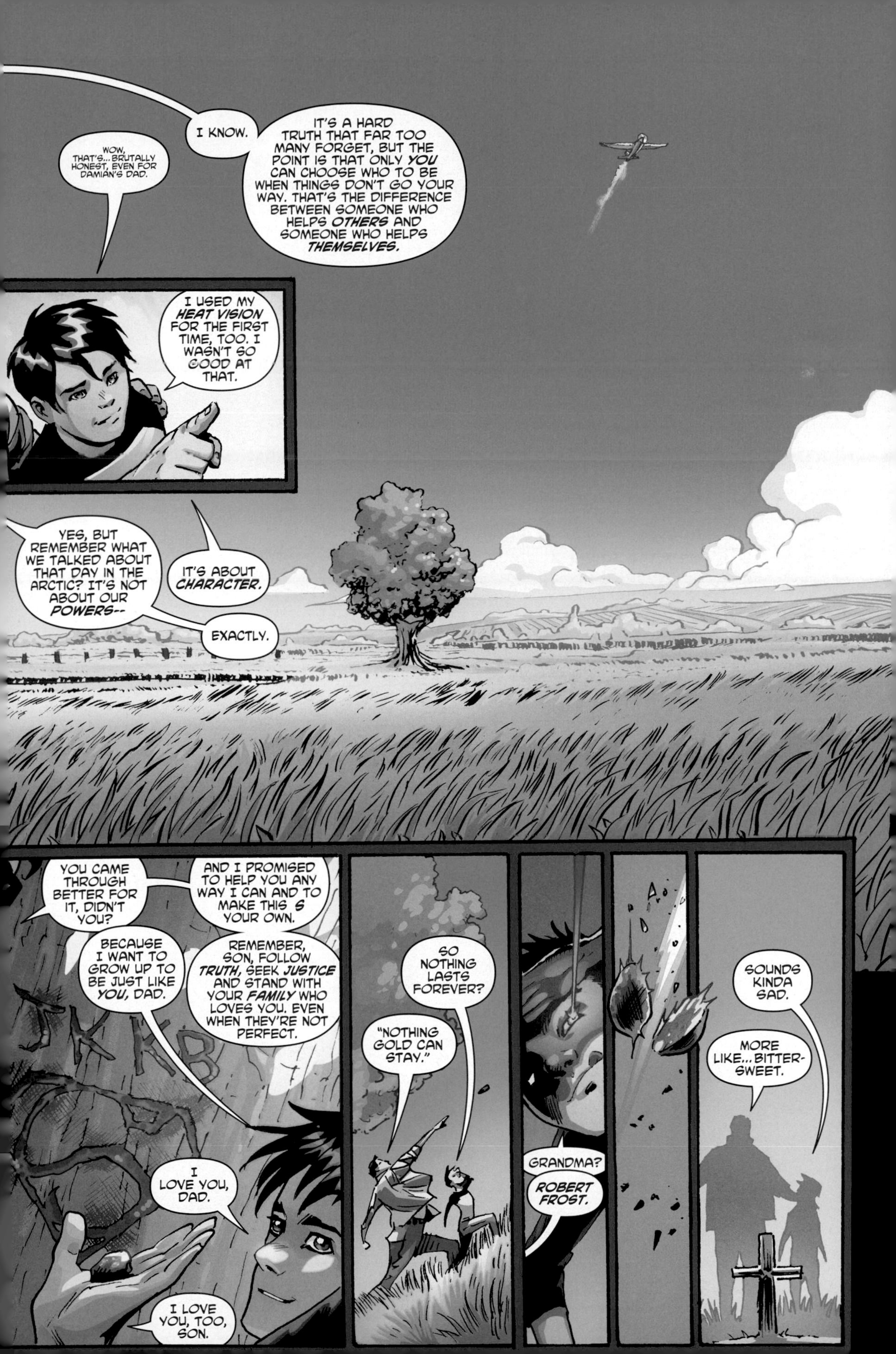
WOW, THAT'S... BRUTALLY HONEST, EVEN FOR DAMIAN'S DAD.
I KNOW.
IT'S A HARD TRUTH THAT FAR TOO MANY FORGET, BUT THE POINT IS THAT ONLY YOU CAN CHOOSE WHO TO BE WHEN THINGS DON'T GO YOUR WAY. THAT'S THE DIFFERENCE BETWEEN SOMEONE WHO HELPS OTHERS AND SOMEONE WHO HELPS THEMSELVES.
I USED MY HEAT VISION FOR THE FIRST TIME, TOO. I WASN'T SO GOOD AT THAT.
YES, BUT REMEMBER WHAT WE TALKED ABOUT THAT DAY IN THE ARCTIC? IT'S NOT ABOUT OUR POWERS--
IT'S ABOUT CHARACTER.
EXACTLY.
YOU CAME THROUGH BETTER FOR IT, DIDN'T YOU?
AND I PROMISED TO HELP YOU ANY WAY I CAN AND TO MAKE THIS S YOUR OWN.
BECAUSE I WANT TO GROW UP TO BE JUST LIKE YOU, DAD.
REMEMBER, SON, FOLLOW TRUTH, SEEK JUSTICE AND STAND WITH YOUR FAMILY WHO LOVES YOU. EVEN WHEN THEY'RE NOT PERFECT.
I LOVE YOU, DAD.
I LOVE YOU, TOO, SON.
SO NOTHING LASTS FOREVER?
"NOTHING GOLD CAN STAY."
GRANDMA?
ROBERT FROST.
SOUNDS KINDA SAD.
MORE LIKE... BITTER-SWEET.

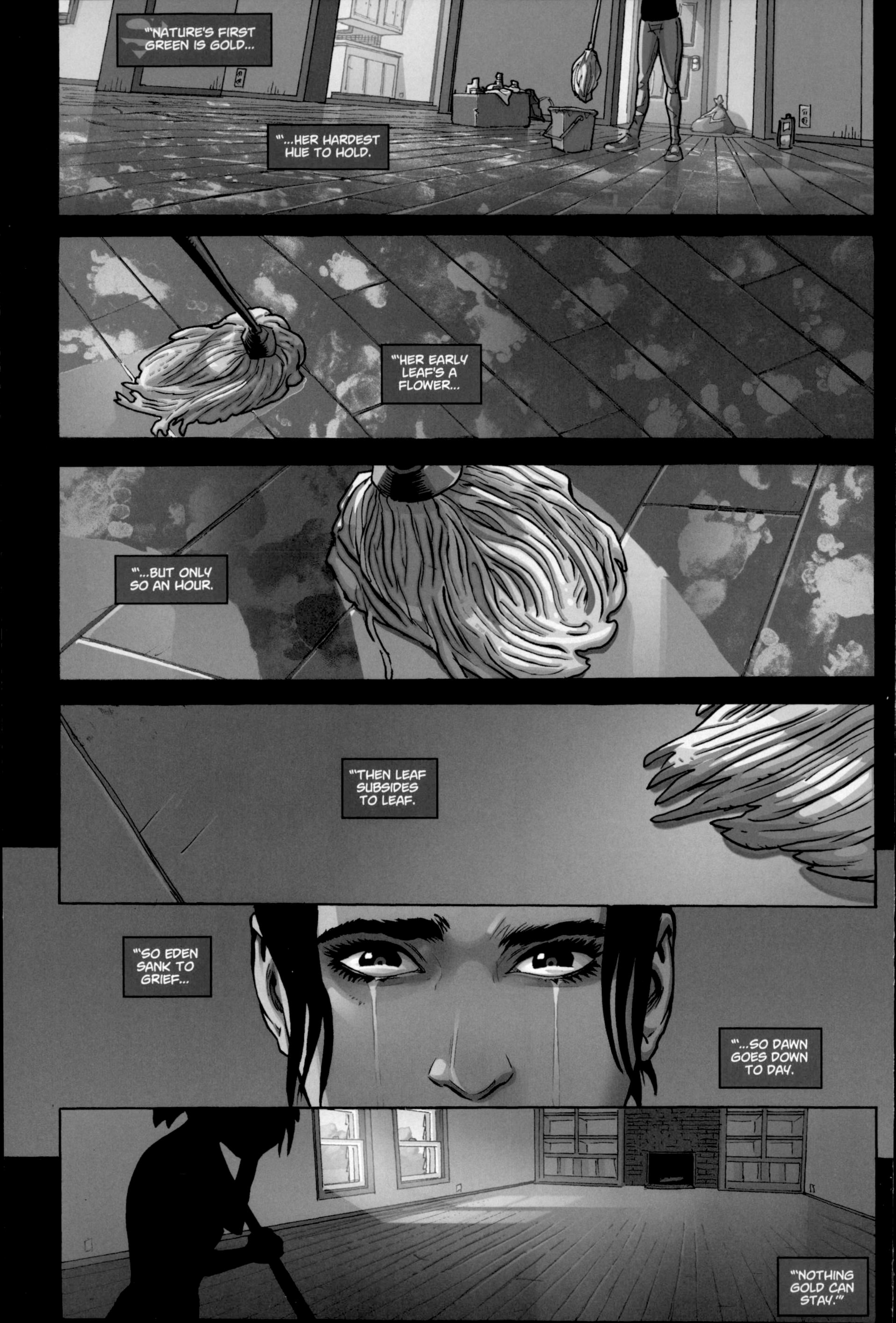
"'NATURE'S FIRST GREEN IS GOLD...
"'...HER HARDEST HUE TO HOLD.
"'HER EARLY LEAF'S A FLOWER...
"'...BUT ONLY SO AN HOUR.
"'THEN LEAF SUBSIDES TO LEAF.
"'SO EDEN SANK TO GRIEF...
"'...SO DAWN GOES DOWN TO DAY.
"'NOTHING GOLD CAN STAY.'"

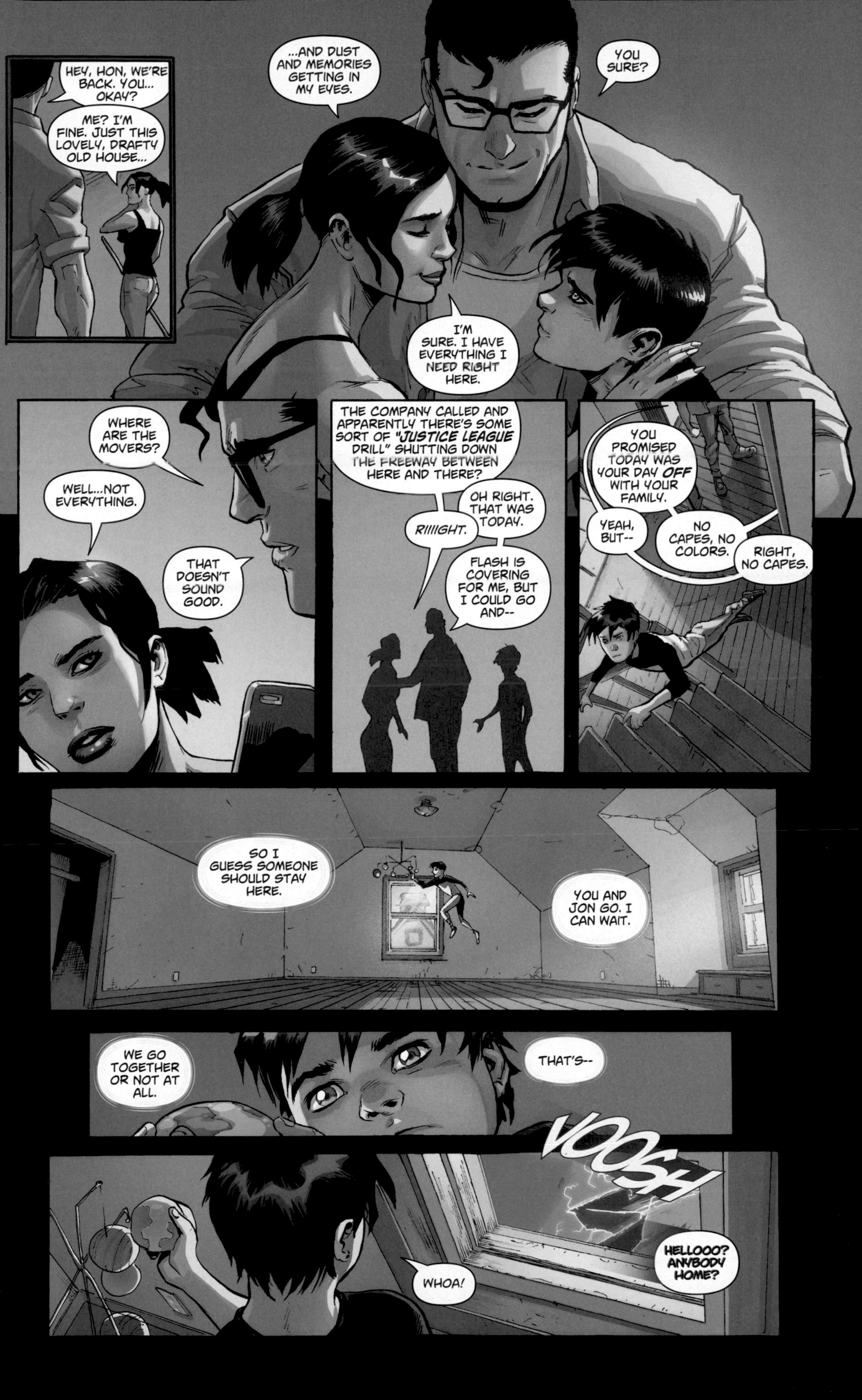
HEY, HON, WE'RE BACK. YOU... OKAY?
ME? I'M FINE. JUST THIS LOVELY, DRAFTY OLD HOUSE...
...AND DUST AND MEMORIES GETTING IN MY EYES.
YOU SURE?
I'M SURE. I HAVE EVERYTHING I NEED RIGHT HERE.
WHERE ARE THE MOVERS?
WELL...NOT EVERYTHING.
THAT DOESN'T SOUND GOOD.
THE COMPANY CALLED AND APPARENTLY THERE'S SOME SORT OF "JUSTICE LEAGUE DRILL" SHUTTING DOWN THE FREEWAY BETWEEN HERE AND THERE?
OH RIGHT. THAT WAS TODAY.
RIIIGHT.
FLASH IS COVERING FOR ME, BUT I COULD GO AND--
YOU PROMISED TODAY WAS YOUR DAY OFF WITH YOUR FAMILY.
YEAH, BUT--
NO CAPES, NO COLORS.
RIGHT, NO CAPES.
SO I GUESS SOMEONE SHOULD STAY HERE.
YOU AND JON GO. I CAN WAIT.
WE GO TOGETHER OR NOT AT ALL.
THAT'S--
VOOSH
WHOA!
HELLOOO? ANYBODY HOME?

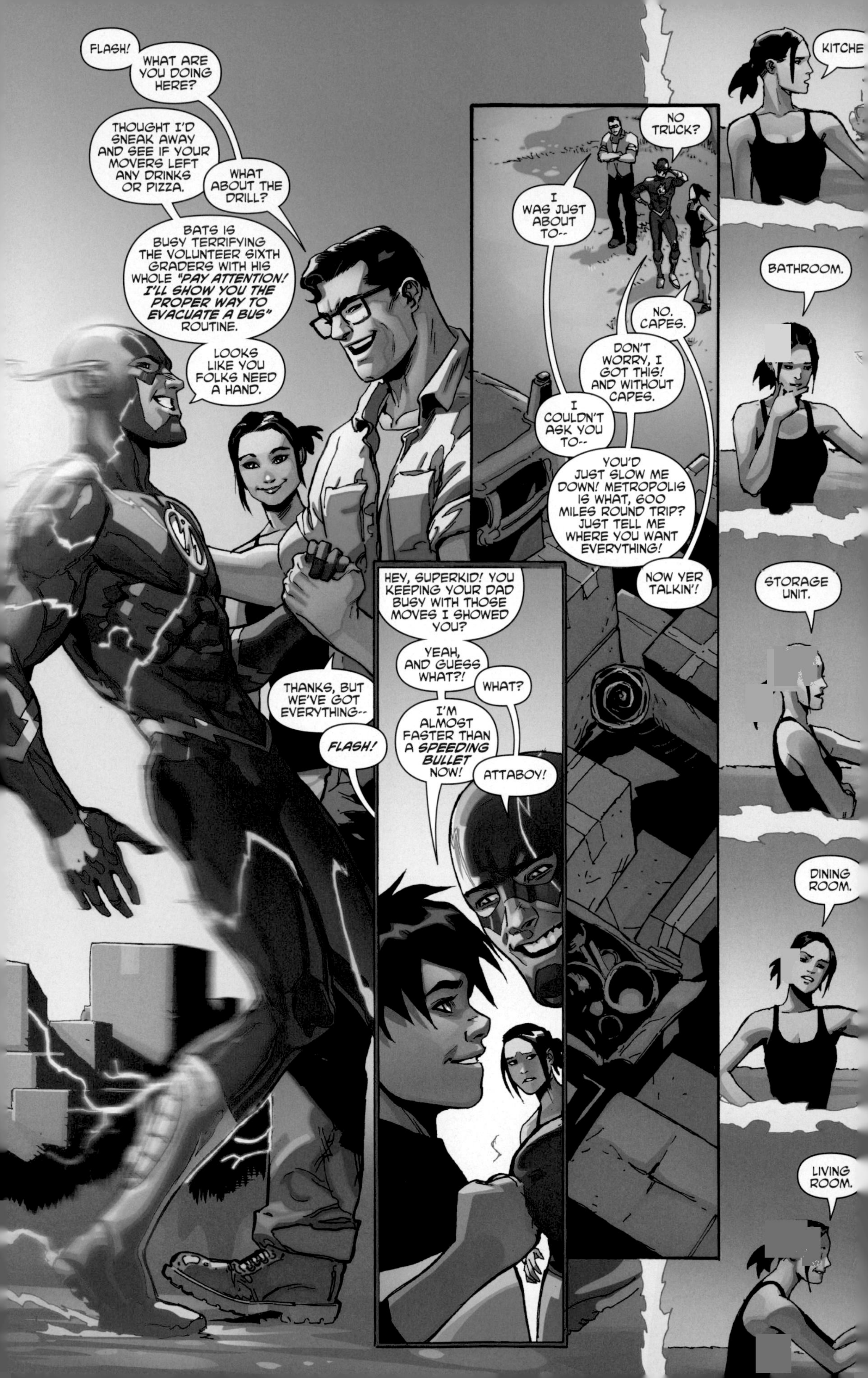
FLASH!
WHAT ARE YOU DOING HERE?
THOUGHT I'D SNEAK AWAY AND SEE IF YOUR MOVERS LEFT ANY DRINKS OR PIZZA.
WHAT ABOUT THE DRILL?
BATS IS BUSY TERRIFYING THE VOLUNTEER SIXTH GRADERS WITH HIS WHOLE *"PAY ATTENTION! I'LL SHOW YOU THE PROPER WAY TO EVACUATE A BUS"* ROUTINE.
LOOKS LIKE YOU FOLKS NEED A HAND.
THANKS, BUT WE'VE GOT EVERYTHING--
*FLASH!*
NO TRUCK?
I WAS JUST ABOUT TO--
NO. CAPES.
DON'T WORRY, I GOT THIS! AND WITHOUT CAPES.
I COULDN'T ASK YOU TO--
YOU'D JUST SLOW ME DOWN! METROPOLIS IS WHAT, 600 MILES ROUND TRIP? JUST TELL ME WHERE YOU WANT EVERYTHING!
NOW YER TALKIN'!
HEY, SUPERKID! YOU KEEPING YOUR DAD BUSY WITH THOSE MOVES I SHOWED YOU?
YEAH, AND GUESS WHAT?!
WHAT?
I'M ALMOST FASTER THAN A *SPEEDING BULLET* NOW!
ATTABOY!
KITCHE
BATHROOM.
STORAGE UNIT.
DINING ROOM.
LIVING ROOM.

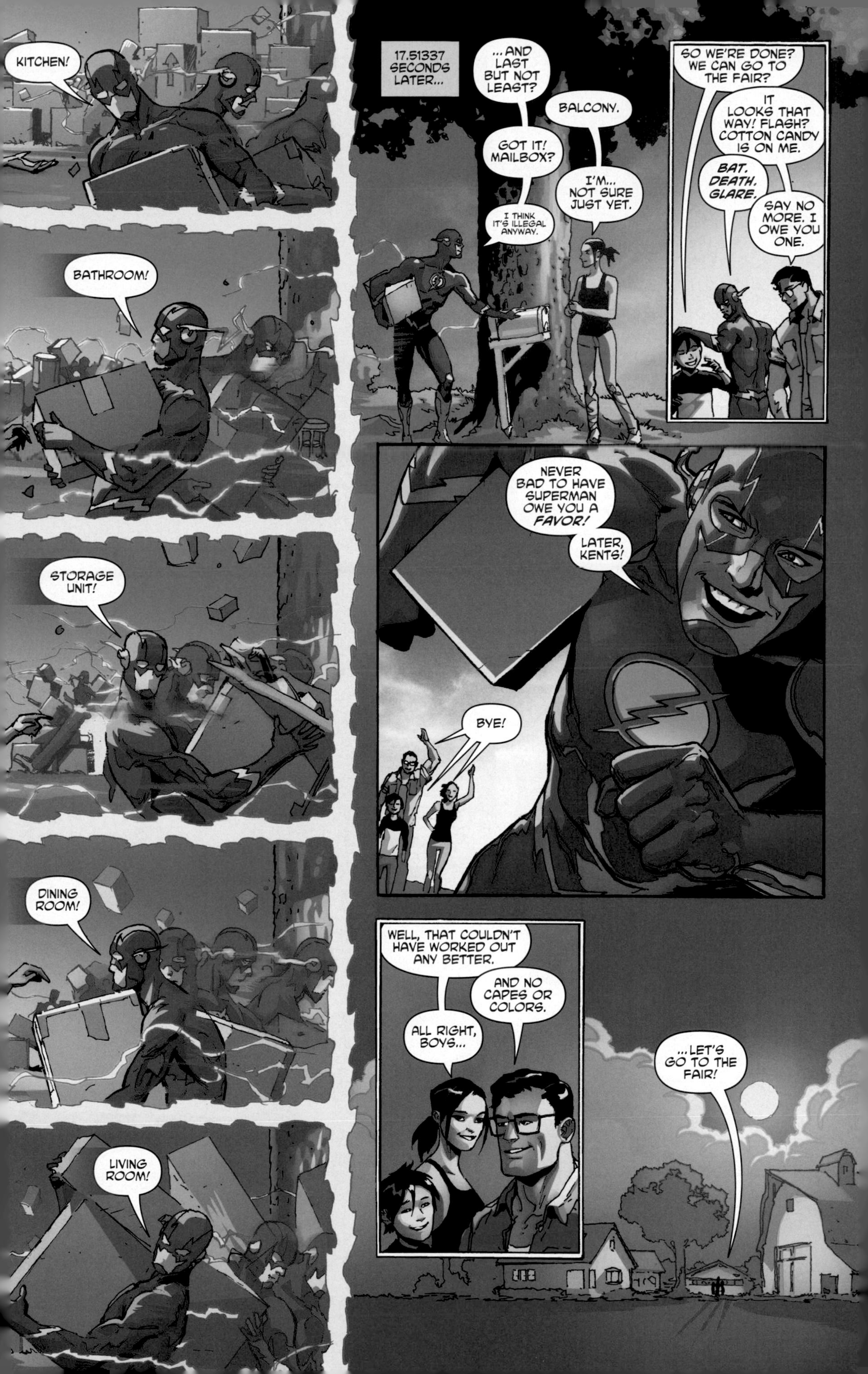
KITCHEN!
BATHROOM!
STORAGE UNIT!
DINING ROOM!
LIVING ROOM!
17.51337 SECONDS LATER...
...AND LAST BUT NOT LEAST?
BALCONY.
GOT IT! MAILBOX?
I'M... NOT SURE JUST YET.
I THINK IT'S ILLEGAL ANYWAY.
SO WE'RE DONE? WE CAN GO TO THE FAIR?
IT LOOKS THAT WAY! FLASH? COTTON CANDY IS ON ME.
BAT. DEATH. GLARE.
SAY NO MORE. I OWE YOU ONE.
NEVER BAD TO HAVE SUPERMAN OWE YOU A FAVOR!
LATER, KENTS!
BYE!
WELL, THAT COULDN'T HAVE WORKED OUT ANY BETTER.
AND NO CAPES OR COLORS.
ALL RIGHT, BOYS...
...LET'S GO TO THE FAIR!

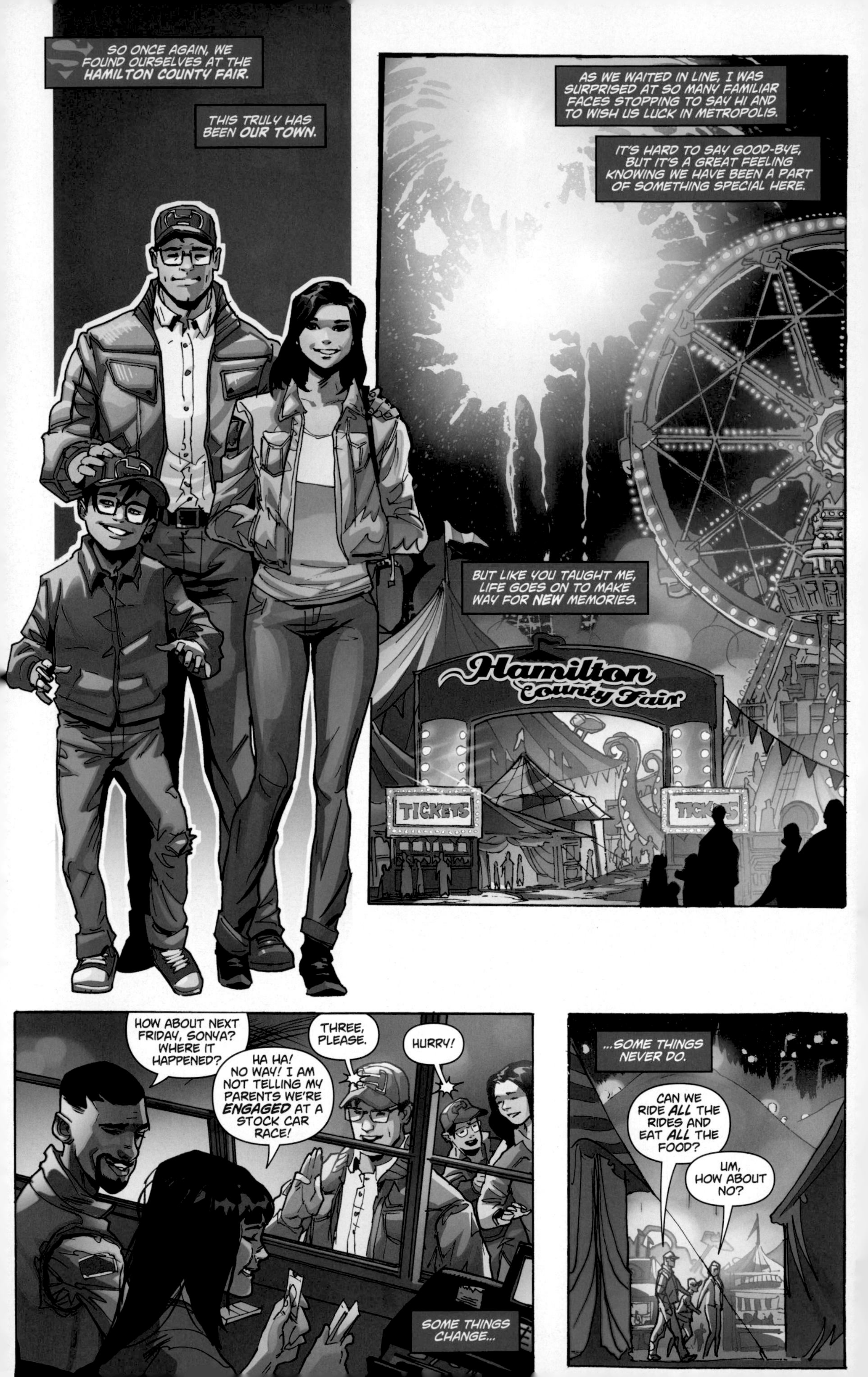
SO ONCE AGAIN, WE FOUND OURSELVES AT THE HAMILTON COUNTY FAIR.
THIS TRULY HAS BEEN OUR TOWN.
AS WE WAITED IN LINE, I WAS SURPRISED AT SO MANY FAMILIAR FACES STOPPING TO SAY HI AND TO WISH US LUCK IN METROPOLIS.
IT'S HARD TO SAY GOOD-BYE, BUT IT'S A GREAT FEELING KNOWING WE HAVE BEEN A PART OF SOMETHING SPECIAL HERE.
BUT LIKE YOU TAUGHT ME, LIFE GOES ON TO MAKE WAY FOR NEW MEMORIES.
Hamilton County Fair
TICKETS
TICKETS
HOW ABOUT NEXT FRIDAY, SONYA? WHERE IT HAPPENED?
HA HA! NO WAY! I AM NOT TELLING MY PARENTS WE'RE ENGAGED AT A STOCK CAR RACE!
THREE, PLEASE.
HURRY!
SOME THINGS CHANGE...
...SOME THINGS NEVER DO.
CAN WE RIDE ALL THE RIDES AND EAT ALL THE FOOD?
UM, HOW ABOUT NO?

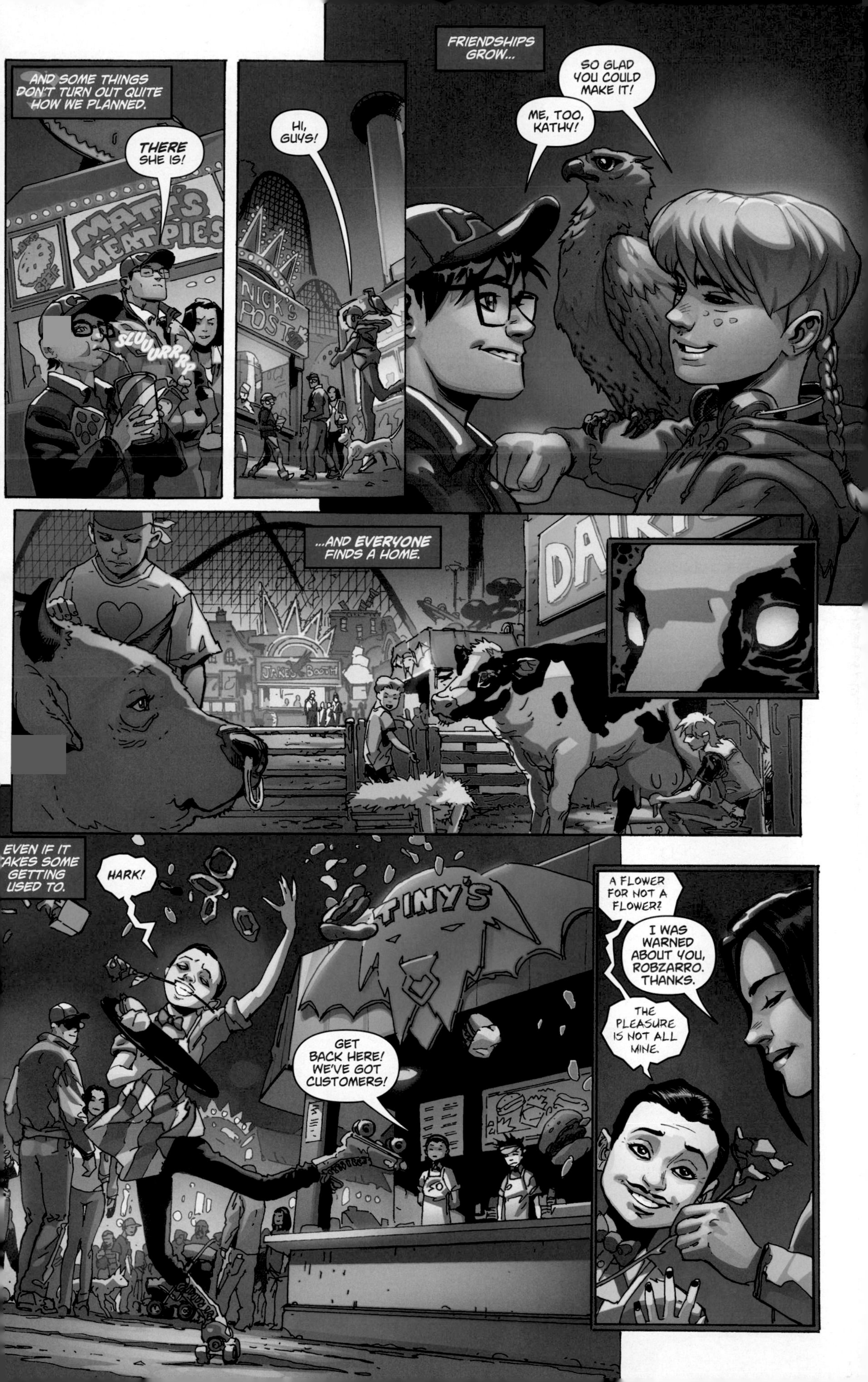

AND SOME THINGS DON'T TURN OUT QUITE HOW WE PLANNED.
THERE SHE IS!
MATT'S MEAT PIES
SLUUURRRRP
HI, GUYS!
NICK'S POST
FRIENDSHIPS GROW...
SO GLAD YOU COULD MAKE IT!
ME, TOO, KATHY!
...AND EVERYONE FINDS A HOME.
JAKE'S BOOTH
EVEN IF IT TAKES SOME GETTING USED TO.
HARK!
TINY'S
GET BACK HERE! WE'VE GOT CUSTOMERS!
A FLOWER FOR NOT A FLOWER?
I WAS WARNED ABOUT YOU, ROBZARRO. THANKS.
THE PLEASURE IS NOT ALL MINE.

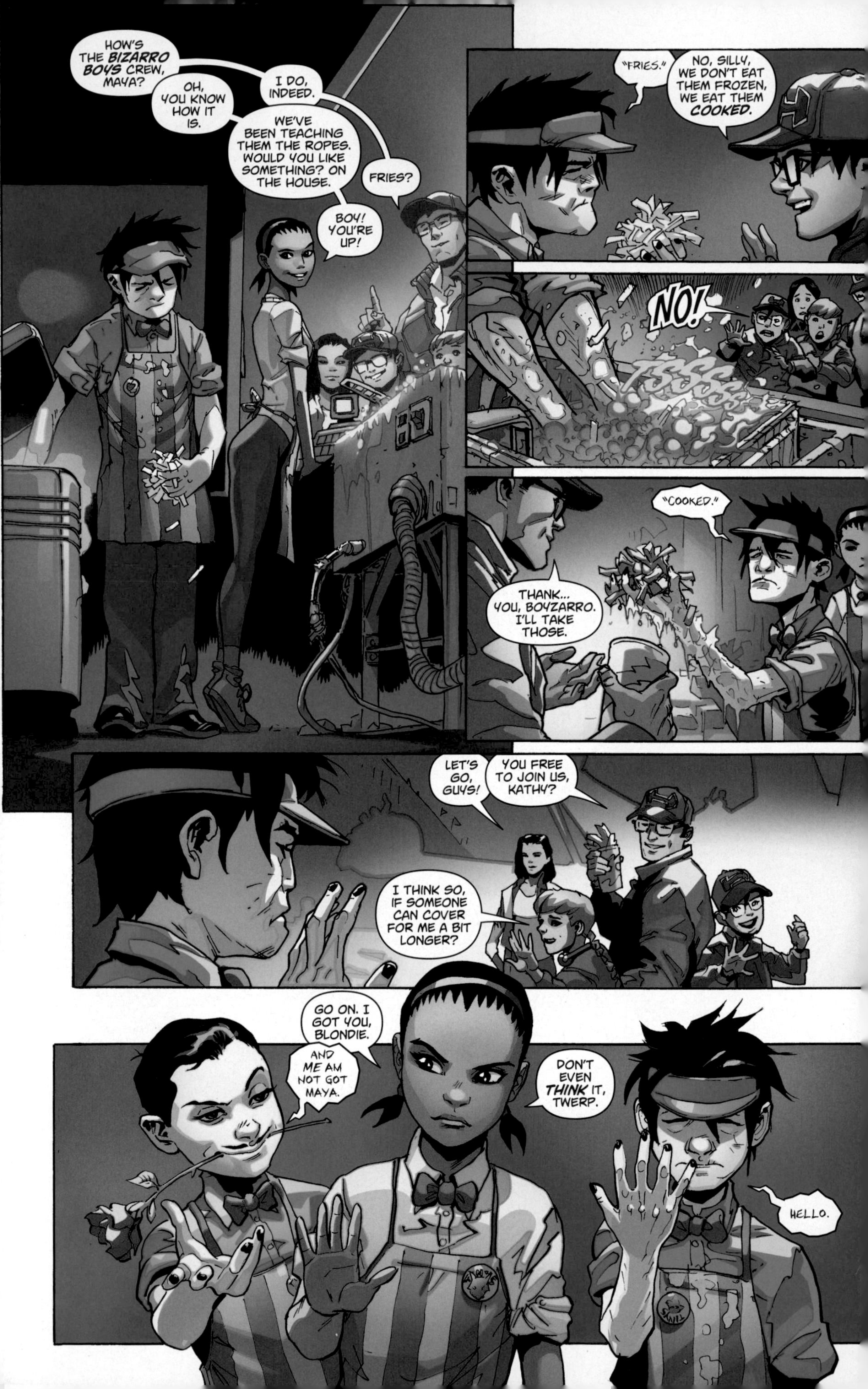
HOW'S THE BIZARRO BOYS CREW, MAYA?
OH, YOU KNOW HOW IT IS.
I DO, INDEED.
WE'VE BEEN TEACHING THEM THE ROPES. WOULD YOU LIKE SOMETHING? ON THE HOUSE.
FRIES?
BOY! YOU'RE UP!
"FRIES."
NO, SILLY, WE DON'T EAT THEM FROZEN, WE EAT THEM COOKED.
NO!
TSSSS
"COOKED."
THANK... YOU, BOYZARRO. I'LL TAKE THOSE.
LET'S GO, GUYS!
YOU FREE TO JOIN US, KATHY?
I THINK SO, IF SOMEONE CAN COVER FOR ME A BIT LONGER?
GO ON. I GOT YOU, BLONDIE.
AND ME AM NOT GOT MAYA.
DON'T EVEN THINK IT, TWERP.
HELLO.

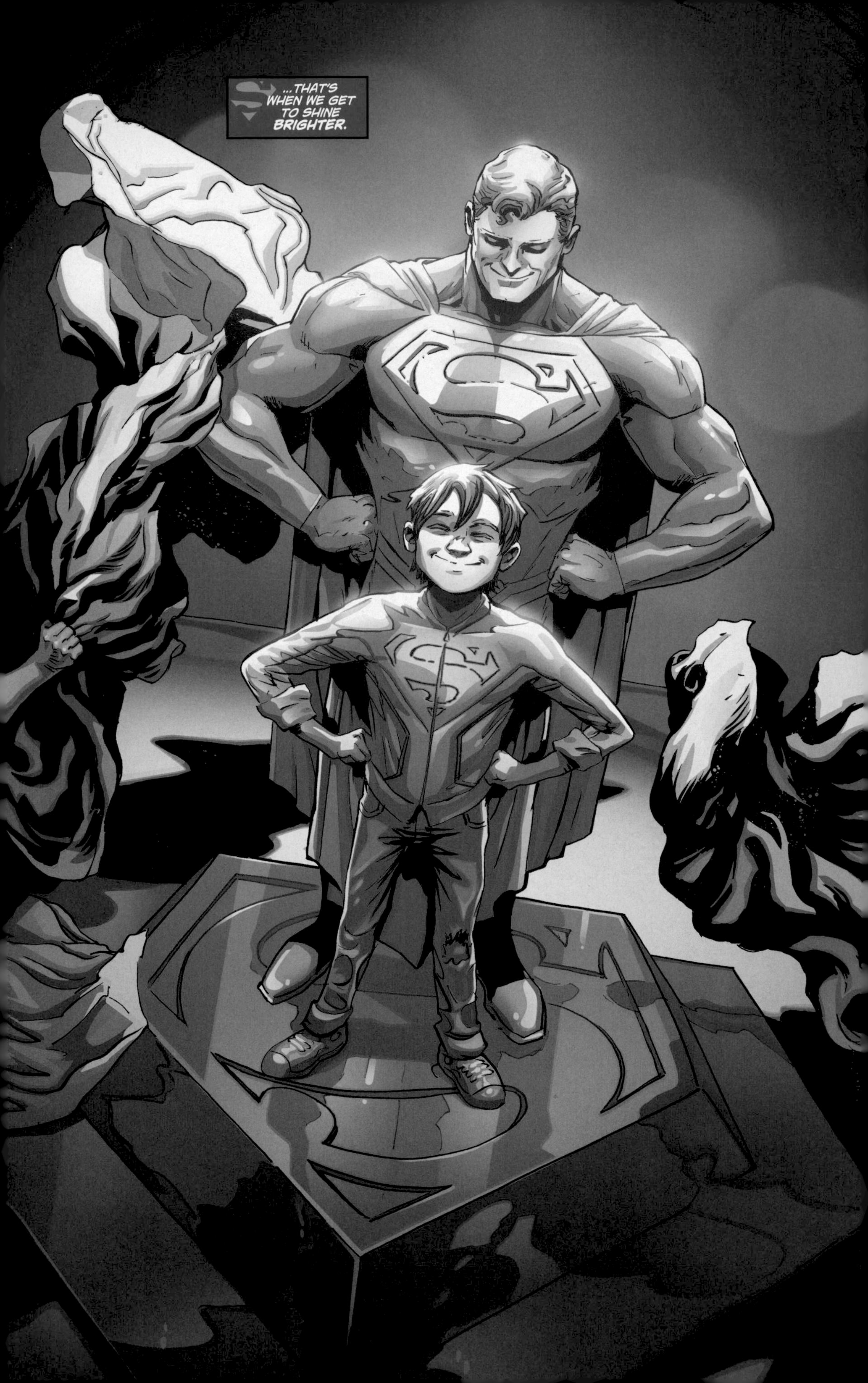
...THAT'S WHEN WE GET TO SHINE BRIGHTER.

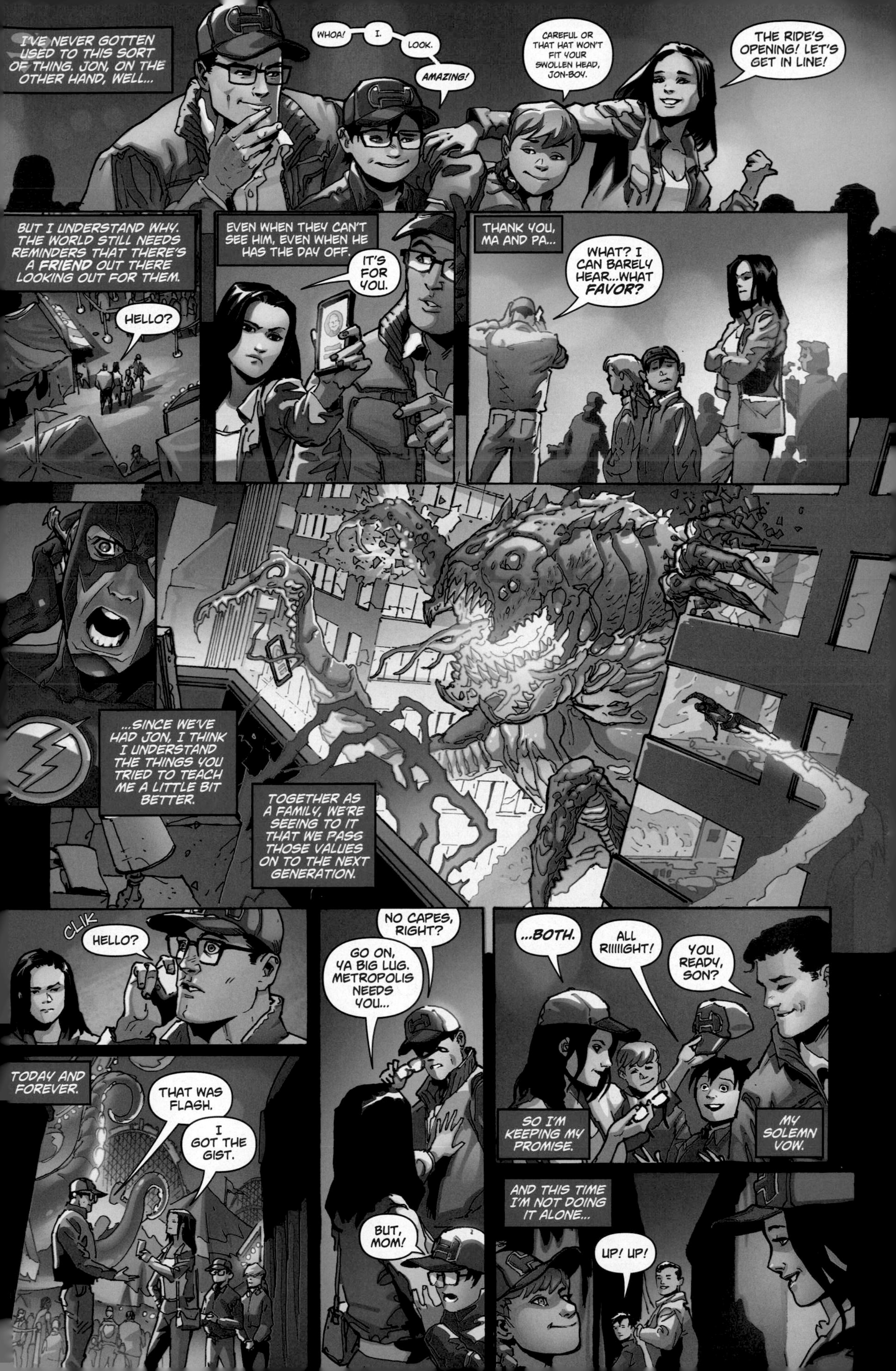

I'VE NEVER GOTTEN USED TO THIS SORT OF THING. JON, ON THE OTHER HAND, WELL...
WHOA!
I.
LOOK.
AMAZING!
CAREFUL OR THAT HAT WON'T FIT YOUR SWOLLEN HEAD, JON-BOY.
THE RIDE'S OPENING! LET'S GET IN LINE!
BUT I UNDERSTAND WHY. THE WORLD STILL NEEDS REMINDERS THAT THERE'S A FRIEND OUT THERE LOOKING OUT FOR THEM.
HELLO?
EVEN WHEN THEY CAN'T SEE HIM, EVEN WHEN HE HAS THE DAY OFF.
IT'S FOR YOU.
THANK YOU, MA AND PA...
WHAT? I CAN BARELY HEAR...WHAT FAVOR?
...SINCE WE'VE HAD JON, I THINK I UNDERSTAND THE THINGS YOU TRIED TO TEACH ME A LITTLE BIT BETTER.
TOGETHER AS A FAMILY, WE'RE SEEING TO IT THAT WE PASS THOSE VALUES ON TO THE NEXT GENERATION.
CLIK
HELLO?
TODAY AND FOREVER.
THAT WAS FLASH.
I GOT THE GIST.
NO CAPES, RIGHT?
GO ON, YA BIG LUG. METROPOLIS NEEDS YOU...
BUT, MOM!
...BOTH.
ALL RIIIIGHT!
YOU READY, SON?
SO I'M KEEPING MY PROMISE.
MY SOLEMN VOW.
AND THIS TIME I'M NOT DOING IT ALONE...
UP! UP!

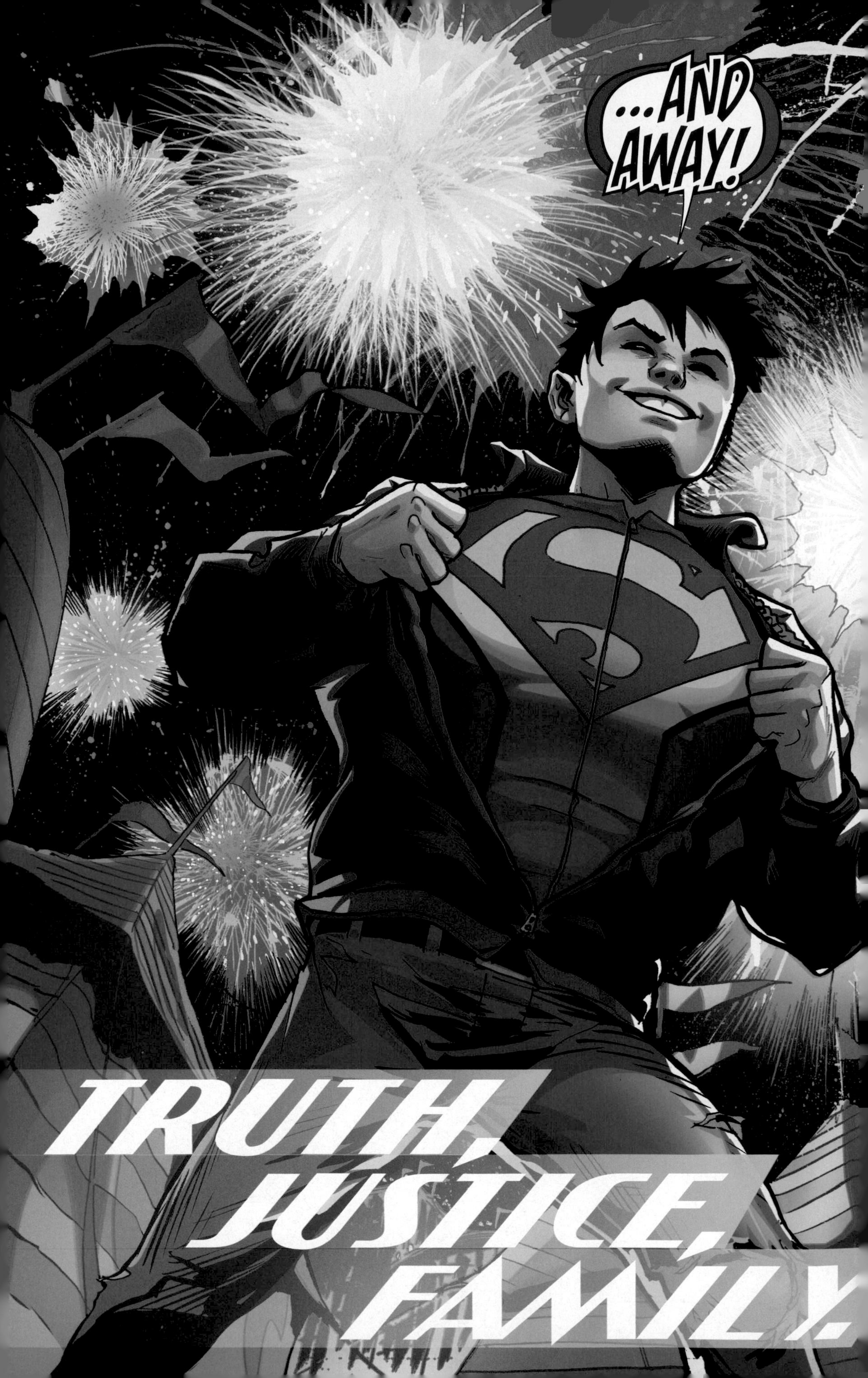
...AND AWAY!
TRUTH, JUSTICE, FAMILY.

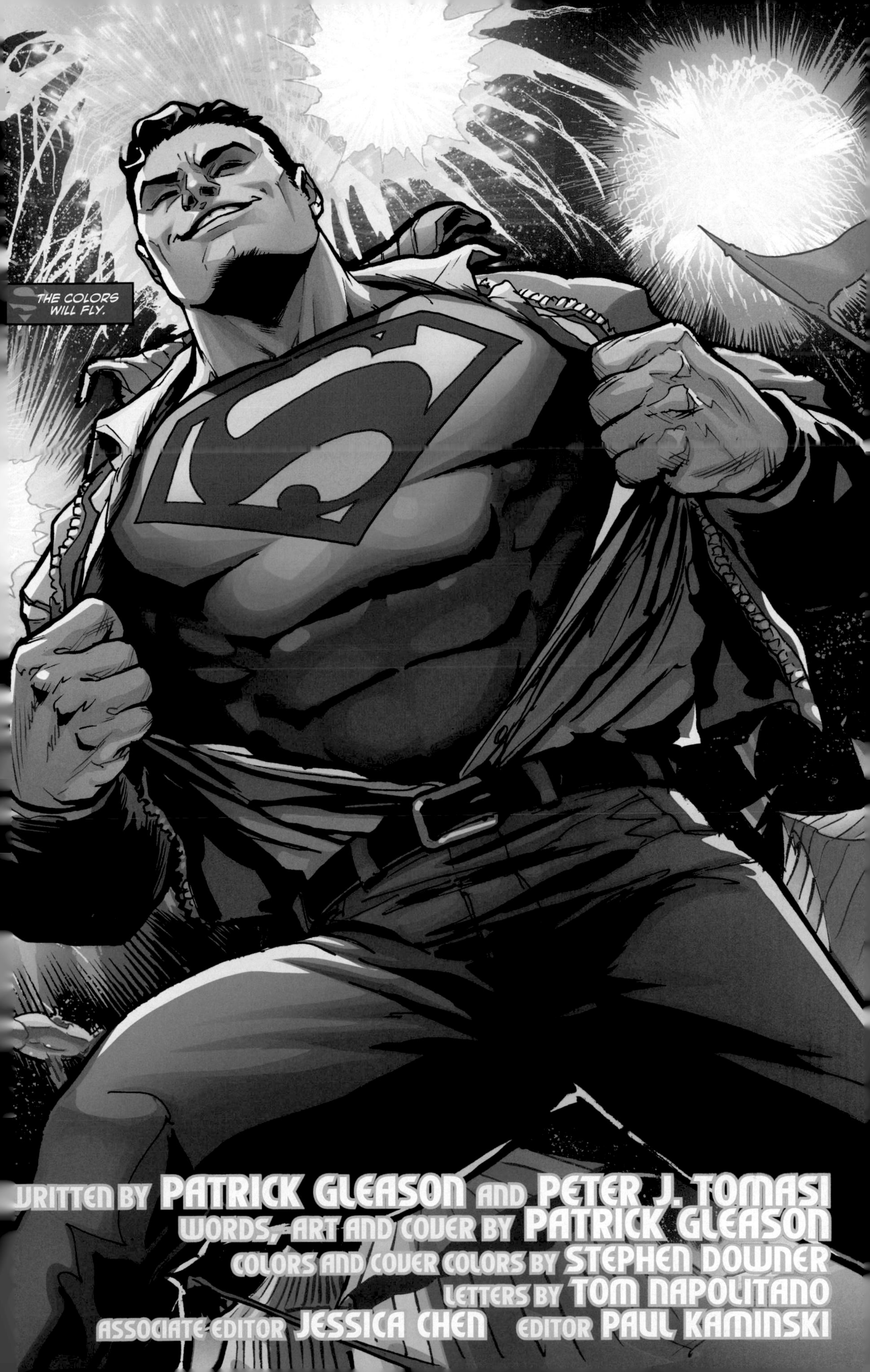
THE COLORS WILL FLY.
WRITTEN BY PATRICK GLEASON AND PETER J. TOMASI
WORDS, ART AND COVER BY PATRICK GLEASON
COLORS AND COVER COLORS BY STEPHEN DOWNER
LETTERS BY TOM NAPOLITANO
ASSOCIATE EDITOR JESSICA CHEN EDITOR PAUL KAMINSKI

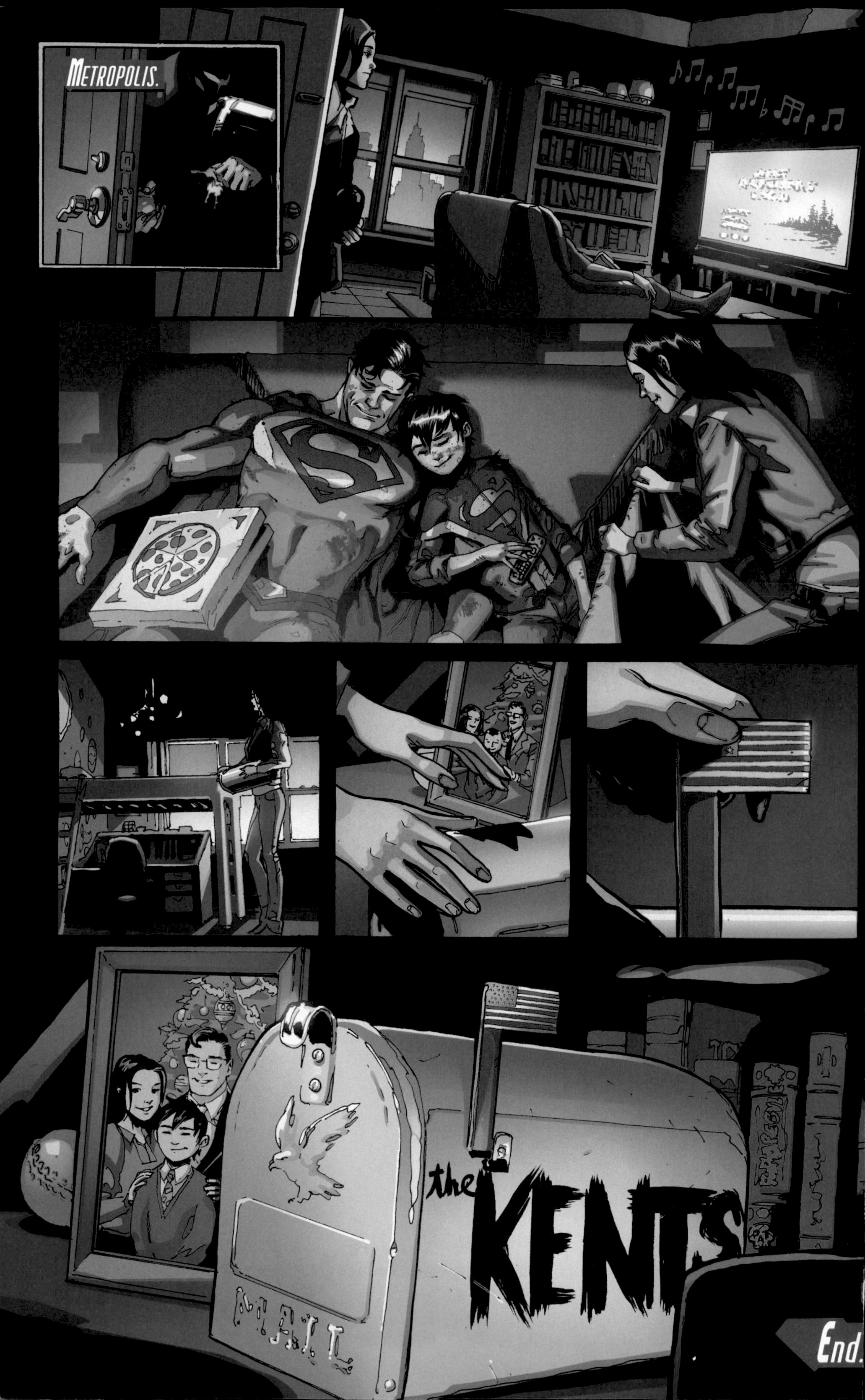
METROPOLIS.
the KENTS
End.

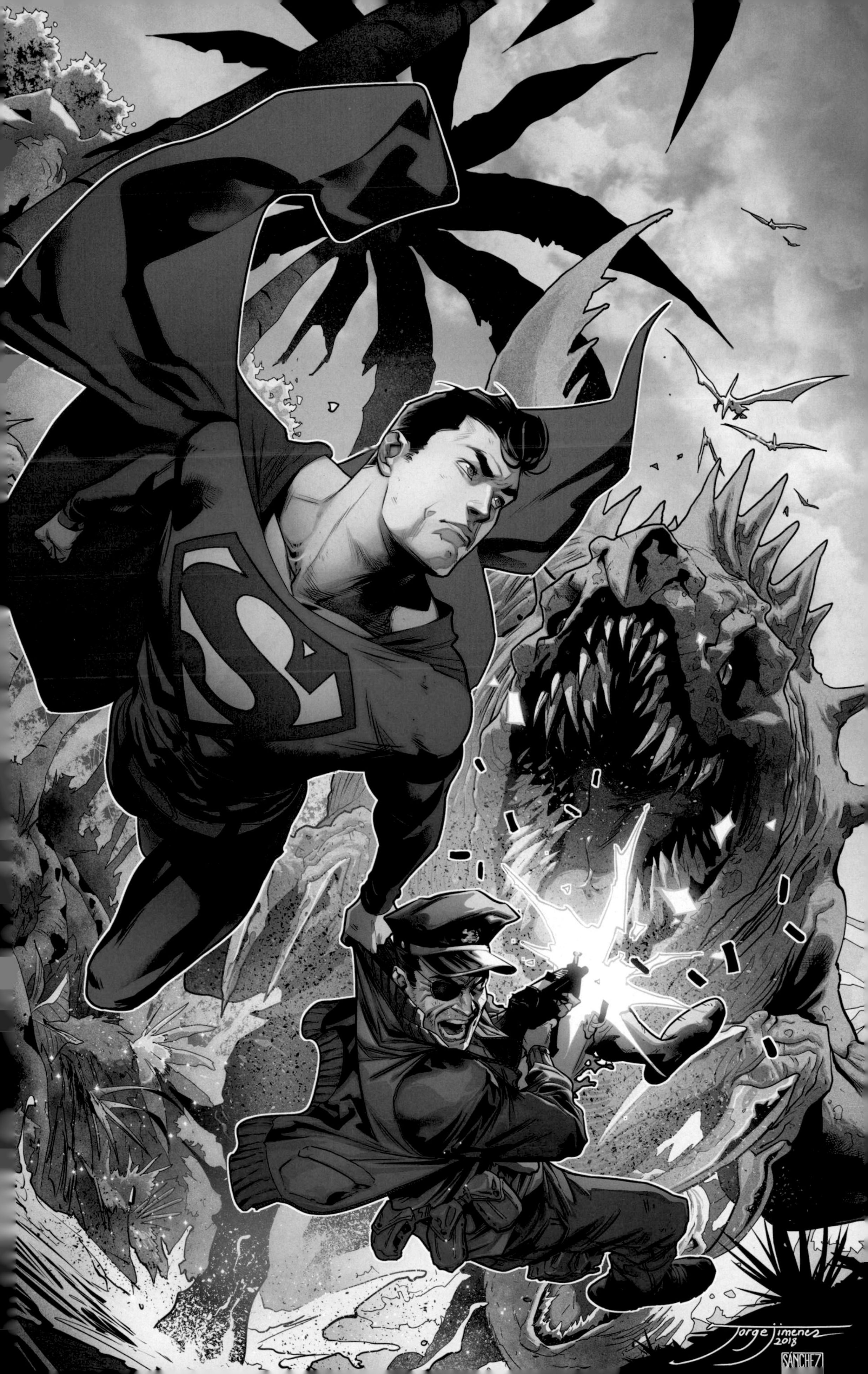

Jorge Jimenez
2018
SÁNCHEZ

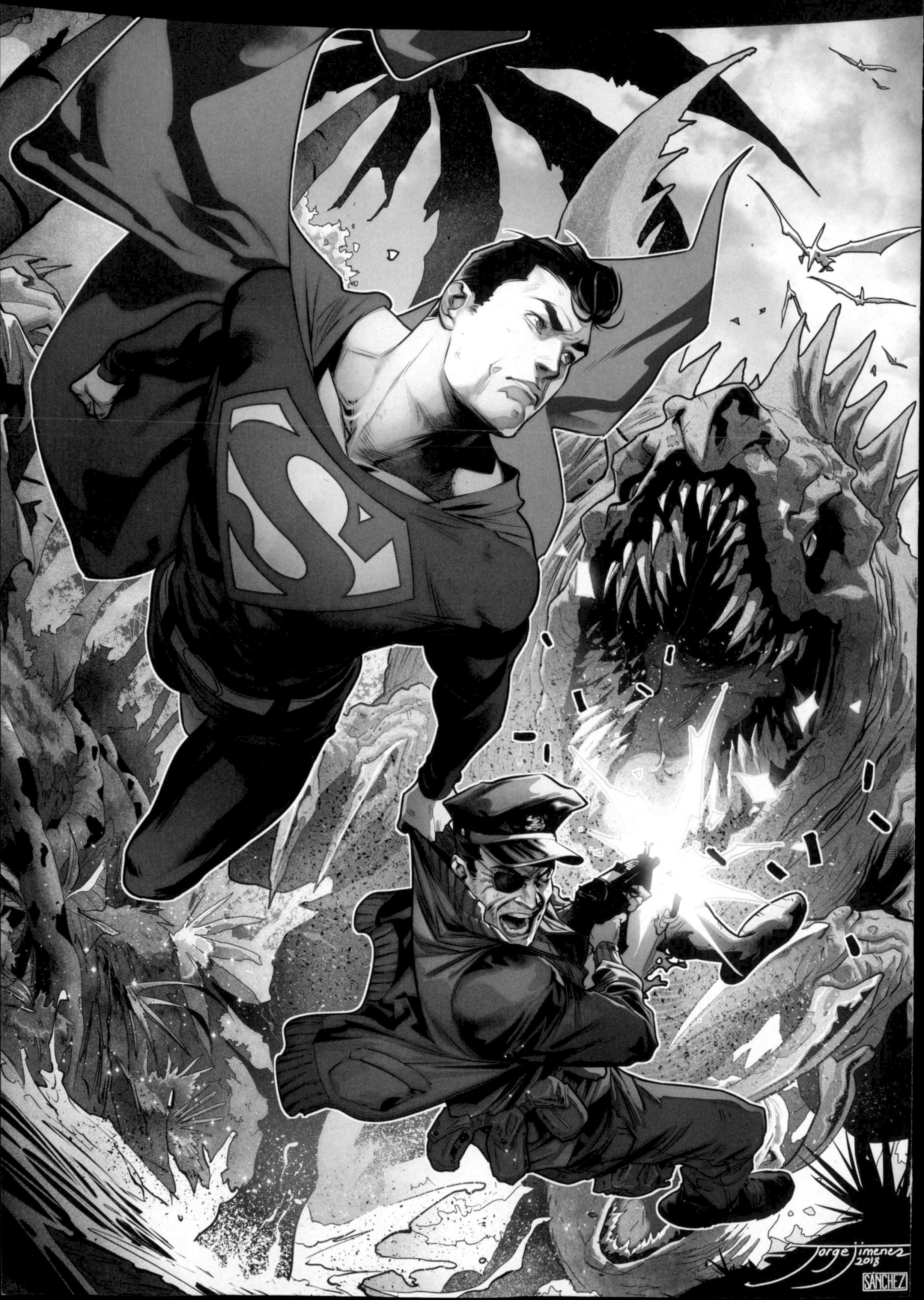
Jorge Jimenez 2018
SANCHEZ

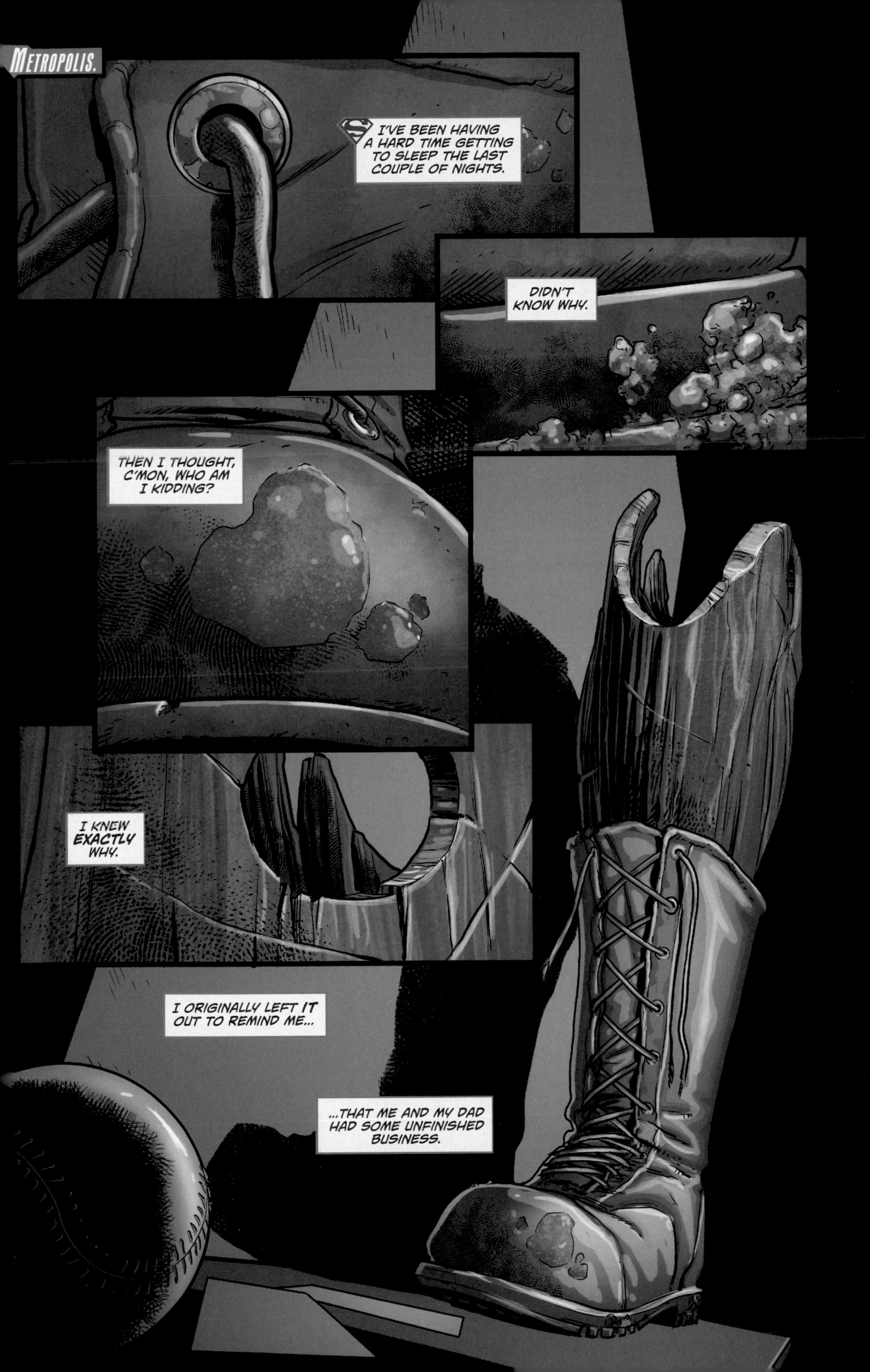
METROPOLIS.
I'VE BEEN HAVING A HARD TIME GETTING TO SLEEP THE LAST COUPLE OF NIGHTS.
DIDN'T KNOW WHY.
THEN I THOUGHT, C'MON, WHO AM I KIDDING?
I KNEW EXACTLY WHY.
I ORIGINALLY LEFT IT OUT TO REMIND ME...
...THAT ME AND MY DAD HAD SOME UNFINISHED BUSINESS.

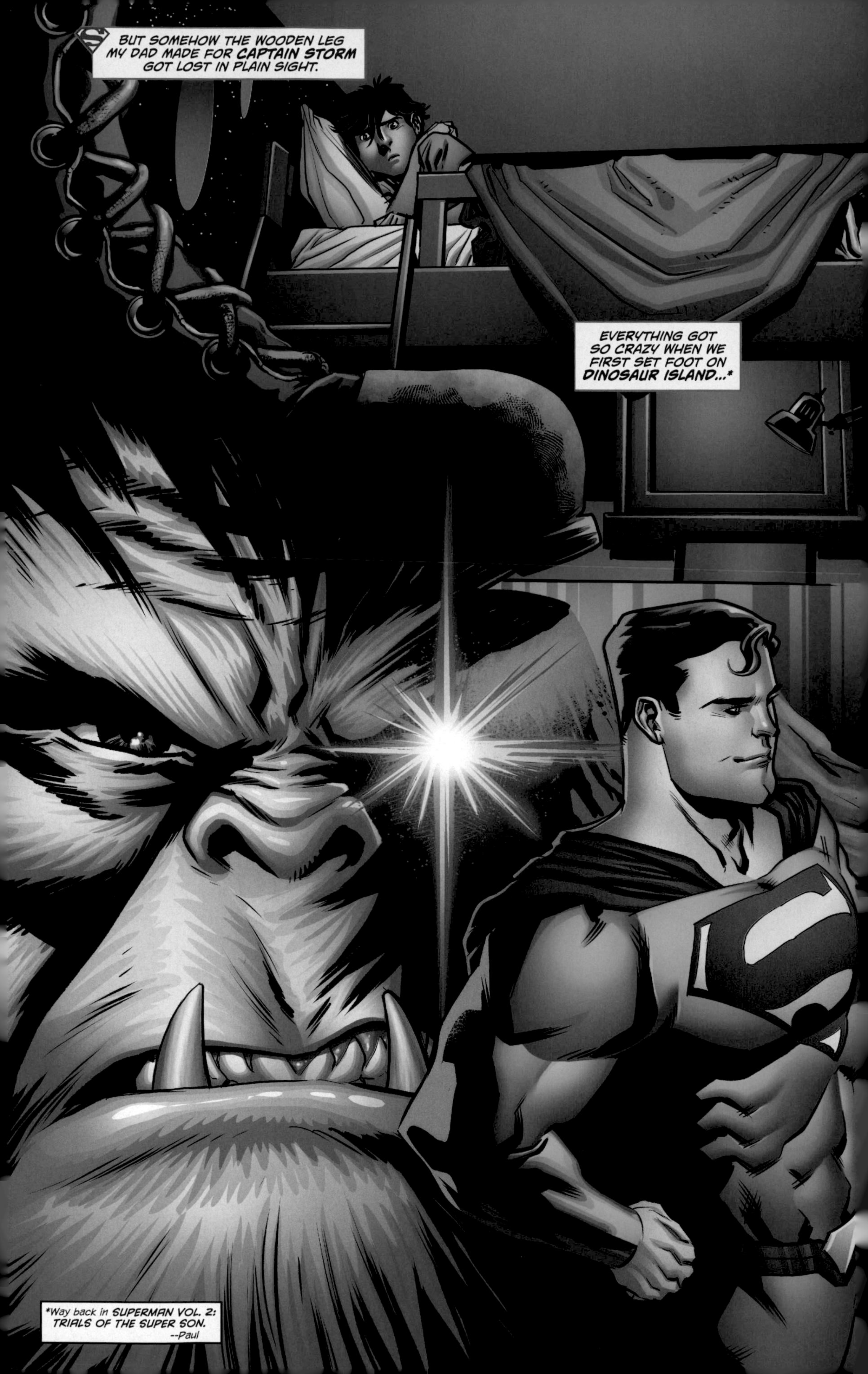

BUT SOMEHOW THE WOODEN LEG MY DAD MADE FOR CAPTAIN STORM GOT LOST IN PLAIN SIGHT.
EVERYTHING GOT SO CRAZY WHEN WE FIRST SET FOOT ON DINOSAUR ISLAND...*
*Way back in SUPERMAN VOL. 2: TRIALS OF THE SUPER SON. --Paul

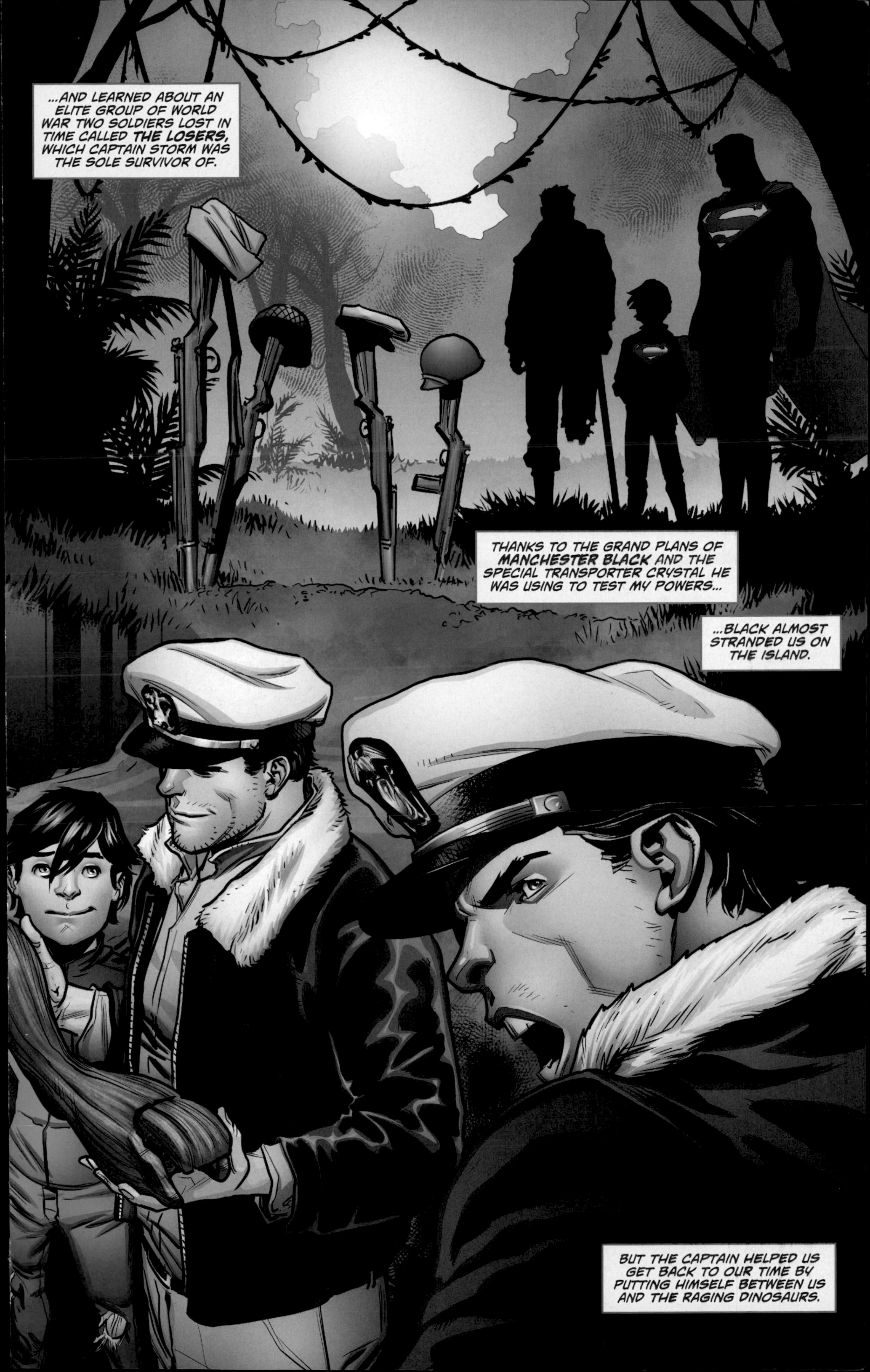
...AND LEARNED ABOUT AN ELITE GROUP OF WORLD WAR TWO SOLDIERS LOST IN TIME CALLED **THE LOSERS**, WHICH CAPTAIN STORM WAS THE SOLE SURVIVOR OF.
THANKS TO THE GRAND PLANS OF **MANCHESTER BLACK** AND THE SPECIAL TRANSPORTER CRYSTAL HE WAS USING TO TEST MY POWERS...
...BLACK ALMOST STRANDED US ON THE ISLAND.
BUT THE CAPTAIN HELPED US GET BACK TO OUR TIME BY PUTTING HIMSELF BETWEEN US AND THE RAGING DINOSAURS.

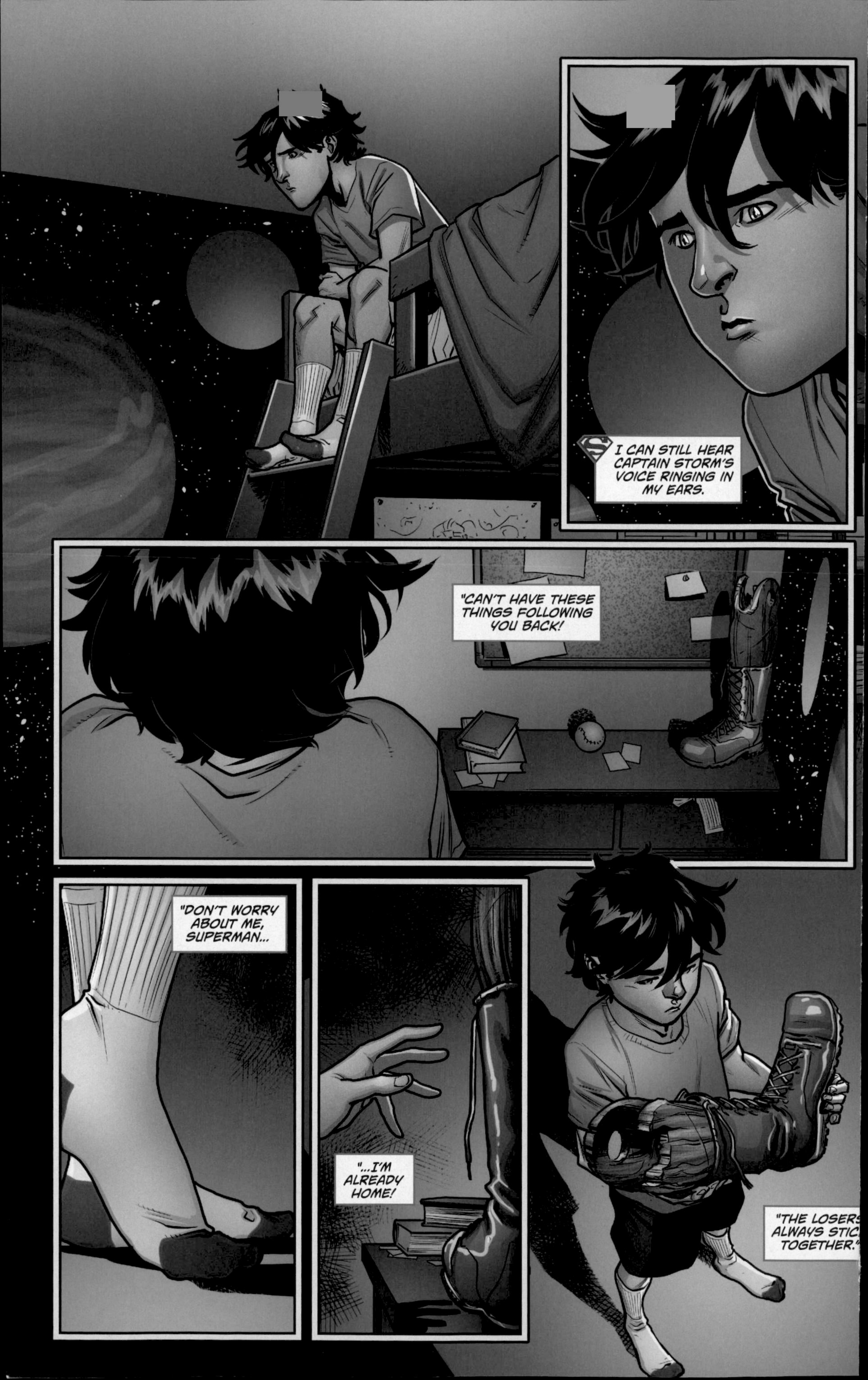
I CAN STILL HEAR CAPTAIN STORM'S VOICE RINGING IN MY EARS.
"CAN'T HAVE THESE THINGS FOLLOWING YOU BACK!
"DON'T WORRY ABOUT ME, SUPERMAN...
"...I'M ALREADY HOME!
"THE LOSERS ALWAYS STIC TOGETHER."

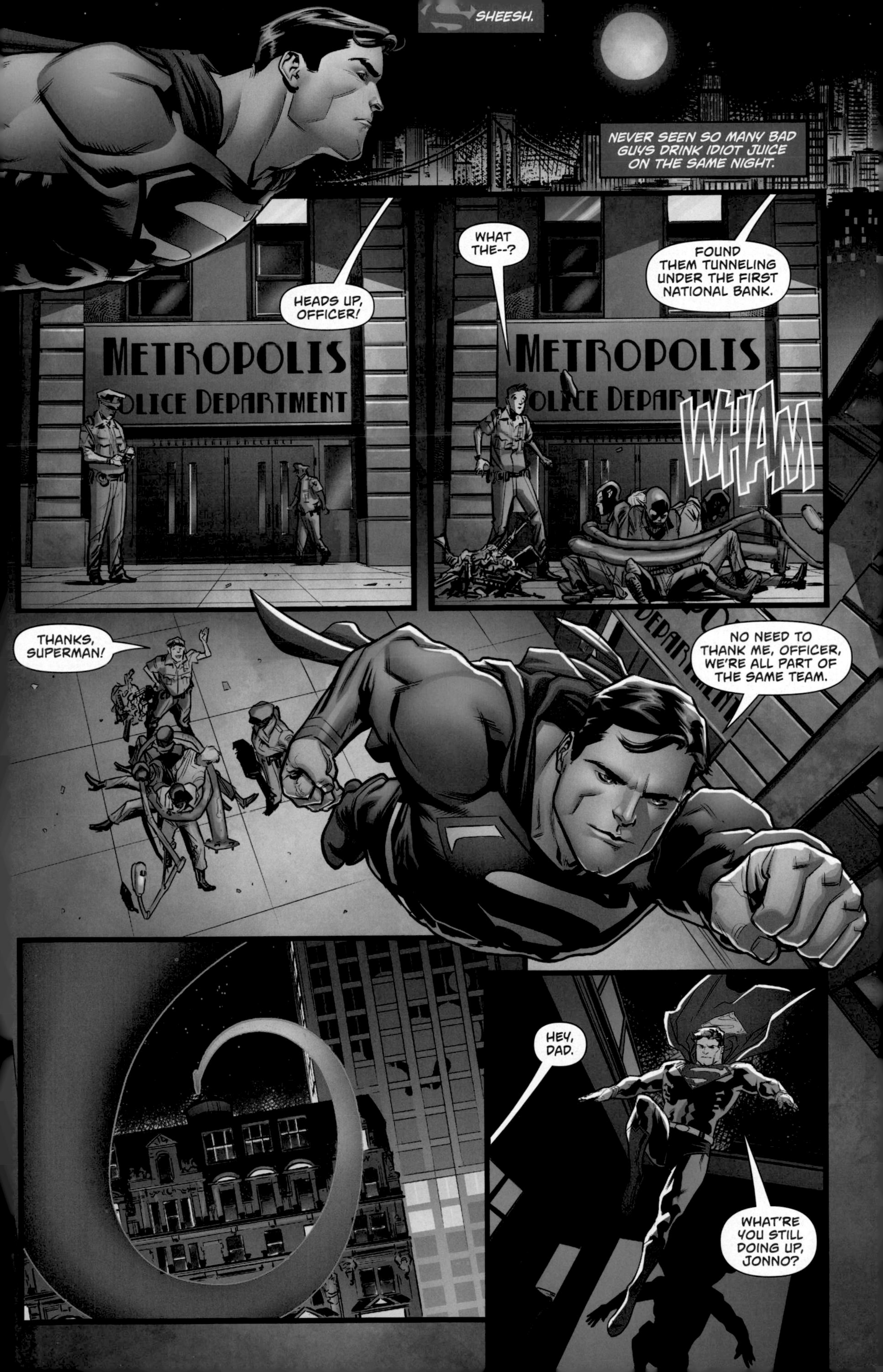
SHEESH.
NEVER SEEN SO MANY BAD GUYS DRINK IDIOT JUICE ON THE SAME NIGHT.
HEADS UP, OFFICER!
METROPOLIS POLICE DEPARTMENT
WHAT THE--?
FOUND THEM TUNNELING UNDER THE FIRST NATIONAL BANK.
WHAM
THANKS, SUPERMAN!
NO NEED TO THANK ME, OFFICER, WE'RE ALL PART OF THE SAME TEAM.
HEY, DAD.
WHAT'RE YOU STILL DOING UP, JONNO?

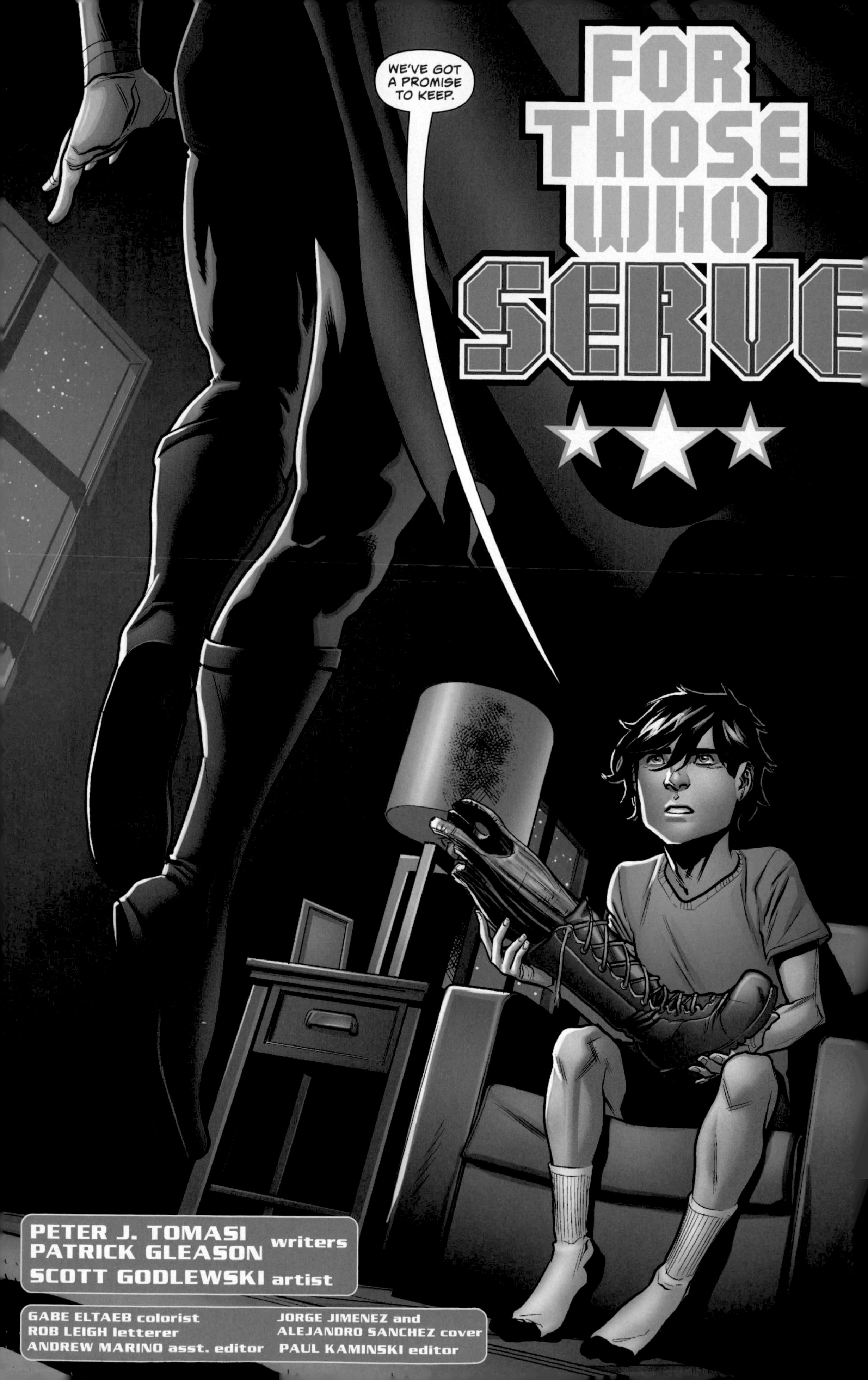
WE'VE GOT A PROMISE TO KEEP.
FOR THOSE WHO SERVE
PETER J. TOMASI PATRICK GLEASON writers
SCOTT GODLEWSKI artist
GABE ELTAEB colorist
ROB LEIGH letterer
ANDREW MARINO asst. editor
JORGE JIMENEZ and ALEJANDRO SANCHEZ cover
PAUL KAMINSKI editor

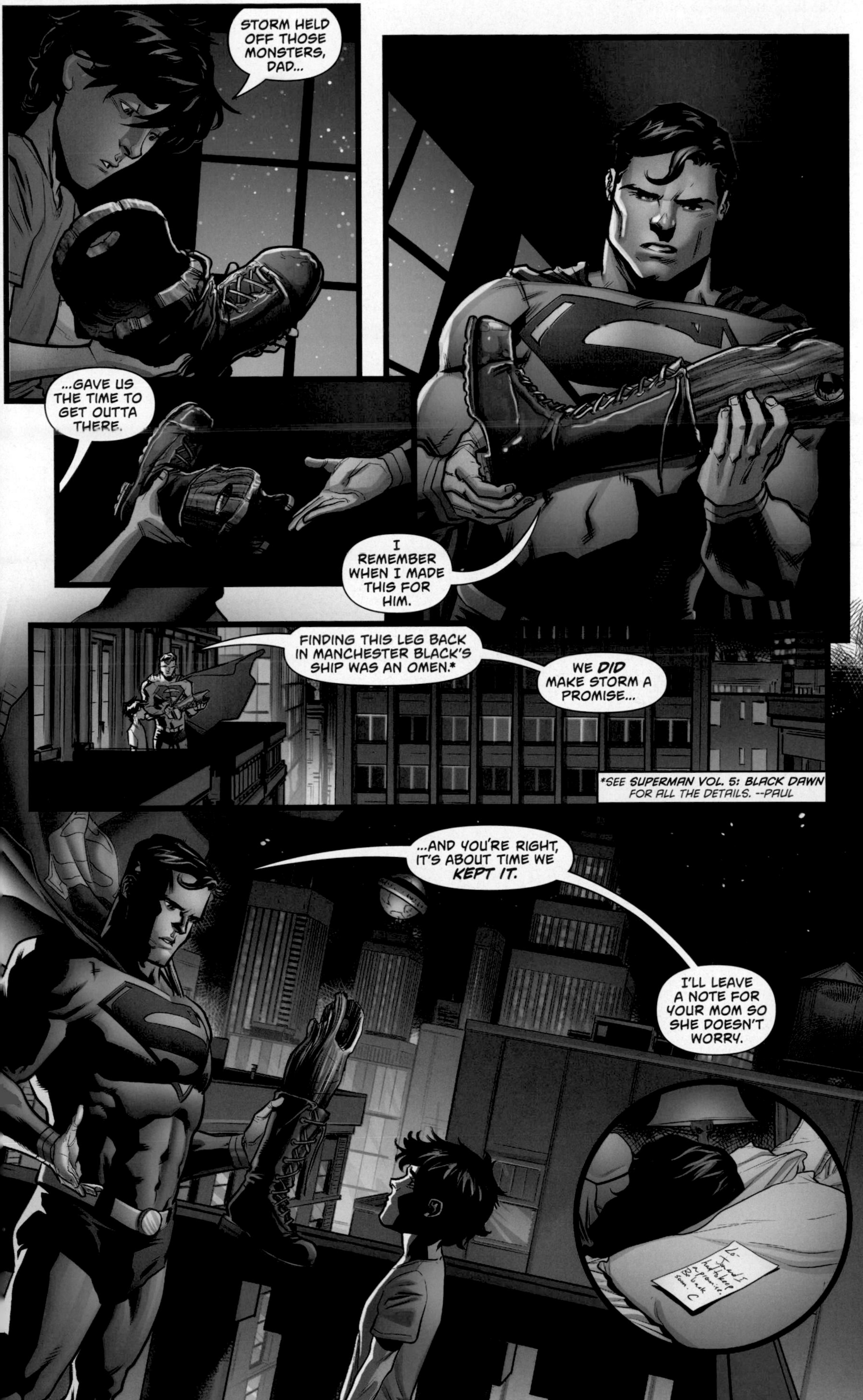
STORM HELD OFF THOSE MONSTERS, DAD...
...GAVE US THE TIME TO GET OUTTA THERE.
I REMEMBER WHEN I MADE THIS FOR HIM.
FINDING THIS LEG BACK IN MANCHESTER BLACK'S SHIP WAS AN OMEN.*
WE *DID* MAKE STORM A PROMISE...
*SEE *SUPERMAN VOL. 5: BLACK DAWN* FOR ALL THE DETAILS. --PAUL
...AND YOU'RE RIGHT, IT'S ABOUT TIME WE ***KEPT IT.***
I'LL LEAVE A NOTE FOR YOUR MOM SO SHE DOESN'T WORRY.

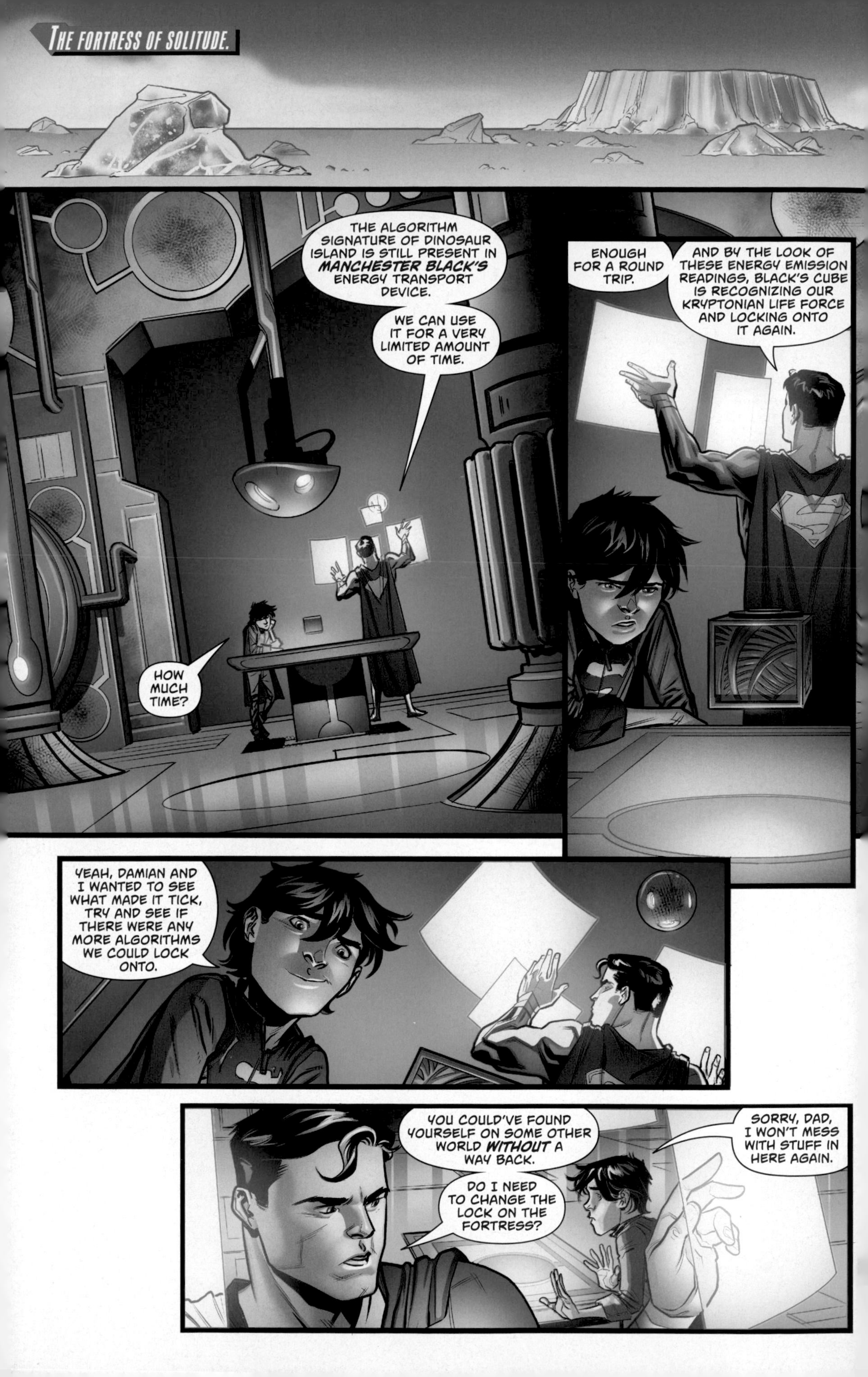
THE FORTRESS OF SOLITUDE.
THE ALGORITHM SIGNATURE OF DINOSAUR ISLAND IS STILL PRESENT IN ***MANCHESTER BLACK'S*** ENERGY TRANSPORT DEVICE.
WE CAN USE IT FOR A VERY LIMITED AMOUNT OF TIME.
HOW MUCH TIME?
ENOUGH FOR A ROUND TRIP.
AND BY THE LOOK OF THESE ENERGY EMISSION READINGS, BLACK'S CUBE IS RECOGNIZING OUR KRYPTONIAN LIFE FORCE AND LOCKING ONTO IT AGAIN.
YEAH, DAMIAN AND I WANTED TO SEE WHAT MADE IT TICK, TRY AND SEE IF THERE WERE ANY MORE ALGORITHMS WE COULD LOCK ONTO.
YOU COULD'VE FOUND YOURSELF ON SOME OTHER WORLD ***WITHOUT*** A WAY BACK.
DO I NEED TO CHANGE THE LOCK ON THE FORTRESS?
SORRY, DAD, I WON'T MESS WITH STUFF IN HERE AGAIN.

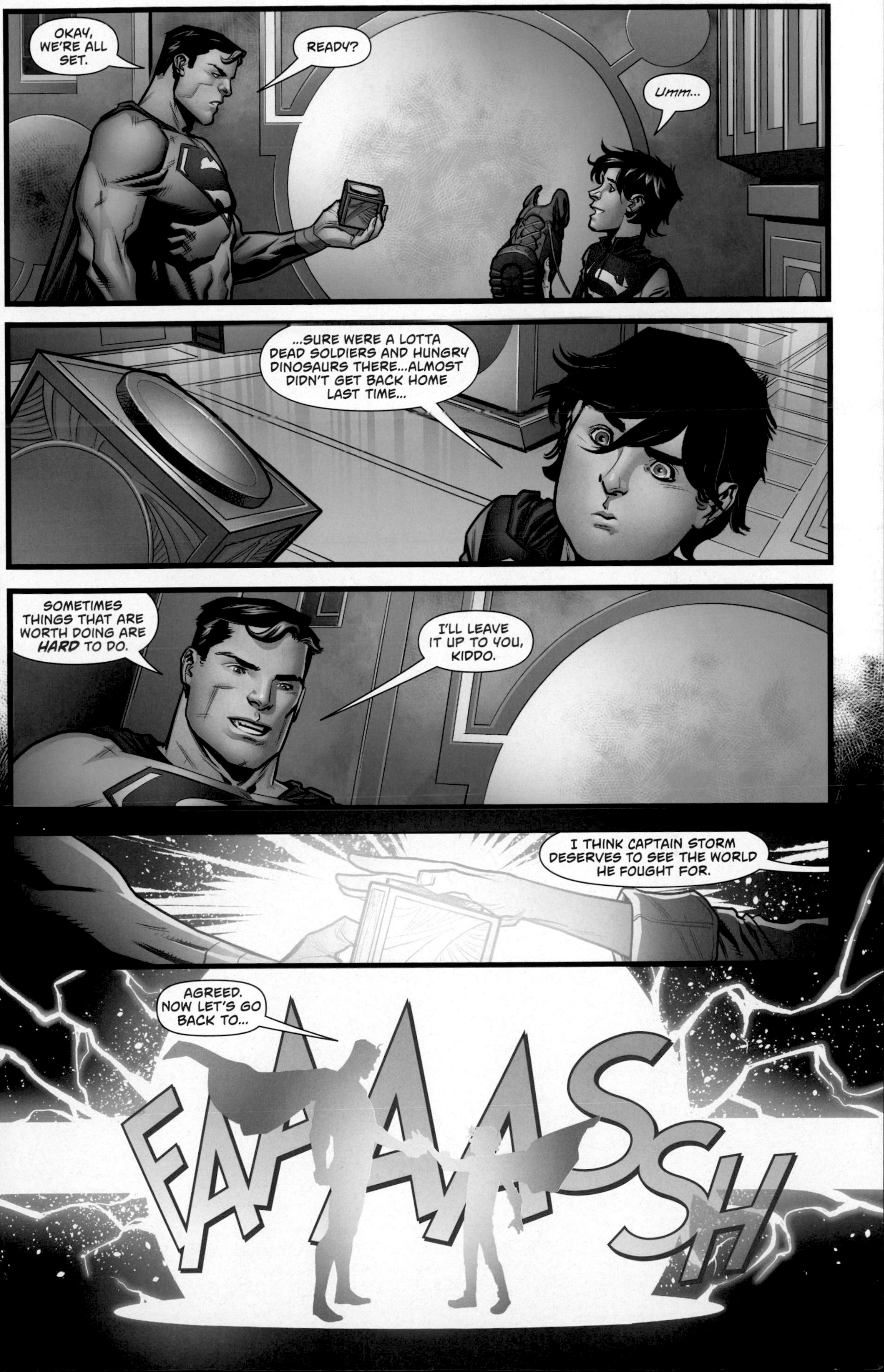
OKAY, WE'RE ALL SET.
READY?
Umm...
...SURE WERE A LOTTA DEAD SOLDIERS AND HUNGRY DINOSAURS THERE...ALMOST DIDN'T GET BACK HOME LAST TIME...
SOMETIMES THINGS THAT ARE WORTH DOING ARE HARD TO DO.
I'LL LEAVE IT UP TO YOU, KIDDO.
I THINK CAPTAIN STORM DESERVES TO SEE THE WORLD HE FOUGHT FOR.
AGREED. NOW LET'S GO BACK TO...
FAAAASSH

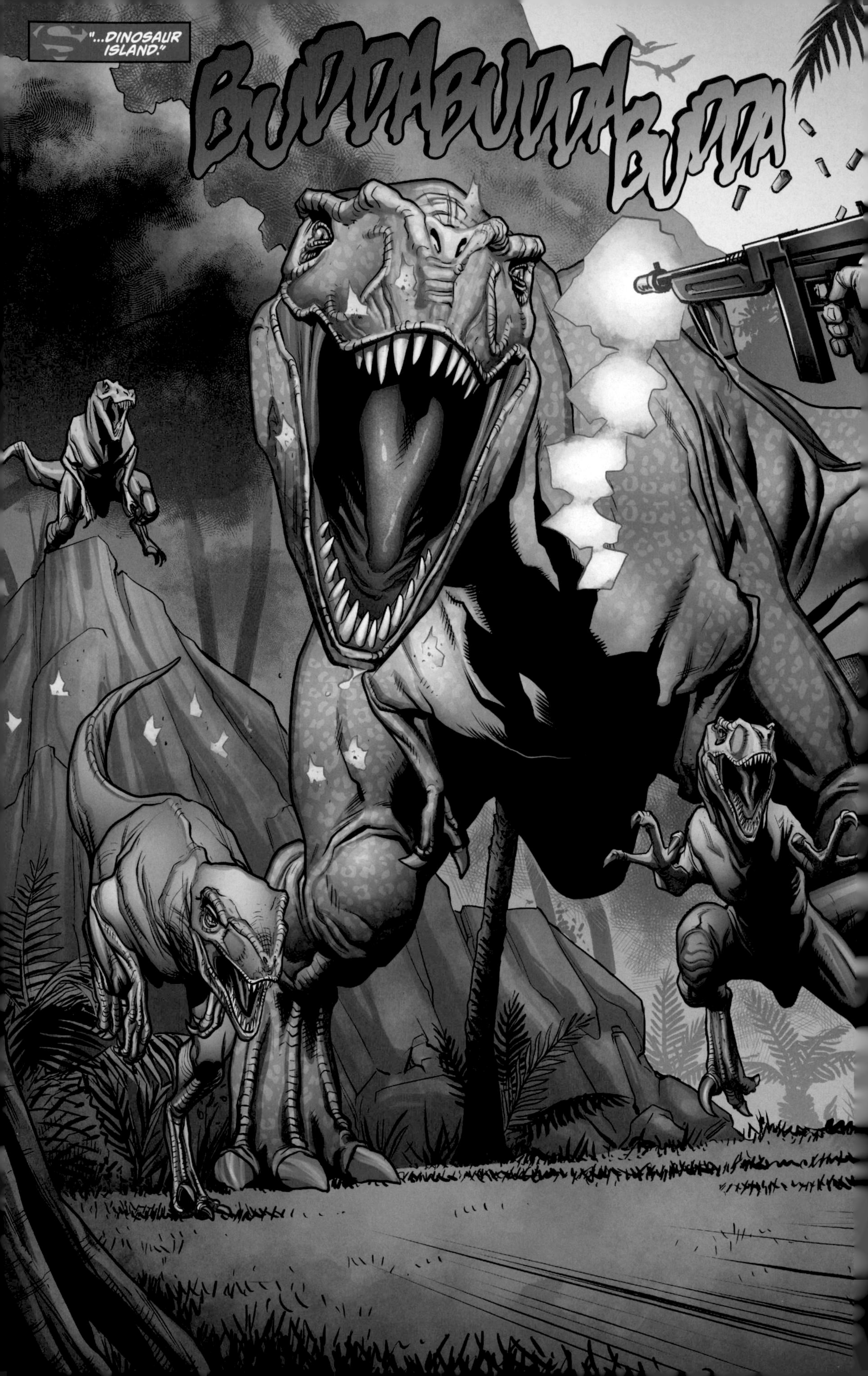
"...DINOSAUR ISLAND."
BUDDABUDDABUDDA

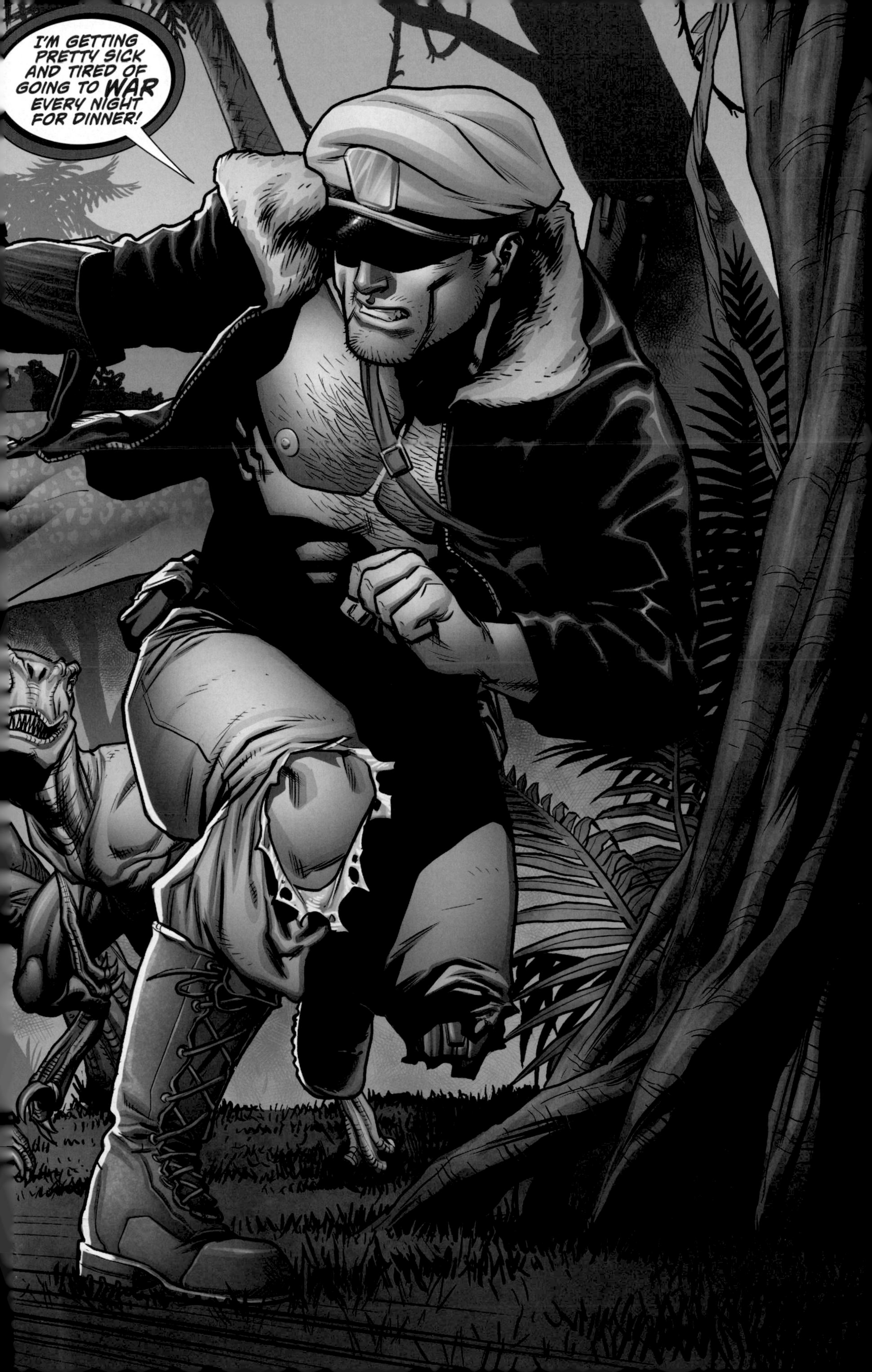
I'M GETTING PRETTY SICK AND TIRED OF GOING TO WAR EVERY NIGHT FOR DINNER!

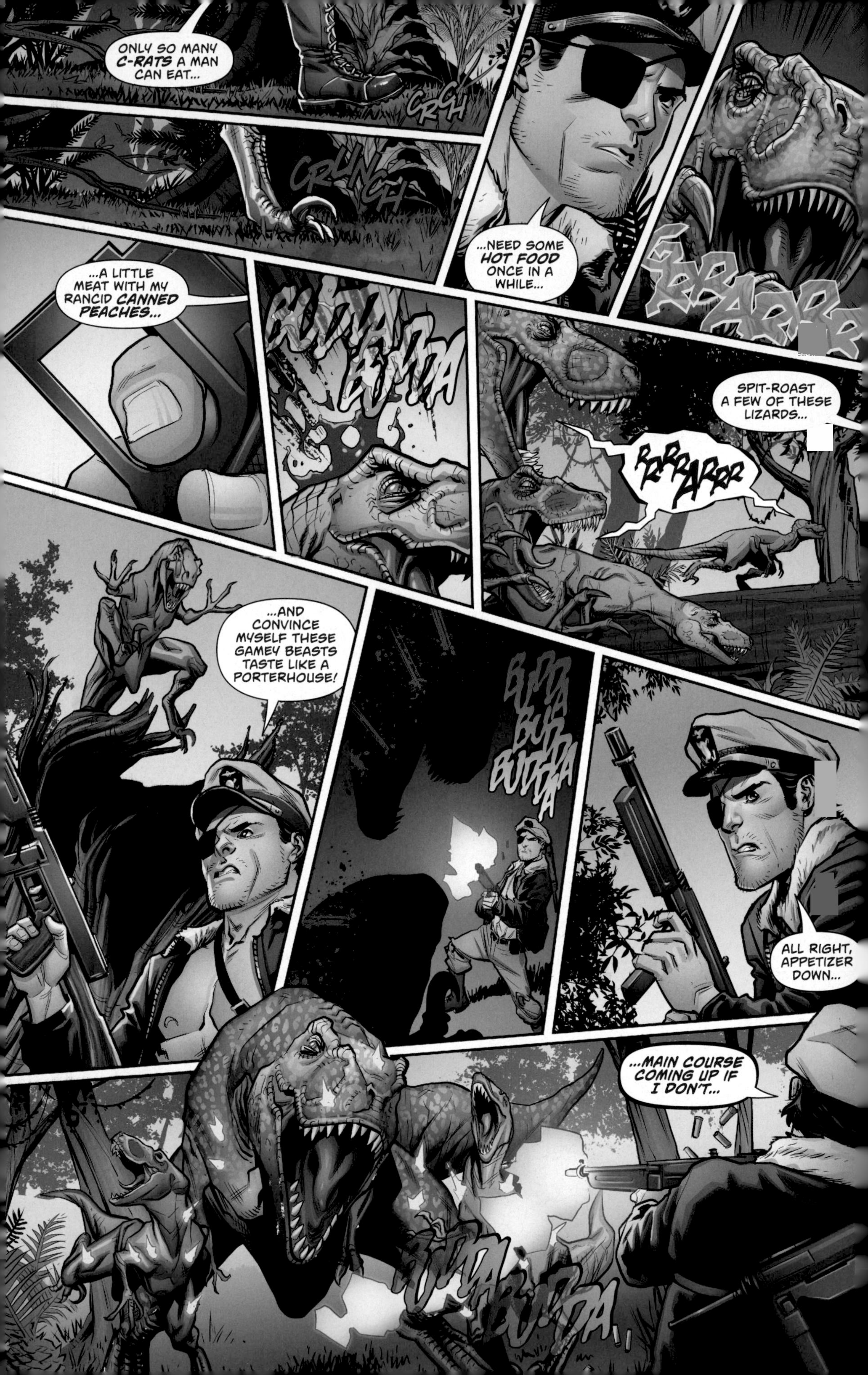
ONLY SO MANY C-RATS A MAN CAN EAT...
CRCH
CRUNCH
...NEED SOME HOT FOOD ONCE IN A WHILE...
...A LITTLE MEAT WITH MY RANCID CANNED PEACHES...
SPIT-ROAST A FEW OF THESE LIZARDS...
RRRRARRR
...AND CONVINCE MYSELF THESE GAMEY BEASTS TASTE LIKE A PORTERHOUSE!
ALL RIGHT, APPETIZER DOWN...
...MAIN COURSE COMING UP IF I DON'T...

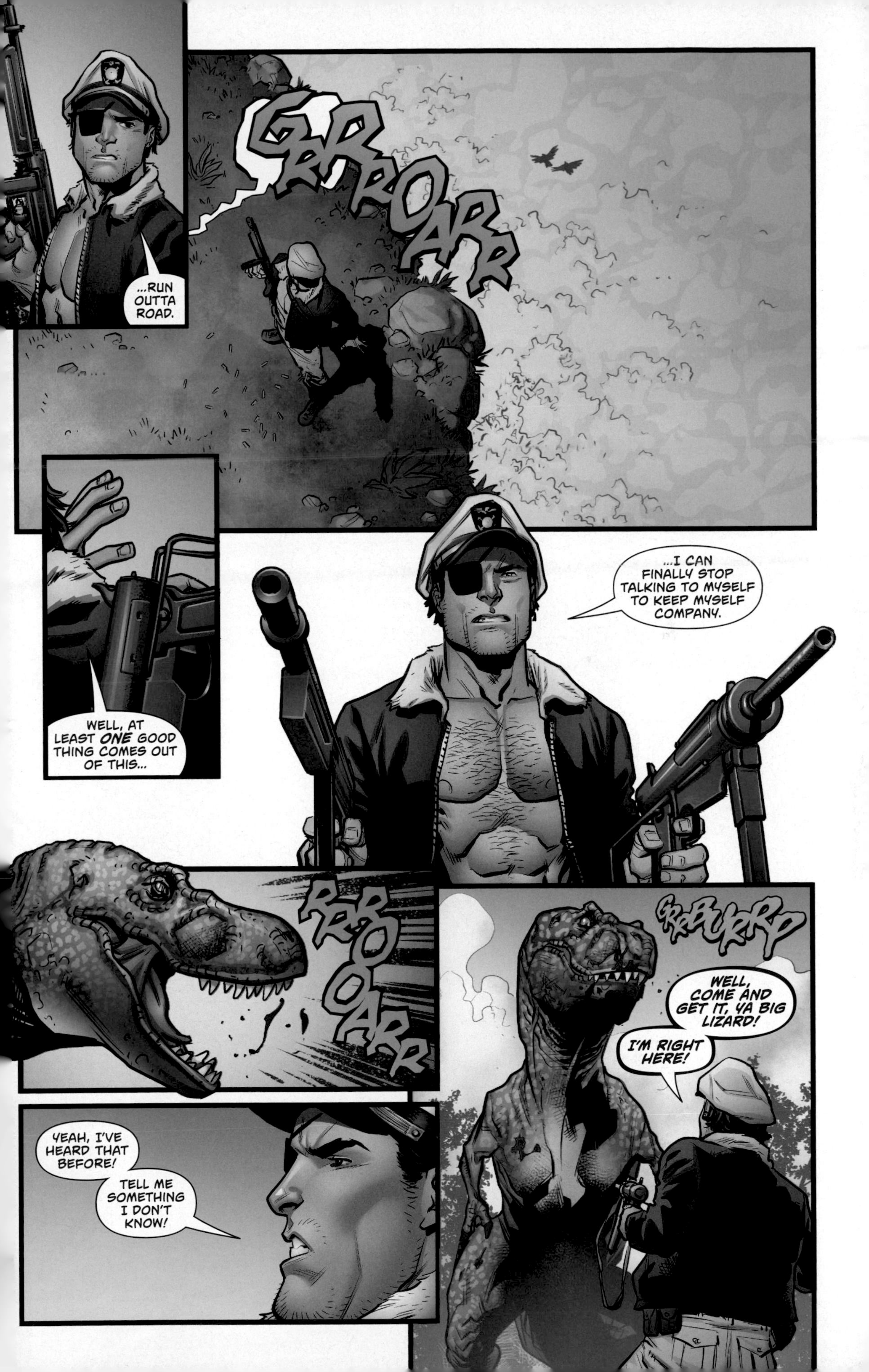
...RUN OUTTA ROAD.
GRRROARR
WELL, AT LEAST ONE GOOD THING COMES OUT OF THIS...
...I CAN FINALLY STOP TALKING TO MYSELF TO KEEP MYSELF COMPANY.
RRROOARR
GRRBURRR
WELL, COME AND GET IT, YA BIG LIZARD!
I'M RIGHT HERE!
YEAH, I'VE HEARD THAT BEFORE!
TELL ME SOMETHING I DON'T KNOW!

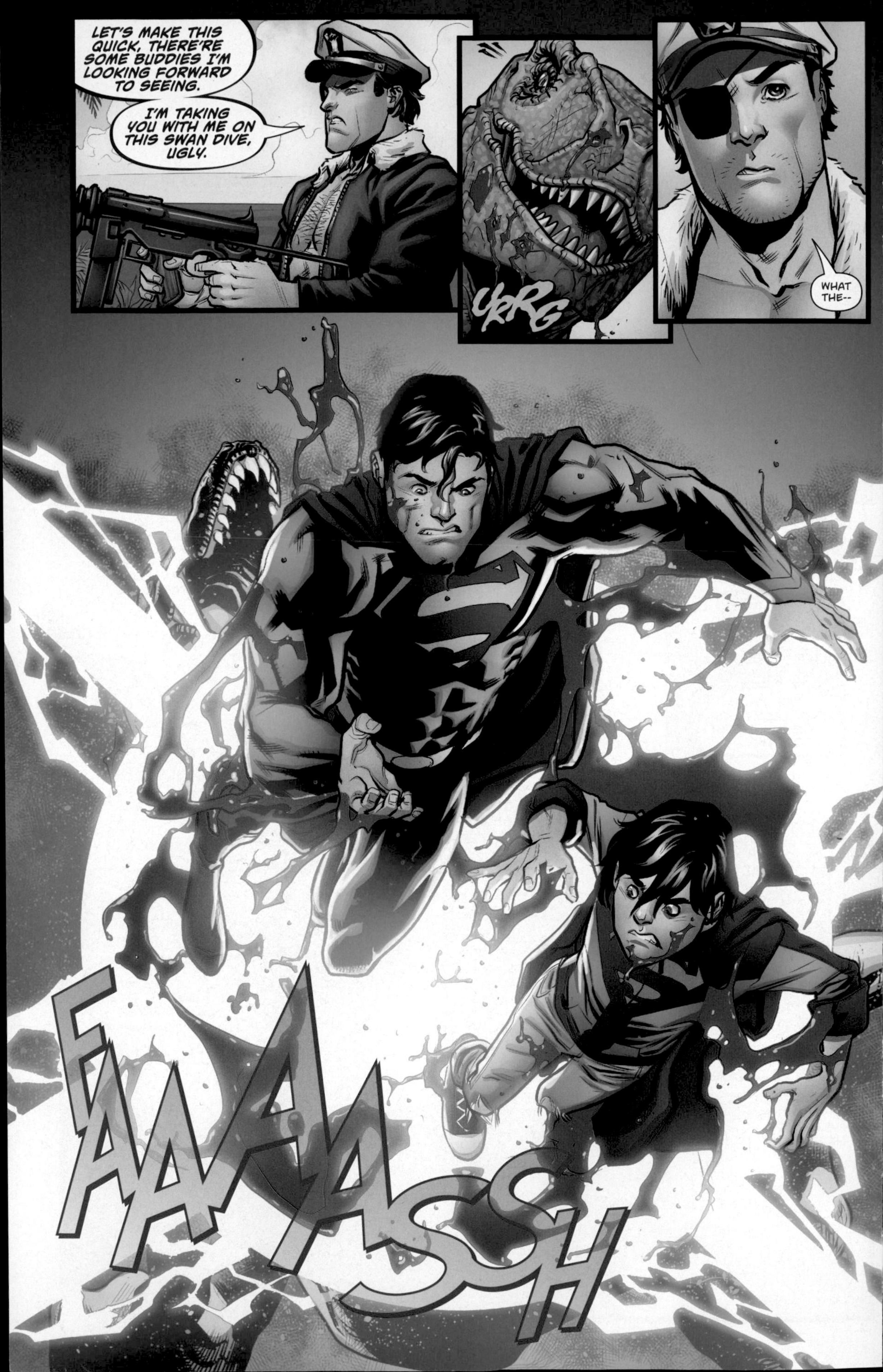
LET'S MAKE THIS QUICK, THERE'RE SOME BUDDIES I'M LOOKING FORWARD TO SEEING.
I'M TAKING YOU WITH ME ON THIS SWAN DIVE, UGLY.
URRG
WHAT THE--
FAAAASSH

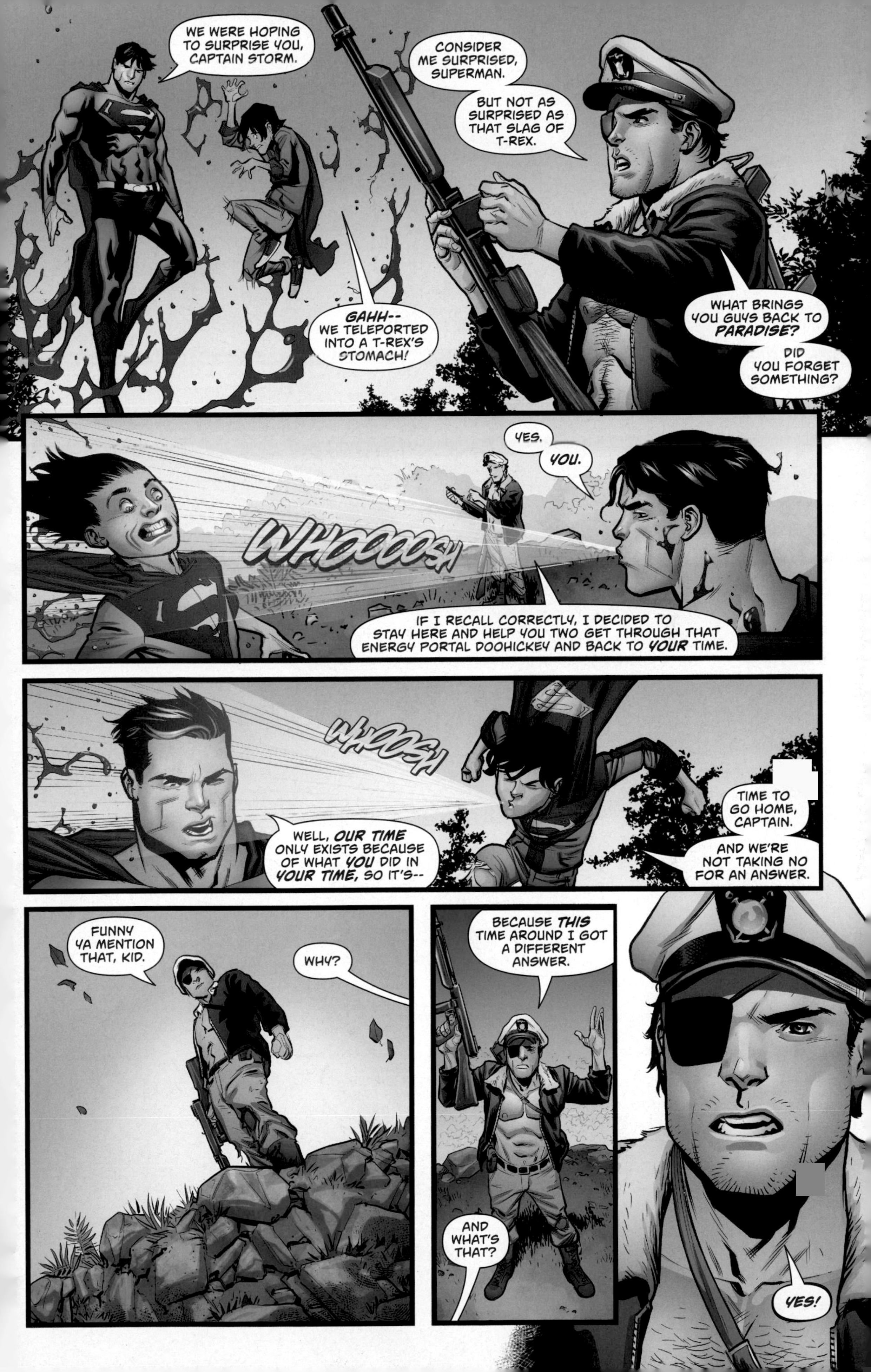
WE WERE HOPING TO SURPRISE YOU, CAPTAIN STORM.
CONSIDER ME SURPRISED, SUPERMAN.
BUT NOT AS SURPRISED AS THAT SLAG OF T-REX.
GAHH-- WE TELEPORTED INTO A T-REX'S STOMACH!
WHAT BRINGS YOU GUYS BACK TO PARADISE?
DID YOU FORGET SOMETHING?
YES.
YOU.
WHOOOOOSH
IF I RECALL CORRECTLY, I DECIDED TO STAY HERE AND HELP YOU TWO GET THROUGH THAT ENERGY PORTAL DOOHICKEY AND BACK TO YOUR TIME.
WHOOSH
WELL, OUR TIME ONLY EXISTS BECAUSE OF WHAT YOU DID IN YOUR TIME, SO IT'S--
TIME TO GO HOME, CAPTAIN.
AND WE'RE NOT TAKING NO FOR AN ANSWER.
FUNNY YA MENTION THAT, KID.
WHY?
BECAUSE THIS TIME AROUND I GOT A DIFFERENT ANSWER.
AND WHAT'S THAT?
YES!

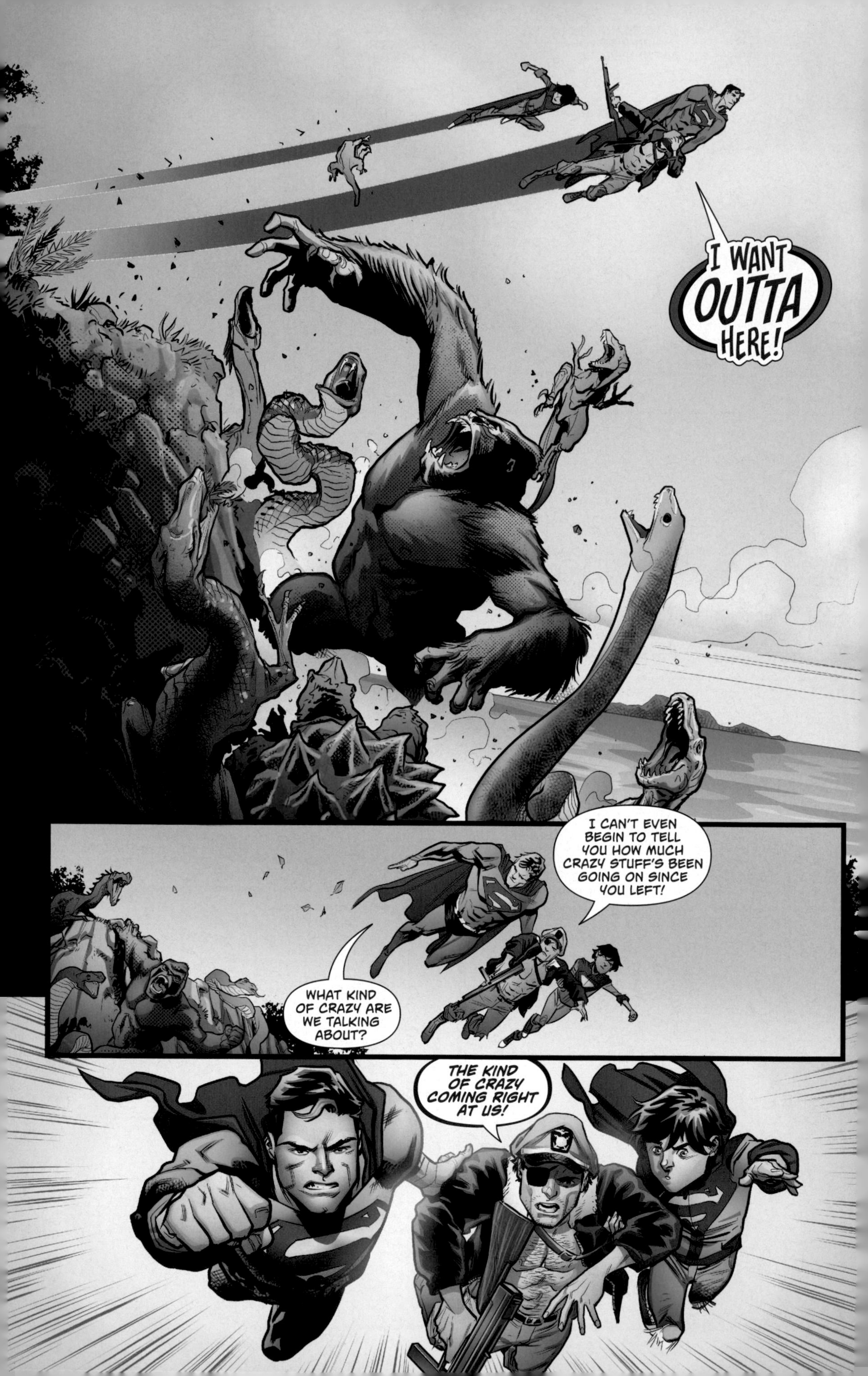
I WANT OUTTA HERE!
I CAN'T EVEN BEGIN TO TELL YOU HOW MUCH CRAZY STUFF'S BEEN GOING ON SINCE YOU LEFT!
WHAT KIND OF CRAZY ARE WE TALKING ABOUT?
THE KIND OF CRAZY COMING RIGHT AT US!

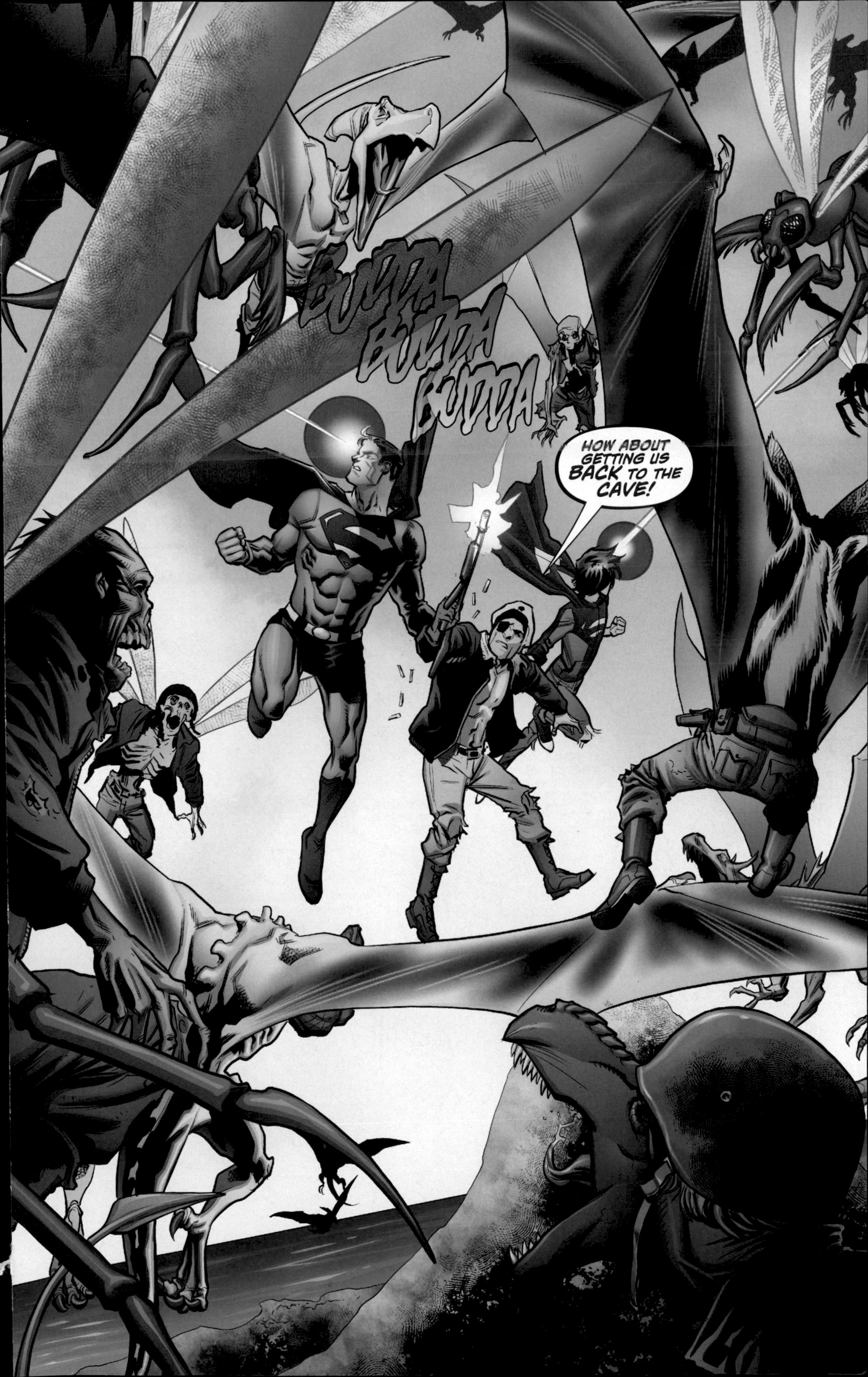
BUDDA BUDDA BUDDA
HOW ABOUT GETTING US BACK TO THE CAVE!

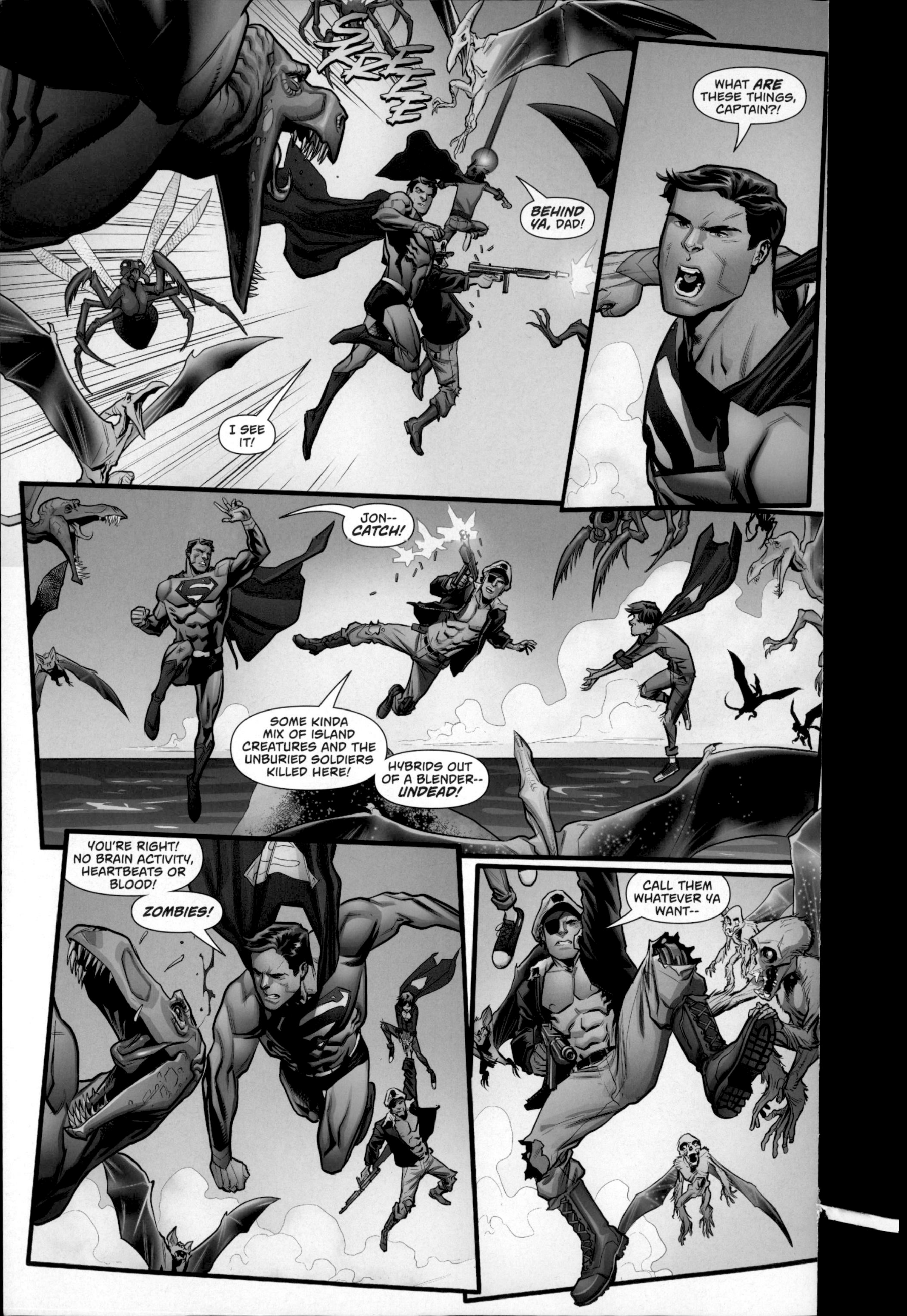
SKREEE
WHAT ARE THESE THINGS, CAPTAIN?!
BEHIND YA, DAD!
I SEE IT!
JON-- CATCH!
SOME KINDA MIX OF ISLAND CREATURES AND THE UNBURIED SOLDIERS KILLED HERE!
HYBRIDS OUT OF A BLENDER-- UNDEAD!
YOU'RE RIGHT! NO BRAIN ACTIVITY, HEARTBEATS OR BLOOD!
ZOMBIES!
CALL THEM WHATEVER YA WANT--

--BUT DON'T LET THEM TAKE A BITE OUT OF YOU!

HOLY MOLEY!

STORM-- YOUR LEG...

YEAH, NOT EXACTLY THE KINDA FOOT I LIKE SEEING IN MY BUSTER BROWNS!

WE DON'T HAVE TO DEAL WITH ALL THIS INSANITY...

...AN ACTIVATION OF THE CRYSTAL AND WE CAN ZAP OUT OF HERE RIGHT NOW.

NOT UNTIL I GET SOMETHING BACK FROM THE CAVE.

WHAT CAN BE SO IMPORTANT THAT--

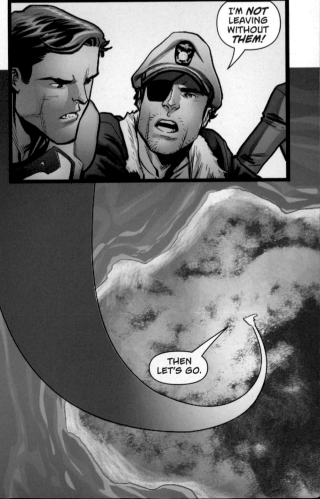

I'M *NOT* LEAVING WITHOUT *THEM!*

THEN LET'S GO.

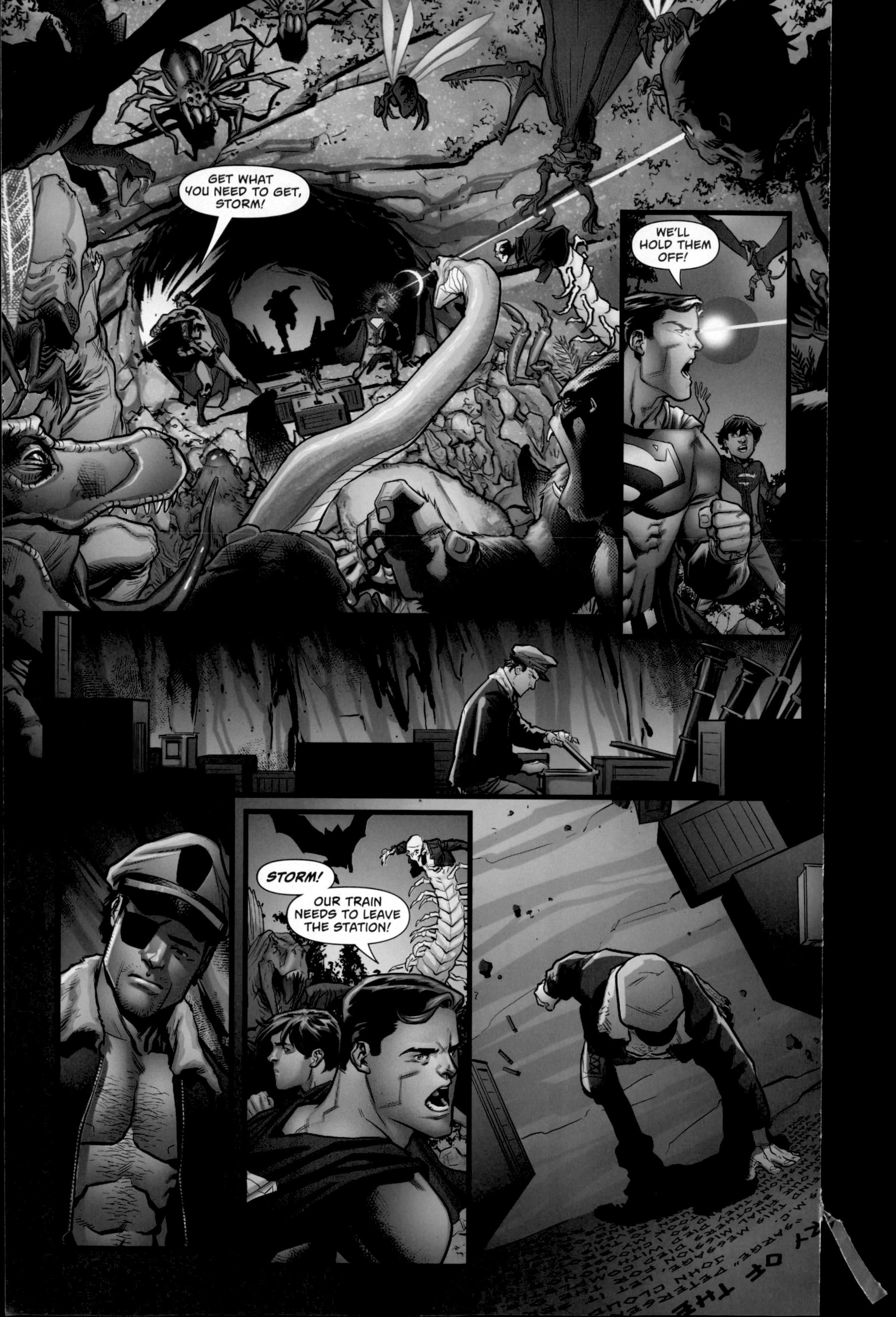
GET WHAT YOU NEED TO GET, STORM!
WE'LL HOLD THEM OFF!
STORM!
OUR TRAIN NEEDS TO LEAVE THE STATION!

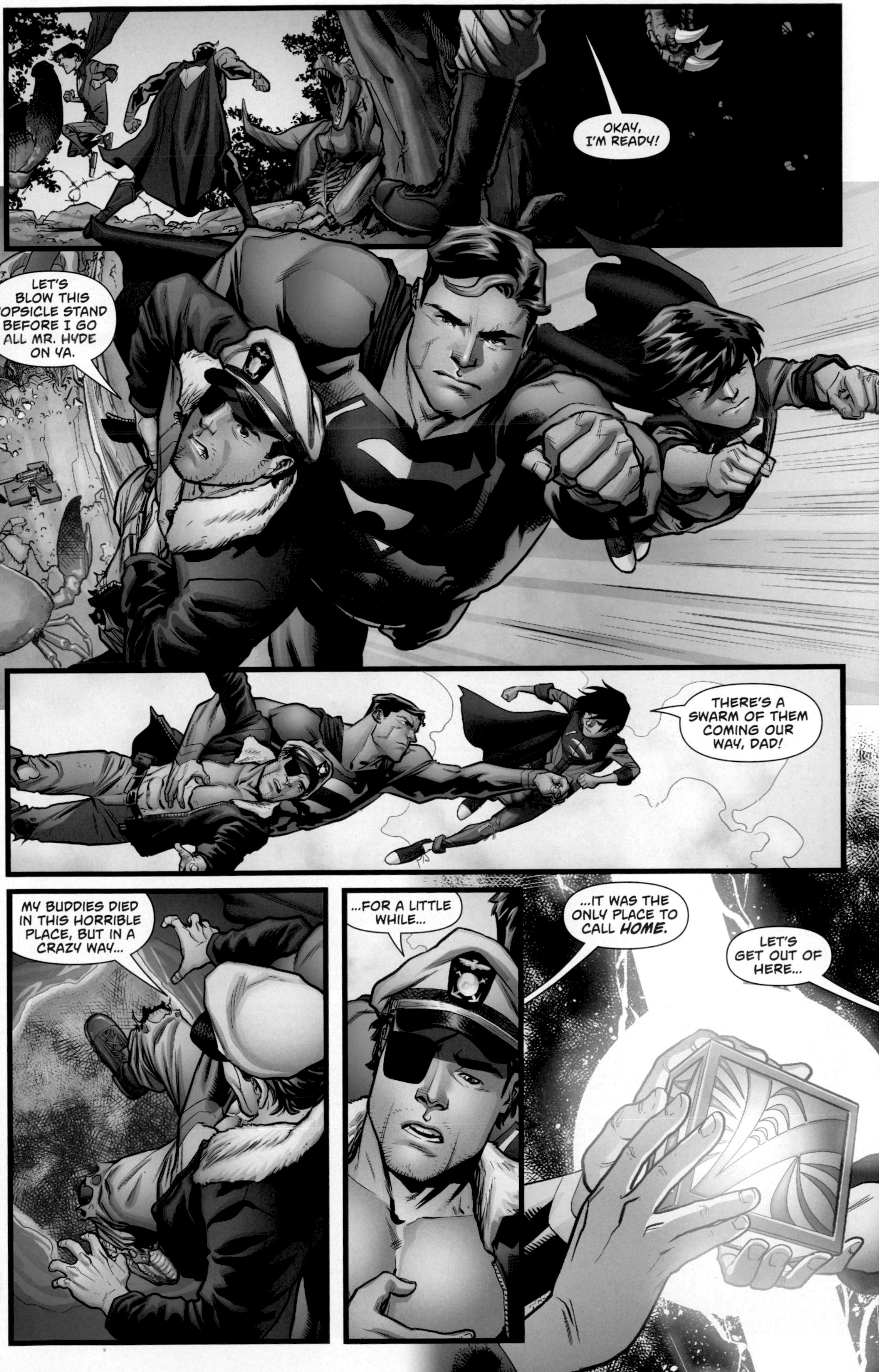

OKAY, I'M READY!
LET'S BLOW THIS POPSICLE STAND BEFORE I GO ALL MR. HYDE ON YA.
THERE'S A SWARM OF THEM COMING OUR WAY, DAD!
MY BUDDIES DIED IN THIS HORRIBLE PLACE, BUT IN A CRAZY WAY...
...FOR A LITTLE WHILE...
...IT WAS THE ONLY PLACE TO CALL HOME.
LET'S GET OUT OF HERE...

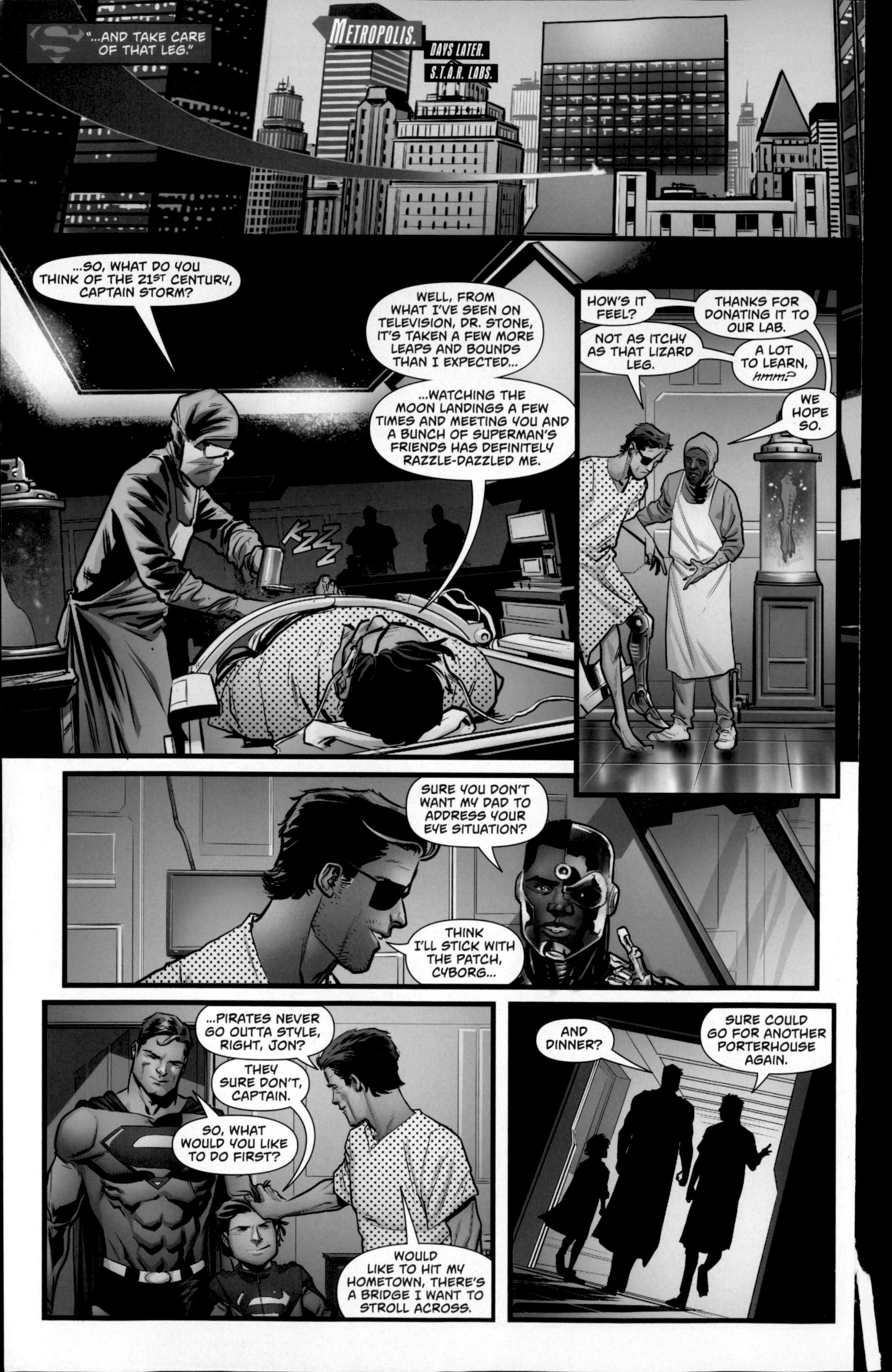

"...AND TAKE CARE OF THAT LEG."
METROPOLIS.
DAYS LATER.
S.T.A.R. LABS.
...SO, WHAT DO YOU THINK OF THE 21ST CENTURY, CAPTAIN STORM?
WELL, FROM WHAT I'VE SEEN ON TELEVISION, DR. STONE, IT'S TAKEN A FEW MORE LEAPS AND BOUNDS THAN I EXPECTED...
...WATCHING THE MOON LANDINGS A FEW TIMES AND MEETING YOU AND A BUNCH OF SUPERMAN'S FRIENDS HAS DEFINITELY RAZZLE-DAZZLED ME.
KZZZ
HOW'S IT FEEL?
NOT AS ITCHY AS THAT LIZARD LEG.
THANKS FOR DONATING IT TO OUR LAB.
A LOT TO LEARN, hmm?
WE HOPE SO.
SURE YOU DON'T WANT MY DAD TO ADDRESS YOUR EYE SITUATION?
THINK I'LL STICK WITH THE PATCH, CYBORG...
...PIRATES NEVER GO OUTTA STYLE, RIGHT, JON?
THEY SURE DON'T, CAPTAIN.
SO, WHAT WOULD YOU LIKE TO DO FIRST?
WOULD LIKE TO HIT MY HOMETOWN, THERE'S A BRIDGE I WANT TO STROLL ACROSS.
AND DINNER?
SURE COULD GO FOR ANOTHER PORTERHOUSE AGAIN.

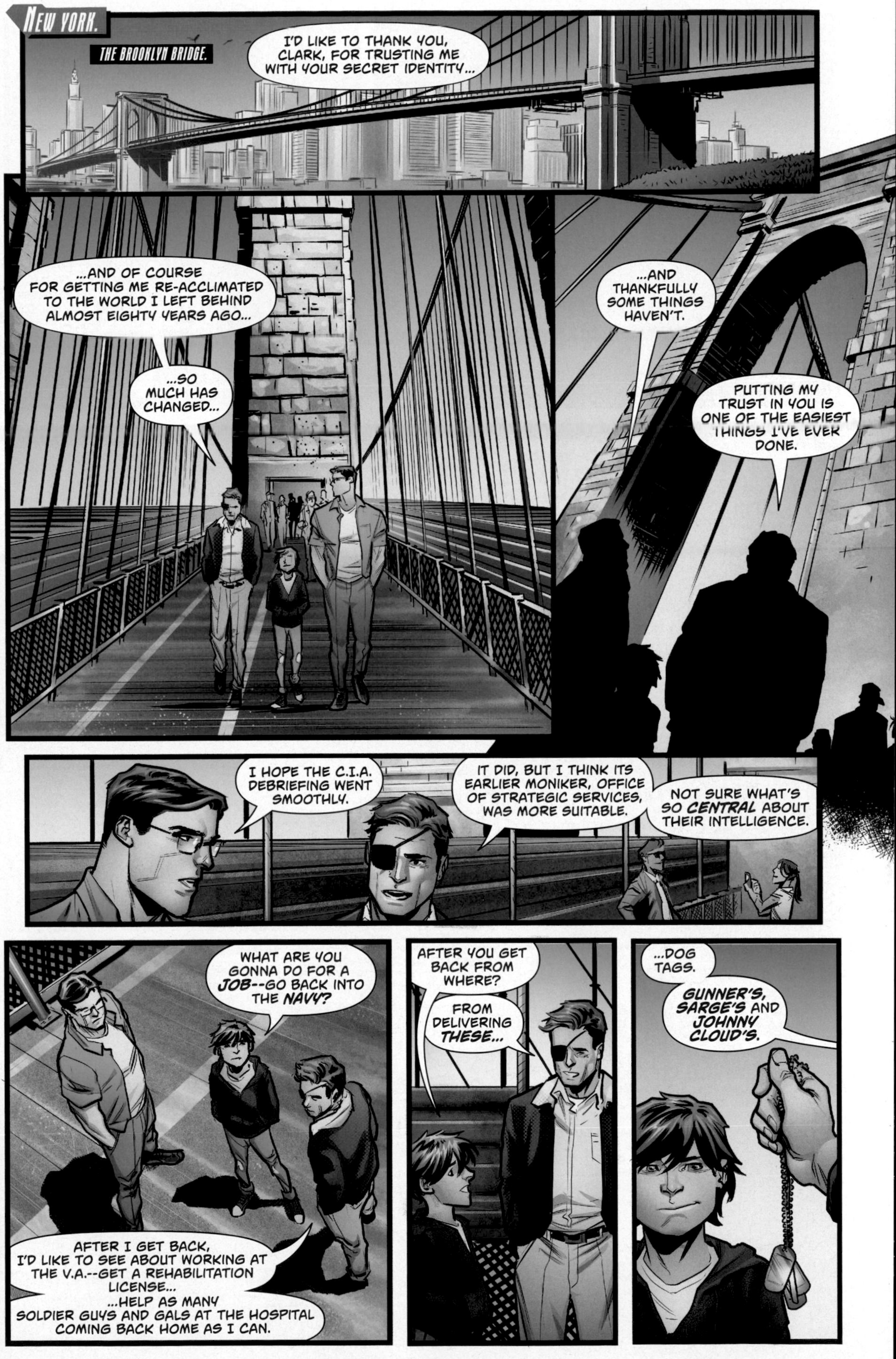
NEW YORK.
THE BROOKLYN BRIDGE.
I'D LIKE TO THANK YOU, CLARK, FOR TRUSTING ME WITH YOUR SECRET IDENTITY...
...AND OF COURSE FOR GETTING ME RE-ACCLIMATED TO THE WORLD I LEFT BEHIND ALMOST EIGHTY YEARS AGO...
...SO MUCH HAS CHANGED...
...AND THANKFULLY SOME THINGS HAVEN'T.
PUTTING MY TRUST IN YOU IS ONE OF THE EASIEST THINGS I'VE EVER DONE.
I HOPE THE C.I.A. DEBRIEFING WENT SMOOTHLY.
IT DID, BUT I THINK ITS EARLIER MONIKER, OFFICE OF STRATEGIC SERVICES, WAS MORE SUITABLE.
NOT SURE WHAT'S SO CENTRAL ABOUT THEIR INTELLIGENCE.
WHAT ARE YOU GONNA DO FOR A JOB--GO BACK INTO THE NAVY?
AFTER I GET BACK, I'D LIKE TO SEE ABOUT WORKING AT THE V.A.--GET A REHABILITATION LICENSE...
...HELP AS MANY SOLDIER GUYS AND GALS AT THE HOSPITAL COMING BACK HOME AS I CAN.
AFTER YOU GET BACK FROM WHERE?
FROM DELIVERING THESE...
...DOG TAGS.
GUNNER'S, SARGE'S AND JOHNNY CLOUD'S.

THAT'S WHY YOU WANTED TO GO BACK TO THE CAVE-- TO GRAB *THEM.*

ONLY RIGHT I TRY AND GET THEM INTO THE HANDS OF A RELATION--SO THEY CAN PUT THEIR BOYS TO REST FOR THE SAKE OF THEIR OWN FAMILIES.

SPEAKING OF FAMILIES, HERE'S THAT LIST OF SURVIVING RELATIVES YOU ASKED FOR, THANKS TO A LITTLE *DETECTIVE* WORK BY A CLOSE FRIEND OF MINE.

I FEEL BAD WE COULDN'T FIND ANYONE ON YOUR SIDE.

WELL, THEY TOLD ME MY WIFE DIED... NEVER REMARRIED OR HAD ANY KIDS... AND I WAS AN ONLY CHILD...BUT TO BE HONEST, I'M NOT READY TO DEAL WITH ALL THAT JUST YET.

YOU'VE GOT A NEW FAMILY IN METROPOLIS THAT YOU CAN ALWAYS VISIT, RIGHT, DAD?

ABSOLUTELY, KIDDO.

OUR DOOR IS ALWAYS OPEN TO YOU, CAPTAIN.

HOW ABOUT WE LOSE THE *CAPTAIN* AND GO WITH *WILLIAM* FROM HERE ON OUT.

HERE, JON, I WANT YOU TO HAVE THIS...

...KEEP THIS ONE SAFE FOR ME.

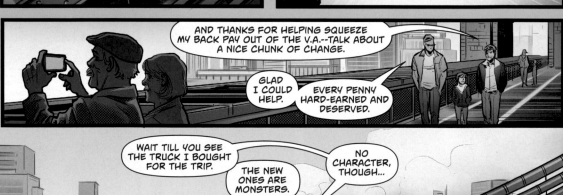

AND THANKS FOR HELPING SQUEEZE MY BACK PAY OUT OF THE V.A.--TALK ABOUT A NICE CHUNK OF CHANGE.

GLAD I COULD HELP.

EVERY PENNY HARD-EARNED AND DESERVED.

WAIT TILL YOU SEE THE TRUCK I BOUGHT FOR THE TRIP.

THE NEW ONES ARE MONSTERS.

NO CHARACTER, THOUGH...

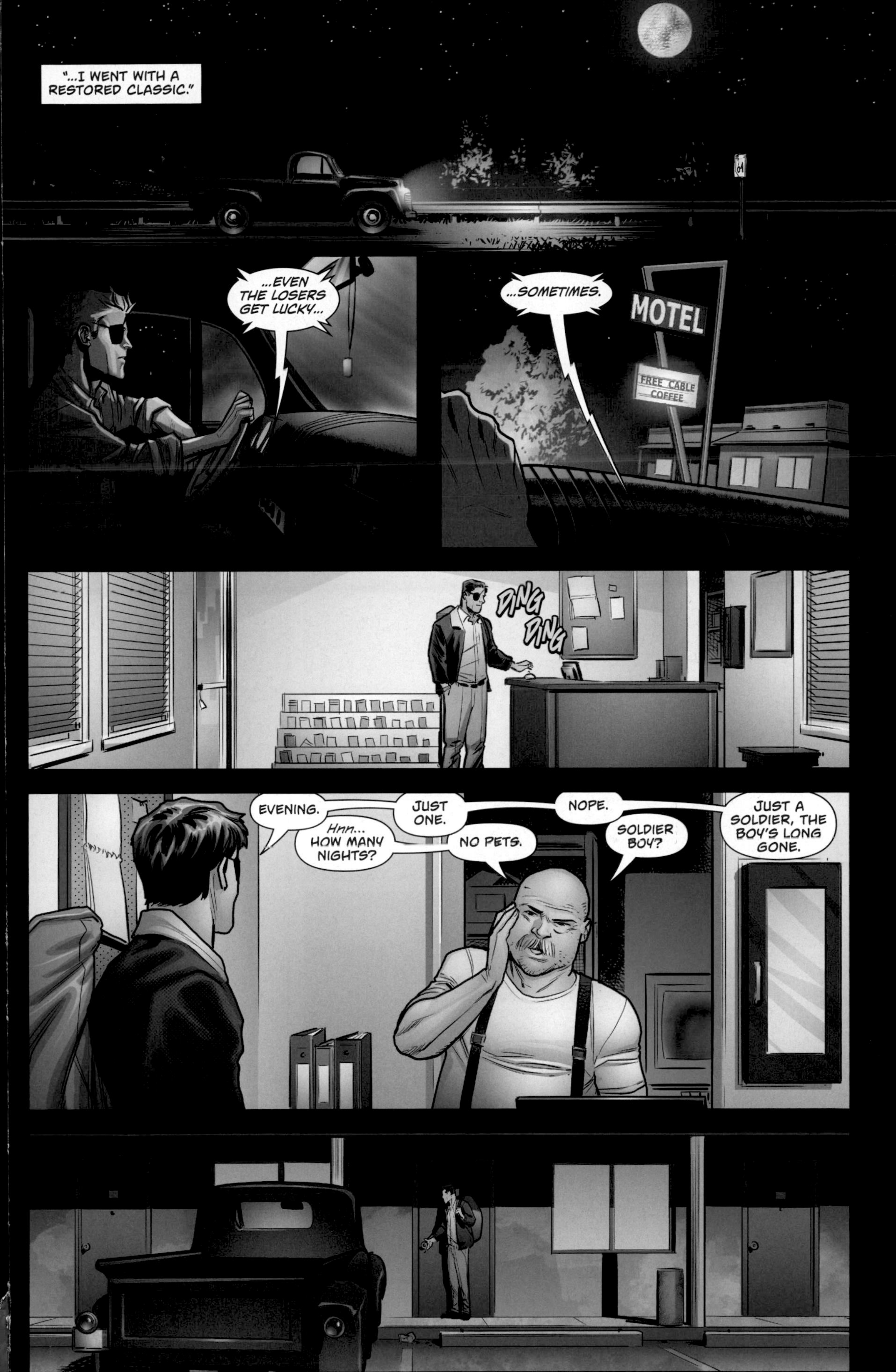
"...I WENT WITH A RESTORED CLASSIC."
...EVEN THE LOSERS GET LUCKY...
...SOMETIMES.
MOTEL
FREE CABLE COFFEE
DING DING
EVENING.
Hnn... HOW MANY NIGHTS?
JUST ONE.
NO PETS.
NOPE.
SOLDIER BOY?
JUST A SOLDIER, THE BOY'S LONG GONE.

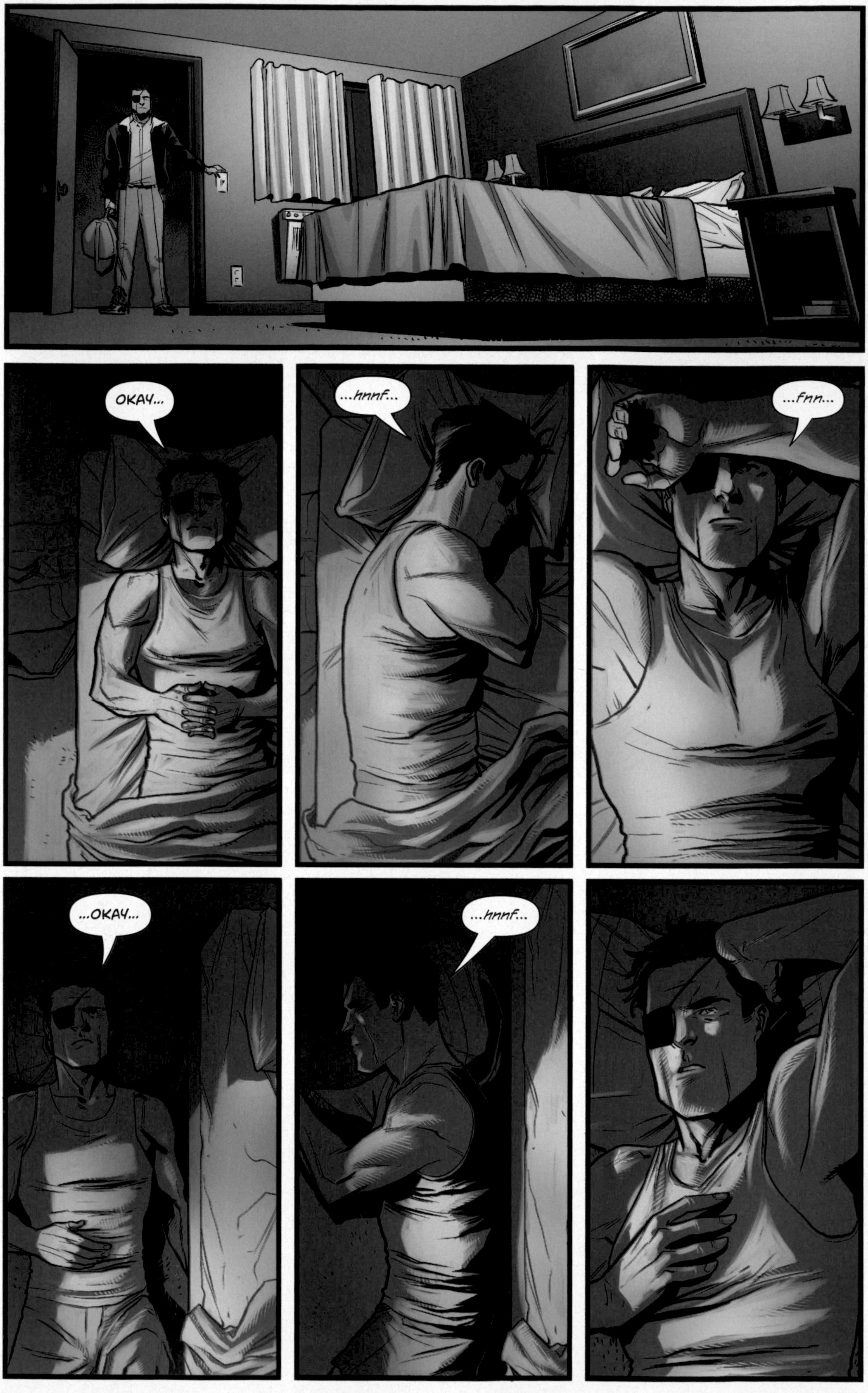
OKAY...
...hnnf...
...fnn...
...OKAY...
...hnnf...

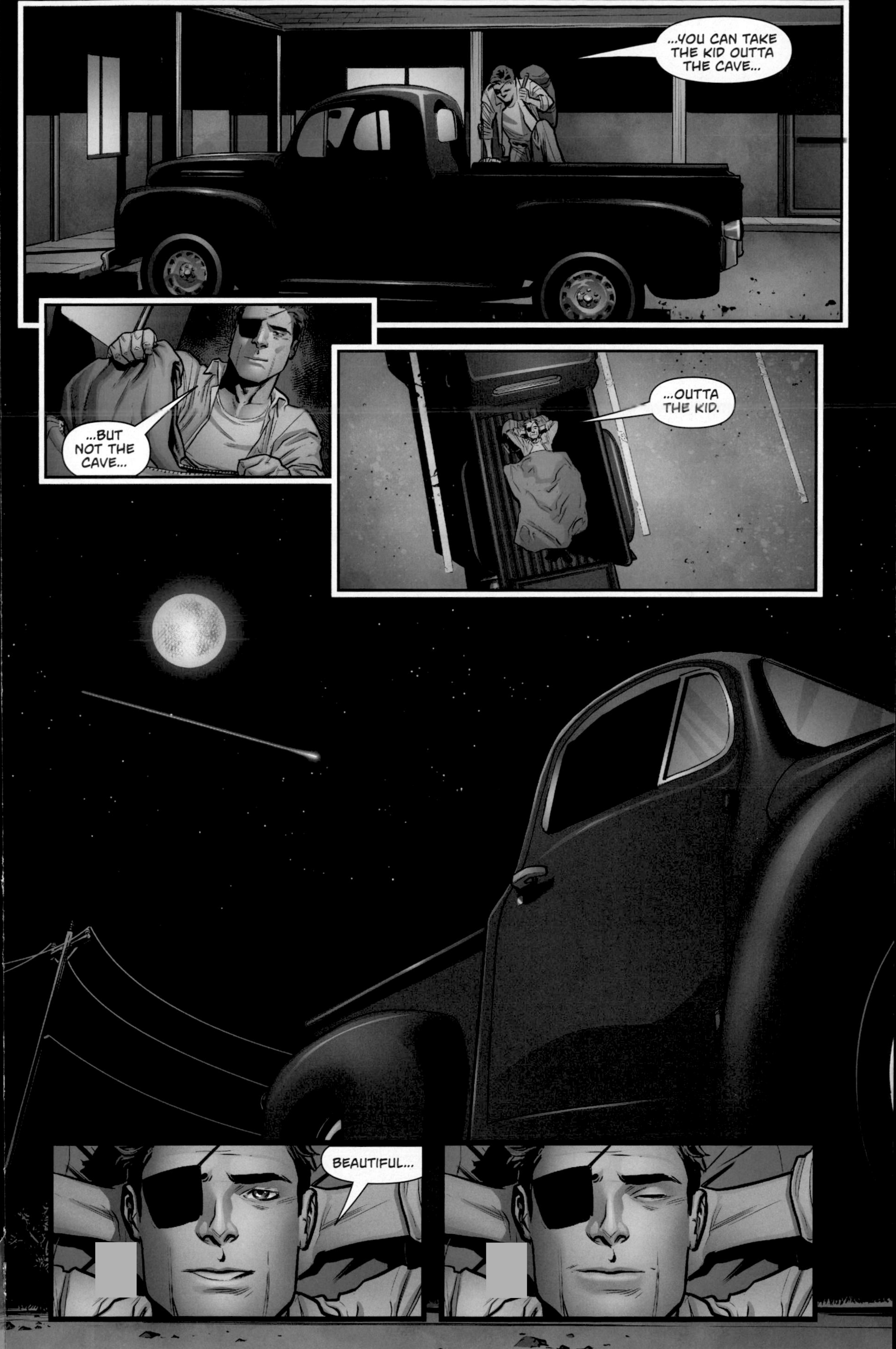
...YOU CAN TAKE THE KID OUTTA THE CAVE...
...BUT NOT THE CAVE...
...OUTTA THE KID.
BEAUTIFUL...

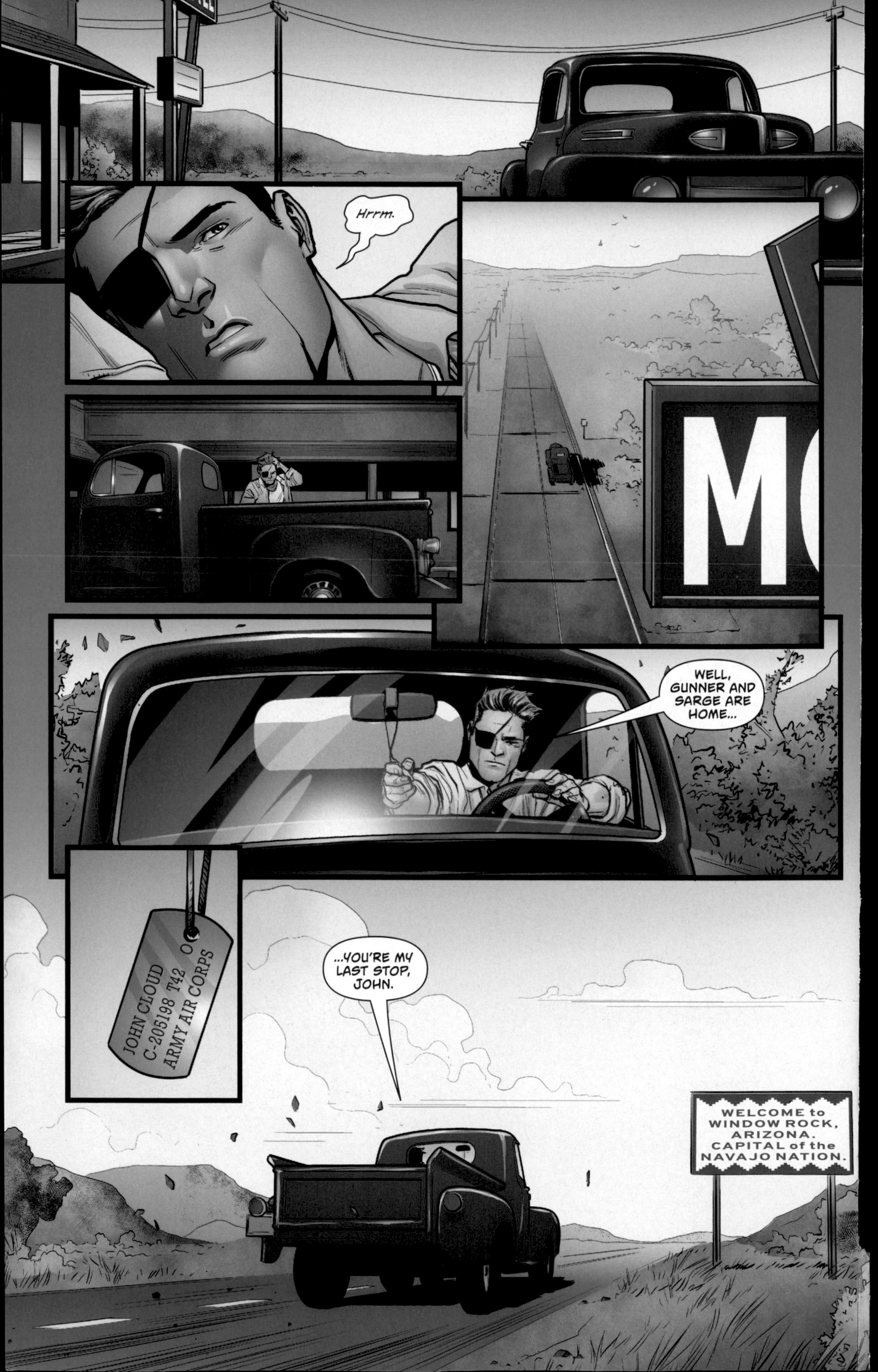
Hrrm.
WELL, GUNNER AND SARGE ARE HOME...
JOHN CLOUD
C-205198 T42
ARMY AIR CORPS
...YOU'RE MY LAST STOP, JOHN.
WELCOME to WINDOW ROCK, ARIZONA. CAPITAL of the NAVAJO NATION.

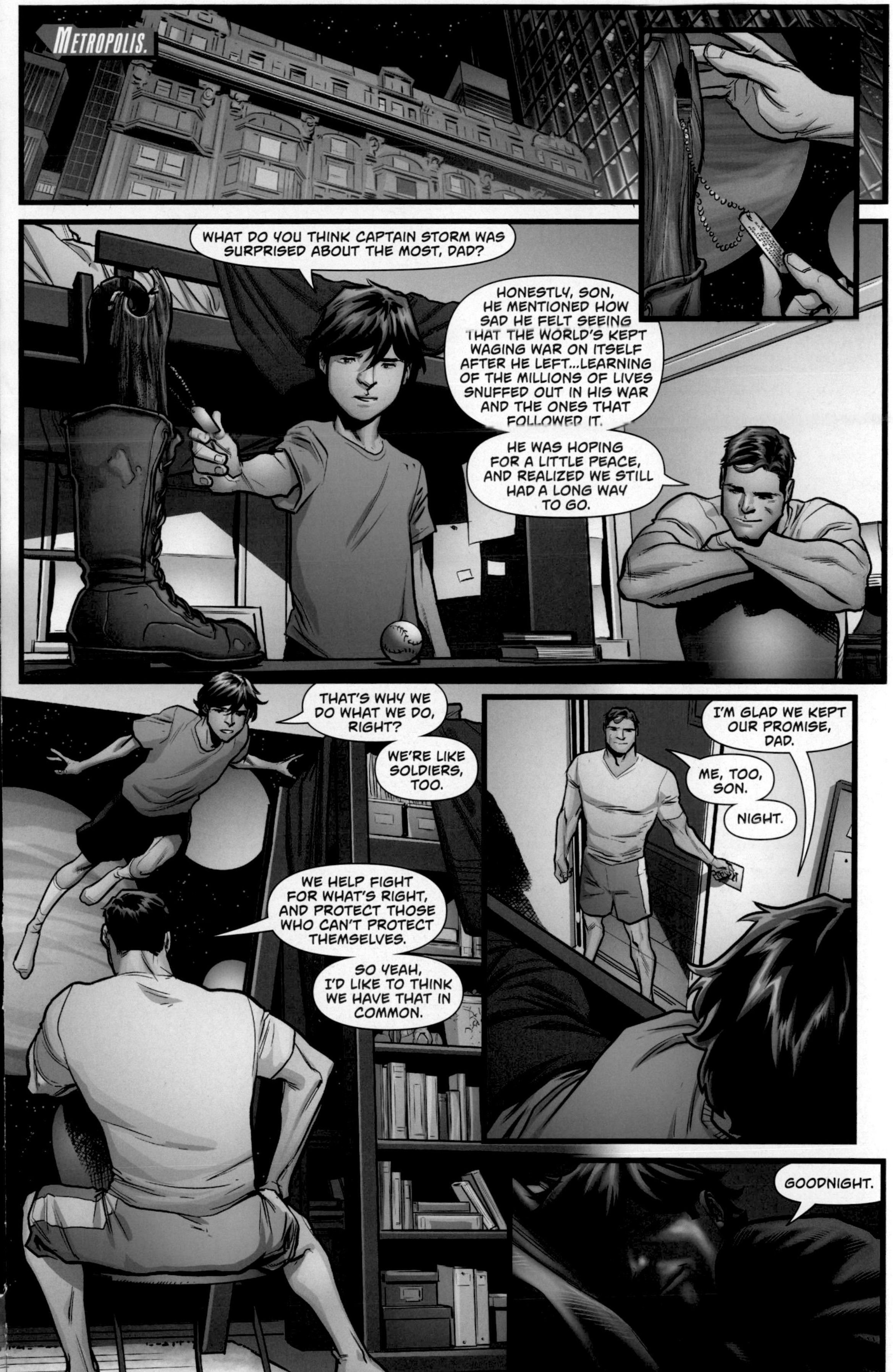
METROPOLIS.
WHAT DO YOU THINK CAPTAIN STORM WAS SURPRISED ABOUT THE MOST, DAD?
HONESTLY, SON, HE MENTIONED HOW SAD HE FELT SEEING THAT THE WORLD'S KEPT WAGING WAR ON ITSELF AFTER HE LEFT...LEARNING OF THE MILLIONS OF LIVES SNUFFED OUT IN HIS WAR AND THE ONES THAT FOLLOWED IT.
HE WAS HOPING FOR A LITTLE PEACE, AND REALIZED WE STILL HAD A LONG WAY TO GO.
THAT'S WHY WE DO WHAT WE DO, RIGHT?
WE'RE LIKE SOLDIERS, TOO.
WE HELP FIGHT FOR WHAT'S RIGHT, AND PROTECT THOSE WHO CAN'T PROTECT THEMSELVES.
SO YEAH, I'D LIKE TO THINK WE HAVE THAT IN COMMON.
I'M GLAD WE KEPT OUR PROMISE, DAD.
ME, TOO, SON.
NIGHT.
GOODNIGHT.

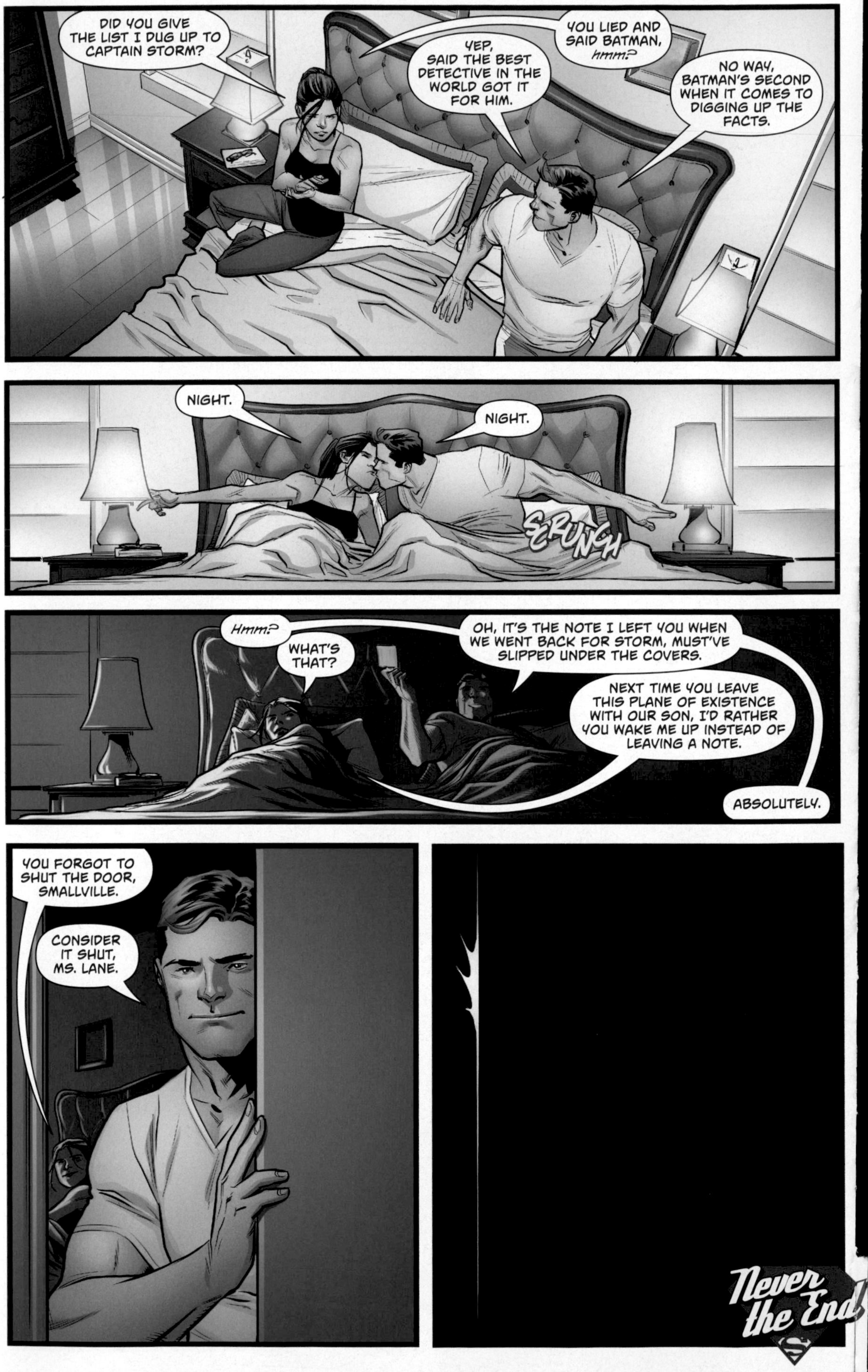
DID YOU GIVE THE LIST I DUG UP TO CAPTAIN STORM?
YEP, SAID THE BEST DETECTIVE IN THE WORLD GOT IT FOR HIM.
YOU LIED AND SAID BATMAN, hmm?
NO WAY, BATMAN'S SECOND WHEN IT COMES TO DIGGING UP THE FACTS.
NIGHT.
NIGHT.
SCRUNCH
Hmm?
WHAT'S THAT?
OH, IT'S THE NOTE I LEFT YOU WHEN WE WENT BACK FOR STORM, MUST'VE SLIPPED UNDER THE COVERS.
NEXT TIME YOU LEAVE THIS PLANE OF EXISTENCE WITH OUR SON, I'D RATHER YOU WAKE ME UP INSTEAD OF LEAVING A NOTE.
ABSOLUTELY.
YOU FORGOT TO SHUT THE DOOR, SMALLVILLE.
CONSIDER IT SHUT, MS. LANE.
Never the End

SUPERMAN #42 variant cover by JONBOY MEYERS

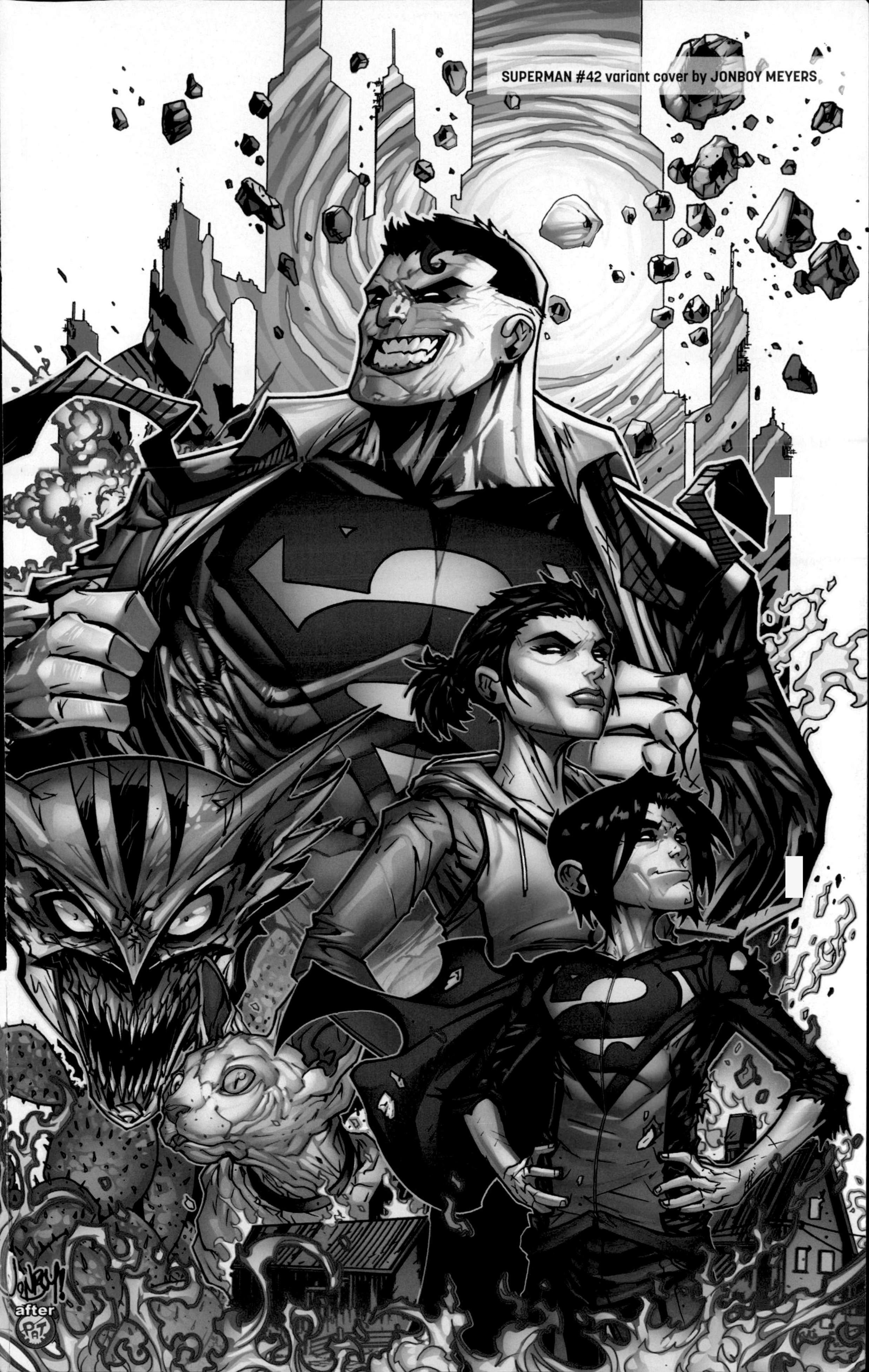

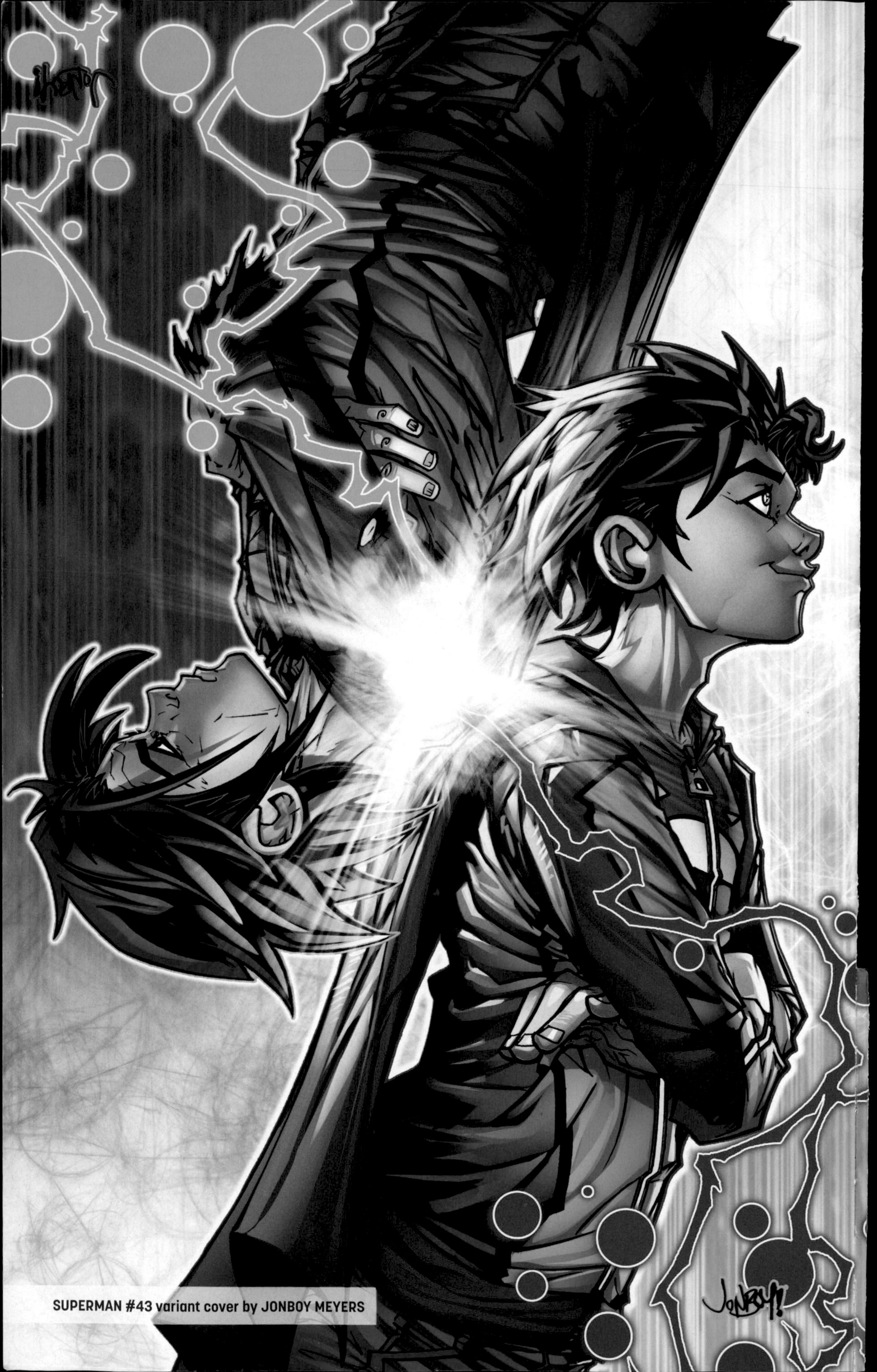

SUPERMAN #43 variant cover by JONBOY MEYERS

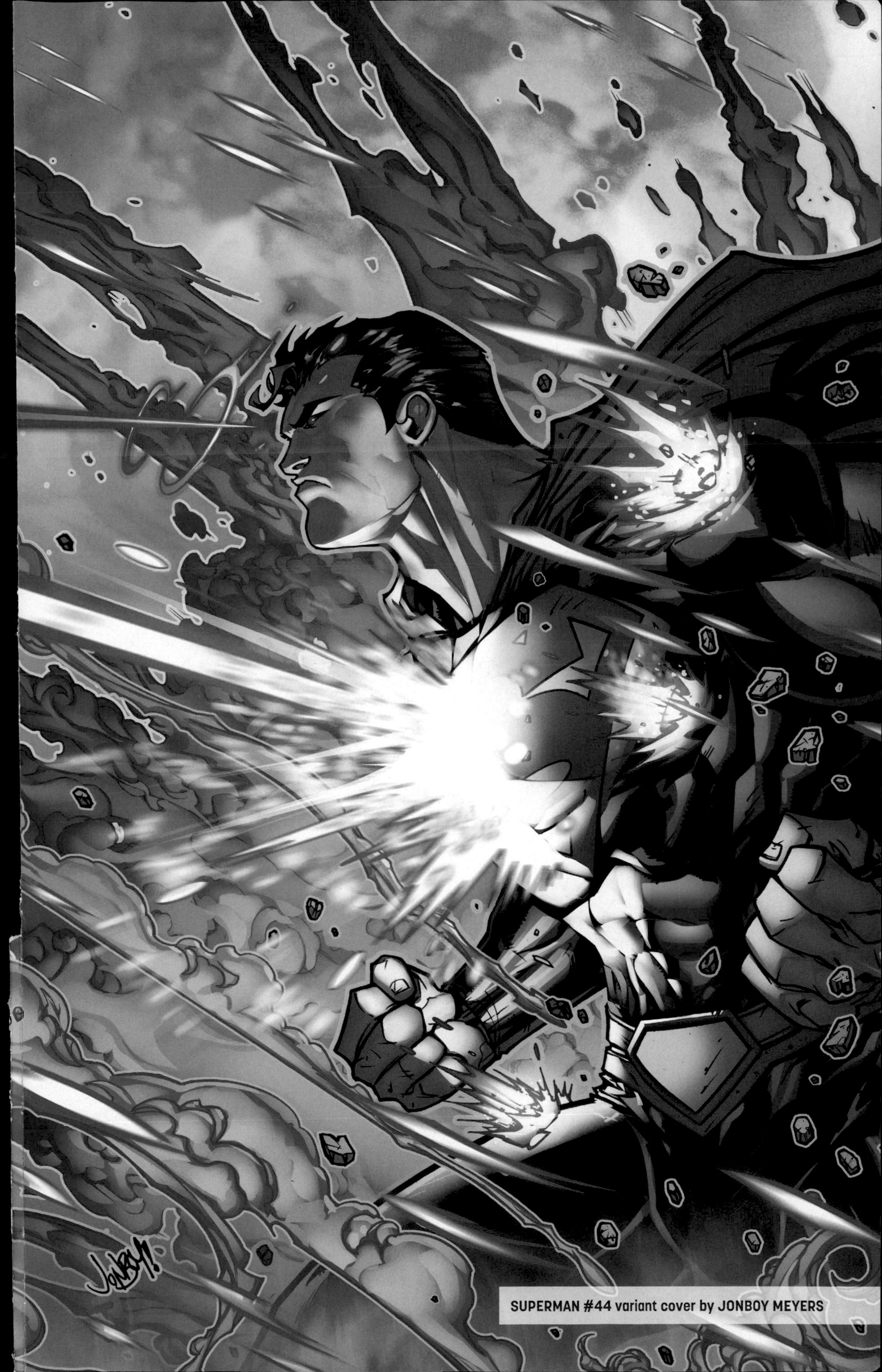
JONBOY!

SUPERMAN #44 variant cover by JONBOY MEYERS

SUPERMAN #45 variant cover by JONBOY MEYERS

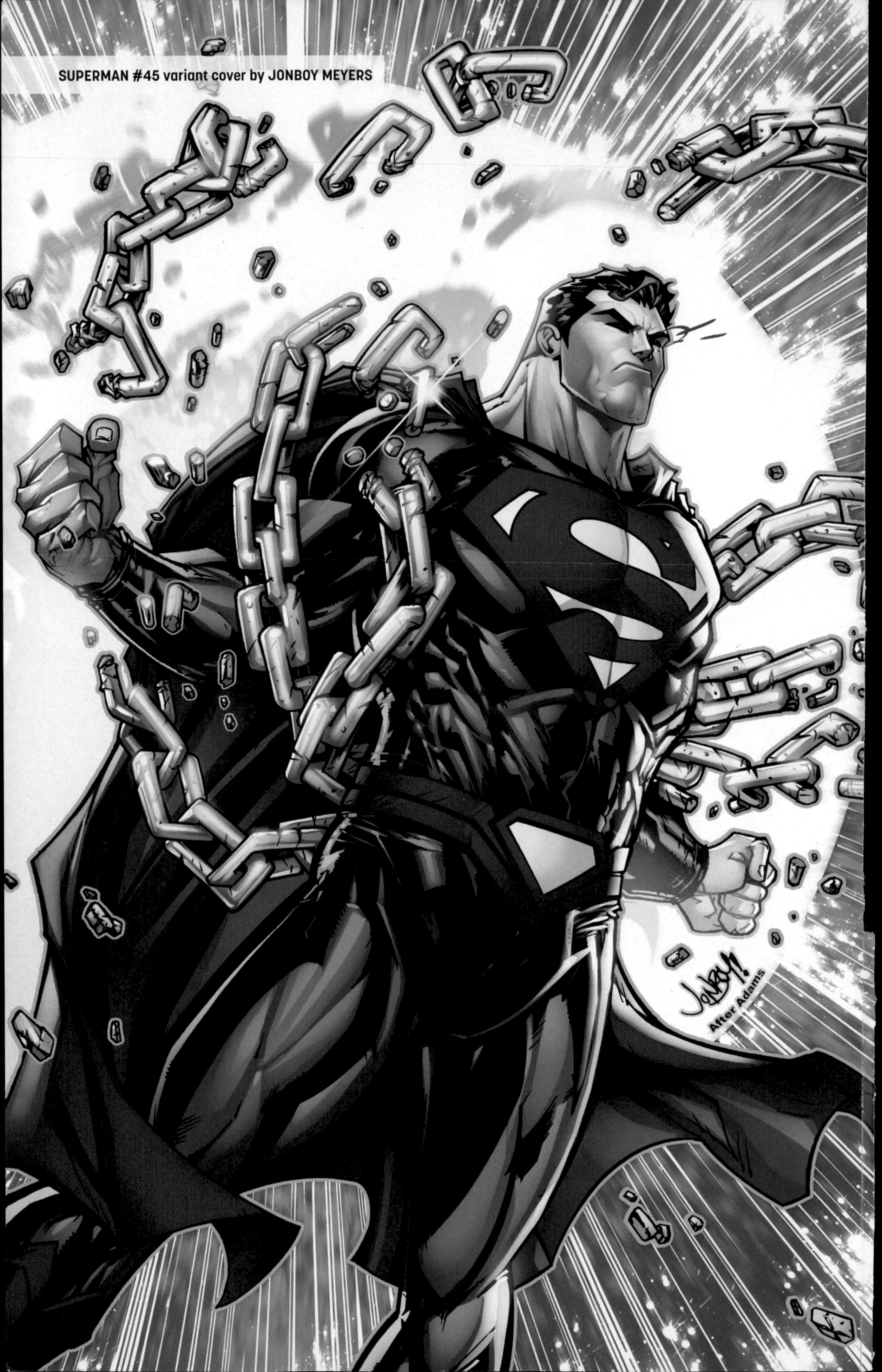
JONBOY!
After Adams

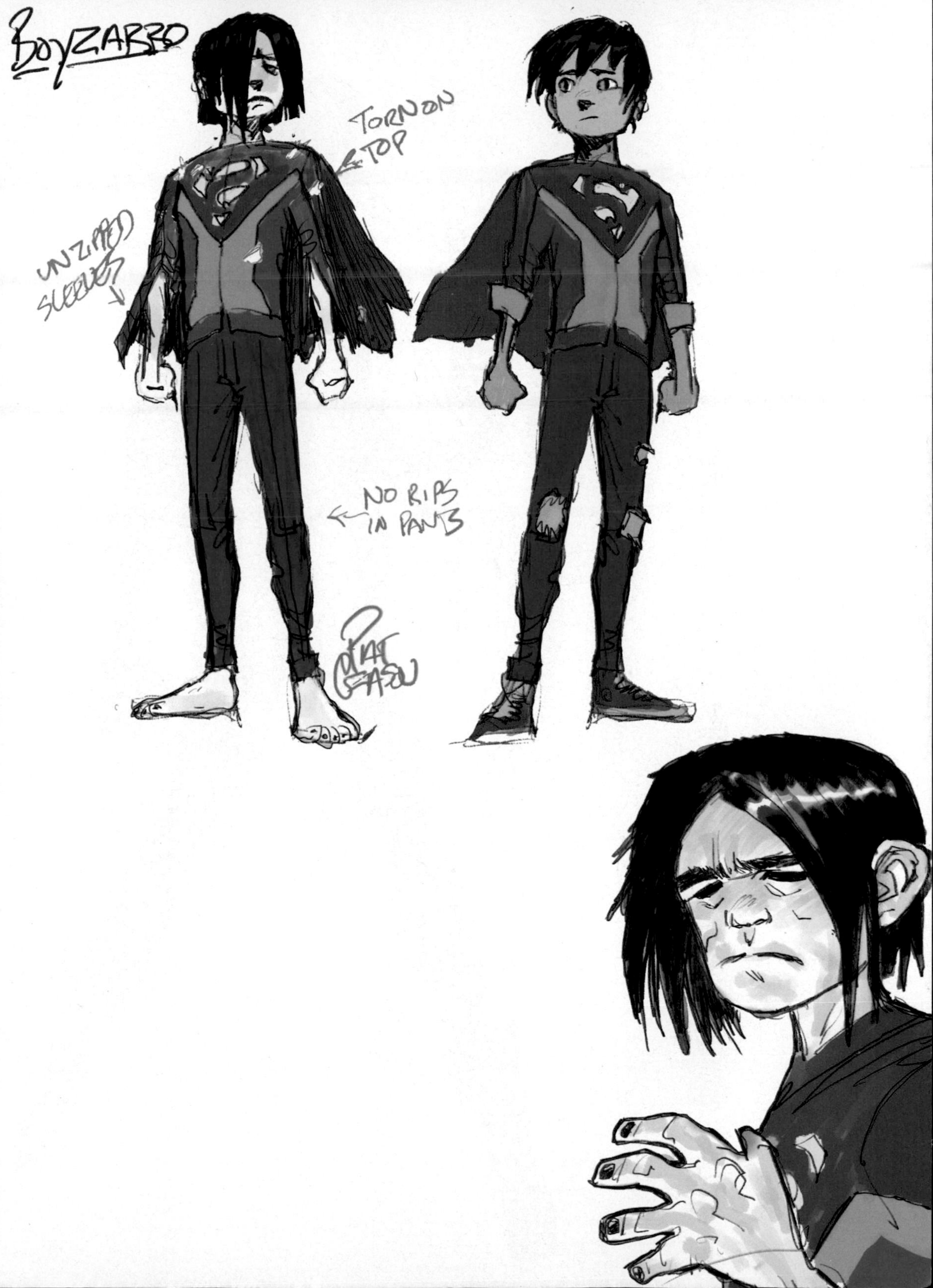
BOYZARRO
TORN ON TOP
UNZIPPED SLEEVES
NO RIPS IN PANTS
PAT GLEASON

KATHY BRANDEN character designs by PATRICK GLEASON

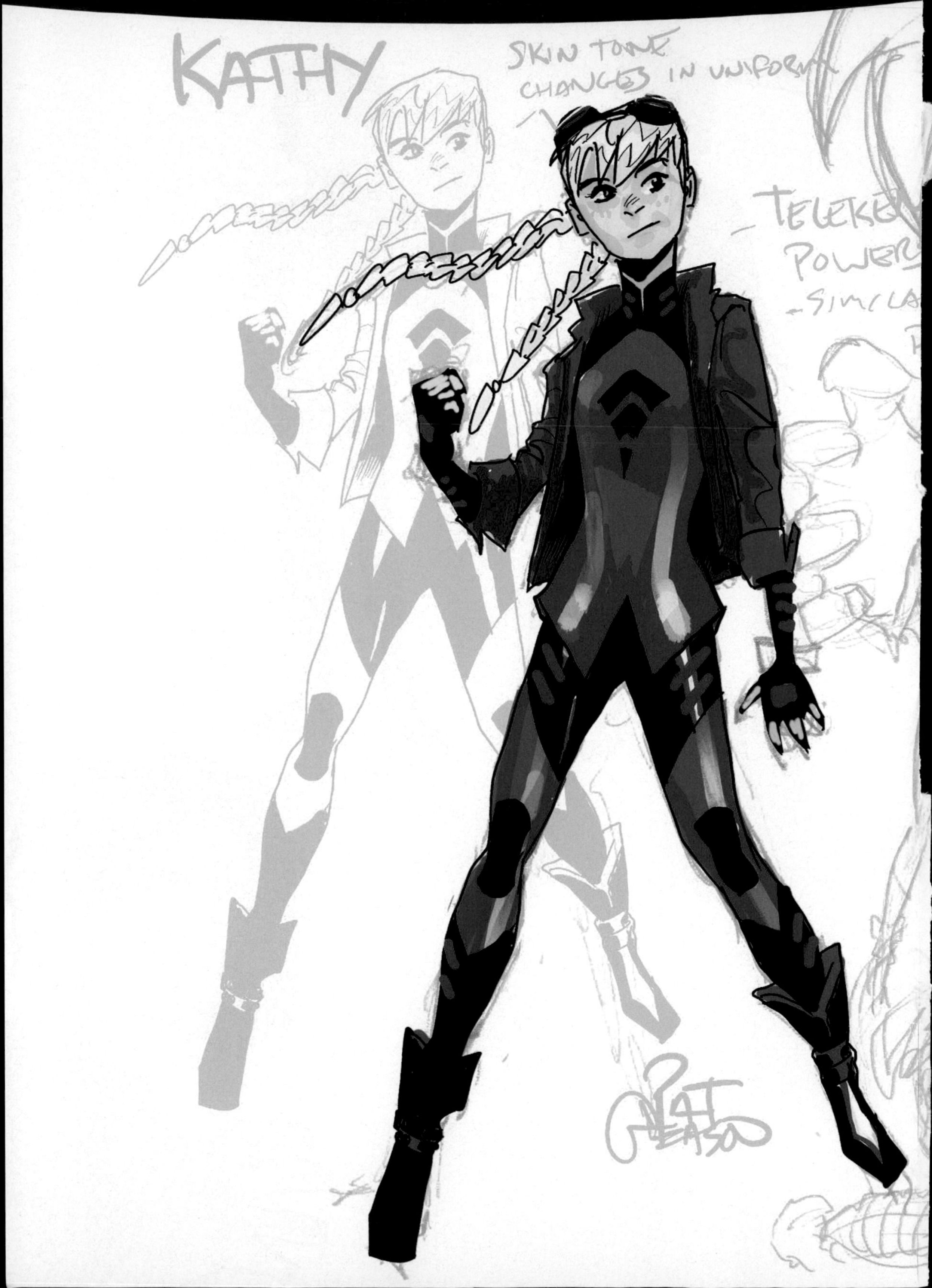
KATHY
SKIN TONE
CHANGES IN UNIFORM
PAT GLEASON

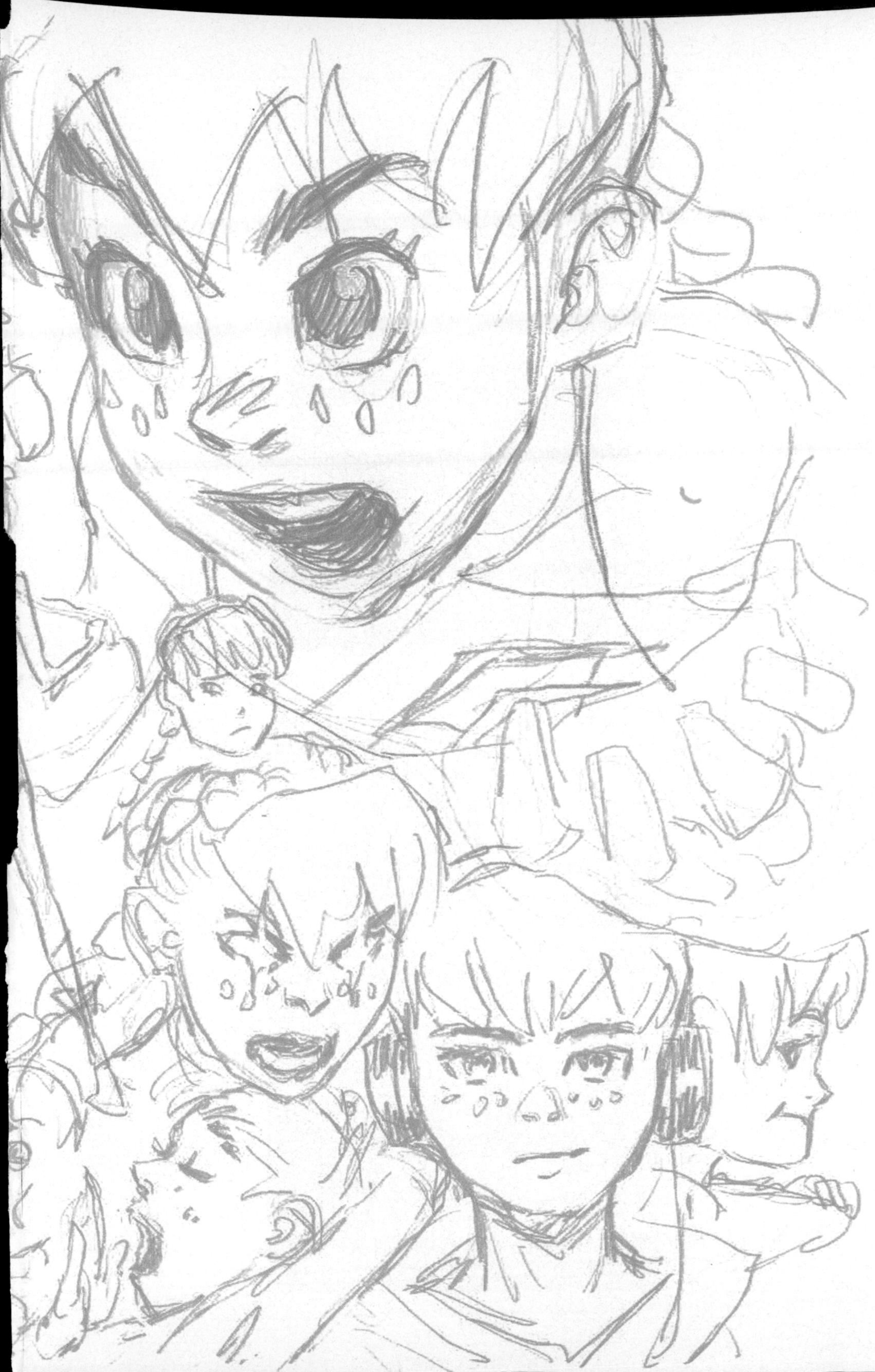

SUPERMAN #42 cover thumbnail and pencils
by PATRICK GLEASON

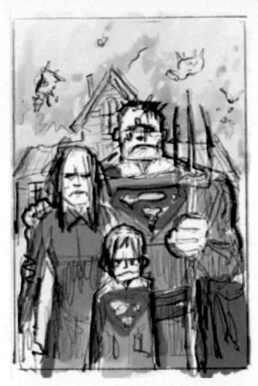

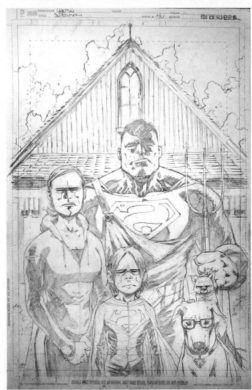